SUNRISE WITH THE SILVER SURFERS

MADDIE PLEASE

Boldwood

First published in Great Britain in 2023 by Boldwood Books Ltd.

Copyright © Maddie Please, 2023

Cover Design by Head Design

Cover Photography: Shutterstock

Every effort has been made to obtain the necessary permissions with reference to copyright material, both illustrative and quoted. We apologise for any omissions in this respect and will be pleased to make the appropriate acknowledgements in any future edition.

A CIP catalogue record for this book is available from the British Library.

Paperback ISBN 978-1-80162-145-8

Large Print ISBN 978-1-80162-144-1

Hardback ISBN 978-1-80162-143-4

Ebook ISBN 978-1-80162-147-2

Kindle ISBN 978-1-80162-146-5

Audio CD ISBN 978-1-80162-138-0

MP3 CD ISBN 978-1-80162-139-7

Digital audio download ISBN 978-1-80162-140-3

Boldwood Books Ltd
23 Bowerdean Street
London SW6 3TN
www.boldwoodbooks.com

For Brian, who took me to Australia.

LYTN&A

1

That morning I entered Heathrow, Terminal 5 with a thrill of excitement. I'd made it this far without anything going wrong; now all I needed was to get on the right plane. With all the security and checks, was it actually possible to get on the wrong plane? Knowing my luck, I probably could.

This time I could enjoy the bustle of people, the sound of the announcements, I could check the departures board as often as I liked without Tom at my elbow, tutting and sighing and telling me to keep a close eye on my case otherwise it would be taken away and blown up.

I know people complain about queues and delays but I love airports. They always make me feel optimistic. Go through those gates and anything could be possible. A week in the South of France. A fortnight in the Greek Islands. A road trip around New England. I particularly liked the sound of that; I'd always wanted to do one.

I hadn't actually travelled very much since coming to England all those years ago. There were school holidays for us all to consider and the resulting and very unfair increase in the price of flights. And of course, worse than that, Tom never fancied the places I suggested we might visit.

We'd managed to take a few package holidays over the years; Tom thought it was important our son Dan should be able to brag to his classmates about visiting Disney or Paris or Venice. But we never explored the places I wanted to see: picturesque French villages with adorable boulangeries, or the soaring beauty of the Italian lakes, or the twinkling Christmas markets of Germany.

Having watched my ex-husband on our last budget flight together to Jersey to celebrate our thirtieth wedding anniversary, it confirmed my belief that the real reason was he was terrified of flying but wouldn't admit it. Even when he almost pulled the arms off the seat when we took off. I swear he was doing little running movements with his feet although he denied that too.

This time it was going to be different. For one thing, I was traveling alone. Without Tom sweating or complaining about the size of the airline seats and couldn't I budge over a bit. Without Dan wanting crayons (aged 8), snacks (aged 14) or more leg room (aged 18).

That morning I was of course far too early; that's just me. I was even early thirty four years ago when Tom and I were married, and I had to sit in the car behind the village hall until my bridesmaid – my younger sister Rowan pretty in Liberty print – told me he had arrived. He'd insisted we were married in Gloucestershire because his mother was 'too frail' to travel to Australia. Sylvia always was 'too frail' to do anything that didn't suit her.

In hindsight I should have done things very differently, but I had been in love with a handsome man who seemed mature, stable, and confident while I was none of those things. Thinking back, I didn't seem to have much of a say in anything. He always claimed to have swept me off my feet. It was only later that I realised this isn't always a good thing.

I wasn't going to think about that, not today. I was single again, back out in the world, and this holiday was going to be different. Slightly scary but very exciting at the same time. I was going on a proper adventure.

After all those years, I was going back to Australia to see my family.

* * *

Joyce was an elderly lady who used to walk her dog in the park next to the house Tom owned, and after my divorce I'd moved to live just down the road from her. My new neighbour Lizzie and I had kept a special watch on her in her last months when she was house bound, doing her shopping, taking her meals, and helping her put her photos into some sort of order.

She had literally thousands, many of them still in the paper envelopes from Timothy Whites or Boots. Black and white pictures of her smiling in front of the pyramids or Machu Pichu or various statues of Buddha in Thailand. And later, colourful snaps of her in Hawaii, Hong Kong and New York. How wonderful to have seen so many places.

'There's a lot of world out there Elin,' she'd said, 'you must see it. And so should Dan. You're a young, healthy, attractive woman in your prime. Make the most of it. Before it's too late.'

Fat chance of that, when my husband hadn't even bothered to renew his passport.

But then, exactly a year after the ink was dry on my divorce from Tom, Joyce died. And much to Tom's frustration, she had left me a considerable amount of money that he couldn't get his hands on. And she left the same for Lizzie so she could get her leaking roof fixed.

Along with my bequest was a letter of wishes from her with

the strict instruction that I must use some of it for travel. So that's what I was doing, standing on a bright June morning having got rid of my big suitcases, hanging on to my cabin bag, reading the notice about things I was not allowed to take on board with me (swords, stews, shaving foam or pepper spray) and plucking up the courage to go through security.

* * *

Evidently I passed the 'looking dangerous and requiring a strip search' test and was allowed through to departures without incident. Then I made my way, heart thumping, to the business class lounge because for the first time in my life I had upgraded my seat. Tom would never have allowed it, not in a million years. When he did travel, he preferred to go for the cheapest airline in the cheapest seats and then complain all the way there and back about the discomfort. I mean it wasn't as though we couldn't have afforded to upgrade to perhaps premium economy, but we never had.

On our ill-fated trip to Jersey, he had complained about having sciatica, a bad back, and possibly a deep vein thrombosis after an hour's flight. And yes, it did rather ruin the mood for the rest of the week as we both anticipated the return trip.

It was absolutely miles to the business class lounge. Perhaps really rich people had the use of the electric carts or perhaps there were special secret entrances somewhere? I had a good look around to see who was coming with me and didn't see anyone remotely famous.

At least the moving pavements were working, and I could stride briskly out, feeling a silly sense of triumph as I passed the people who had chosen to just walk. I resisted the impulse to walk backwards on it, or pretend to be swimming, something I'd seen on social media once. Perhaps it wouldn't be so amusing if I fell over and got my clothes tangled up in the slats.

Heathrow airport declares incident as woman eaten by travelator.

I eventually found myself in a calm, quiet, armchair-strewn lounge with a wonderful view of the runway and the ground crew.

There is always one man in a high-viz jacket and ear defenders standing around next to the plane apparently not doing anything. I was delighted to see he was still there, still apparently doing nothing.

There were free meals. And drinks. Okay, it was only eleven thirty in the morning but would madam like some champagne? Yes, indeed madam jolly well would.

I collected a glass and went and sat in one of the squishy leather armchairs overlooking the runway. I looked around. Had anyone noticed I was travelling alone? Did they wonder about me in the same way I wondered about other people? Or had I just disappeared into the background as a lone, middle aged woman? Everyone else seemed to have someone to talk to, there were even a few children rushing about, seemingly used to this sort of thing. I wondered what Dan would think if he could see me. But then I began to enjoy myself. No one needed anything from me or couldn't find their car keys or wanted to know where I was. Until I was half way down the glass of bubbly and my mobile pinged.

Tom. Of course it was Tom. The reality of our divorce didn't seem to make any difference to him now he was dissatisfied with his new life and sleep deprived. Ashley had smugly announced her pregnancy with astonishing speed after their wedding. Considering it had taken me six years to get pregnant, I didn't know Tom had it in him. Nor did he, I suspect. Starting again at the age of sixty with a new baby, a thirty-five year old wife and with a twenty-eight-year-old son to explain himself to can't have been easy.

Where are you? I was hoping to catch up.

I ignored him; recently I've decided it's the best way. Why my ex-husband still thought I wanted anything to do with him after the way he behaved is a mystery. It was like I was some sort of comfort blanket for him.

Another ping.

Elin, I need to speak to you.

Are you at home, I might pop in?

I sighed and replied. I think like most women my age, I'm a people-pleaser. It can be a real problem, but in a strange kind of way I wanted him to know that I was doing something. Something exciting.

I'm at Heathrow drinking champagne.

Very funny. So is five thirty ok? Maybe closer to six.

I won't be in.

So when will you be in?

No idea.

I went to look at the food displays and was suddenly hungry. It was nearly three hours until the flight and I had been up since before dawn, so I might as well have a little something. Rude not to really when they'd gone to all that trouble.

I decided on a smoked salmon and cream cheese bagel, (low-fat – I do need to keep an eye on my cholesterol) and a chocolate brownie, washed down with more champagne. Outside I could see the white and gold bulk of a huge plane being loaded with suitcases and pallets of stuff. Food perhaps? Sparkly, exciting things?

Ping.

Elin, what time will you be home?

Foolishly – perhaps it was the champagne – I relented and replied again.

No idea. What exactly do you want Tom?

You see, my impulse to show off was backfiring on me. I was opening up a conversation with him when I didn't want one.

I'm in the middle of some really serious stuff here and I've had about ten minutes sleep in the last week. I think Josie is teething or something. I don't remember Daniel making such a song and dance about it. Or about sleeping. I could do with a bit of sympathy and a strong gin and tonic.

Then have one.

I shouldn't have replied. I should have turned my phone off. I should have blocked his number months ago. But I'll admit occasionally seeing his increasing dissatisfaction with his new 'soulmate' gave me a certain *schadenfreude*. Perhaps that's not very kind of me?

I don't suppose you'd make lasagne for me this evening would you?

Extra special pretty please? Ashley is having a go at being a vegan and it's killing me. She says its healthy but I feel quite faint half the time.

Oh dear.

I smiled to myself, how simply frightful. Tom had always said a meal without a chunk of meat on his place was merely a starter. Perhaps Ashley wasn't quite as amenable as I had been.

What are you doing Elin?

I told you. I'm at Heathrow. I'm going to Australia for two months. I'm in the Business Class Lounge at Terminal 5 drinking champagne.

Tom assumed radio silence. I wouldn't be surprised if he had fainted. I raised my glass in a silent toast to myself and my adventure.

* * *

The room was busier now with people sitting by the window, drinking coffee and chatting. A few were working on their laptops; a couple were on their mobiles, a tiny Japanese woman at a nearby table was eating noodles with chopsticks as though her life depended on it, some people were dozing. It was all very pleasant. No one was shouting or pacing about, or asking me for anything.

Ping.

Business Class? Are you completely mad? Why would you want to go back to Australia after all this time? Elin, when are you back?

I sighed.

1) No I'm not completely mad 2) because I want to see my family again. And 3) MYOB.

The little dots at the bottom of the screen to show a reply was on the way appeared and then disappeared. Evidently Tom was offended. Or outraged. Well tough. I might have been 'swept off my feet' once, but my size fives were firmly back on the ground now.

* * *

A very nice-looking man who had been standing looking out of the window came to sit opposite me. Not that I usually take notice of these things, but he was tall and tanned and rather lovely. Business Class travellers could certainly be eye catching.

He leaned towards me and I gave him a nervous smile.

'You don't mind?' he said with a broad, white grin.

He had great teeth and a faint Australian accent. What did he want? Perhaps he was going to be on my plane. Maybe he had spotted me across the room and taken a shine to me for some reason. If he was attracted to short sighted (recently acquired contact lenses) fifty eight year old women who perhaps should have fitted in a haircut before their holiday? No, he wanted something didn't he? Men always use charm and smiles when they want something.

'Mind what?' I said, a bit flustered.

He smiled again and pointed to the wall next to me.

'I hate to disturb you, but I need the power socket. My laptop's nearly out of charge.'

'Oh of course not. Help yourself,' I said flushing a bit and he messed about with cables before he started typing. I wondered what he was doing.

I allowed myself the sort of fantasy that had always irritated Tom when he saw I wasn't paying proper attention to him but had zoned out.

Perhaps the Australian was a high-powered businessman on his way to an important board meeting. In Sydney, in an office with a fabulous view over the harbour through the floor to ceiling windows. He would have changed out of his chinos and t-shirt obviously. Perhaps he would be outlining some impending business reshuffle, or takeover? The room would be filled with steely eyed men in dark suits, all drinking iced water out of crystal tumblers. He'd have an impressive PowerPoint proposal to go through and the others would nod and make notes in leather...

Ping.

Mum, I'm thinking of coming over to do my washing this weekend. Our machine has packed up.

Dan, I told you. I'm going to Australia.

Bloody hell. I'd forgotten. Skye is working all weekend at the wine bar. I'll have to go to dad's and Ashley has the wrong sort of washing powder. It brings me out in a rash.

God forbid Ashley had the wrong sort of washing powder. Don't use it, buy your own washing powder. Here's an idea. Go to a laundrette? Do your washing there?

Are you really going to Australia?

I'm at Heathrow.

Definitely on my way to Australia.

Why didn't you remind me?

I did. Several times.

The last time was two days ago.

I forgot.

Mum, I haven't got a key for your house.

No I know.

So how am I going to get in?

You can't. You don't actually need to get in.

Tiger mother, that's me, sending my cub out into the wilds with only a degree in maths, a teaching certificate, and a rudimentary knowledge of domestic appliances.

Flipping heck, Mum. Well have a nice time.

I intended to have a nice time. With any luck I'd have bloody marvellous time.

I gave a snort of laughter and realised the nice-looking man sitting opposite me had stopped typing and was watching me. I felt my face flush. What must he think?

'Everything okay?' he said; he was obviously trying hard not to laugh.

'Fine,' I said, straightening my face. I have a habit of muttering when I'm texting, and sometimes have a conversation with myself, voicing the things I don't actually type. What on earth had I been saying?

'Just a few last-minute things to clear up.'

'Sounds like it. So where are you off to?'

'I'm going to Sydney to visit my aunt and uncle and my sister,' I looked at my watch, and felt a sizzle of anticipation, 'in an hour and a half.'

'That sounds exciting. I'll be on your plane,' he said, 'I live on the outskirts of Sydney.'

'Amazing!'

This was going surprisingly well. Perhaps we would strike up a conversation about Australia and he would tell me something about himself and I would be interesting and engaging and he would find me unexpectedly fascinating, and I would make him laugh. I pushed my fringe out of my eyes and sat up a bit straighter.

'The washing powder could be a problem though,' he said thoughtfully.

Bugger. I could feel my face getting hot again. What else had I said?

He typed for a few minutes and then snapped his laptop shut.

'First trip to Australia?'

'I was born there. But I haven't been back for ages. My parents died years ago; we are only a small family, and my sister and I were brought up by my father's sister. My aunt Maggie. She was ten years younger than my dad. She and my uncle Banjo have been to visit me a couple of times and so has my sister.'

'Is his name really Banjo?'

'It's Bernard but no one ever calls him that.'

'Great name!'

'We have Zoom calls and WhatsApp and Skype...'

He shook his head. 'But it's not the same, is it?'

I smiled and relaxed a bit, glad that he understood.

'No, it's not the same. My ex-husband hated flying and just refused. But now I'm single again and my son has his own flat and is reasonably independent, well I can.'

I was talking far too much. And saying the word sister a lot. All those years of keeping my opinions to myself had started to wear off in the time since Tom and I had separated and then divorced. Even so, I was being a bit garrulous, even by my standards. Did he need to know I was divorced? That I had a son? A sister? That my parents had died? That my aunt had been to visit me? No, I was being far too free with my personal details. He could be anyone.

Australian businessman didn't seem to mind. He appeared to be listening with interest.

'That's excellent. Good for you. I hope you have fun. It's quite a trip, and I warn you the jet lag is just as bad as it ever was.'

'And you?' I said, realising we were just talking about me. And I wanted to know more about him; he seemed really nice. And rather handsome. It was a long time since an attractive man like this had noticed me. Or any man for that matter.

He ran one hand over his hair, which was dark, shot through with streaks of silver.

'I make this trip quite frequently. Far more often than I actually want to. Business. New South Wales is a beautiful part of the world, and Sydney is a wonderful city. Make sure you see the Rocks area and the Opera House. And Darling Harbour. You won't recognise it. There's been an incredible amount of development there since you left. Not to mention all the roads that have been built. It's very impressive.'

'I will, I certainly will,' I said eagerly.

He gave me another smile and then he stood up.

'I've just remembered, I have a couple of phone calls I must make, and I tend to shout and pace about. Enjoy your champagne and have a good trip,' he said.

He unplugged the cable again and loaded up his laptop bag.

'You too,' I said.

Had I said something to put him off? Pity, I was actually enjoying talking to him.

I watched him walk away, and then went back to my drink.

Ping. Tom again.

I know we have had our disagreements, but you could at least be civil.

I sent a last text to Lizzie telling her I had got to the airport safely, and then one each to my aunt and sister telling them the same thing, and then I turned my phone off.

Getting on the plane was very exciting indeed. The cabin crew were all helpful and smiling and there was so much space. I couldn't believe it. I had my own little pod to sit in, slanted towards the window too, which made a change because on the few other flights I have known, Tom always insisted on sitting in the window seat so he could point out things I couldn't see and wonder aloud if the wings were strong enough. That sort of thing. Then if Dan was with us, he would insist on the aisle seat, leaving me crushed in the middle between two man-spreaders and no arm rest.

What is the etiquette on arm rests anyway? Surely I should have access to one if not occasionally one and a half in a fair world. This time I had two to myself. And shortly after that, a steward with a pair of tongs brought me a hot face towel in case getting on the plane had made me grubby. I happily wiped it over my face, forgetting I had carefully applied make up that morning. Now the rest of the cool, hip business class travellers would see that my complexion was probably blotchy with the champagne I'd knocked back.

Oh well. I'd never see any of them again. I bet I wasn't the only one.

I accepted a chilled bottle of mineral water and another glass of champagne while outside, the ground crew disappeared and the corridor connecting the plane to English air was pulled back.

The captain introduced himself over the intercom and told us all about the cabin crew who apparently spoke lots of languages and would attend to all our needs on the flight to Dubai. His voice was smooth and calm, and he sounded tall and capable, and he was probably very handsome too, with a finely chiselled jaw and a noble nose. Marvellous.

For the first time since a school trip to Canberra, I was thoroughly enjoying myself on a plane. I could listen to the safety briefing, appreciate the massive thrust of the wheels on the tarmac, the stomach swooping moment when we took off, and the sight of London disappearing beneath the clouds.

Down there, people were getting on with their lives, their problems, sitting fuming in traffic jams on the M25 while I was soaring away above them with my mobile turned off and about five hundred films to watch on the entertainment system in front of me.

It did feel strange after a while because I had no one to share this with. I hadn't really thought about that part. I had no companion to turn to and say how excited I was. Discuss the meal choices or the wine we were served, no one to agree on the comfort of the seats, the marvellous amount of leg room, the abundance of arm rests. After so many years, I was going to see my childhood home again. It was seven years since I'd seen my family and I was fizzing with excitement. I had no one with me to share my delight at going back to Australia. That sort of thing.

What time was it anyway? I had no idea. Apart from everything else, the blinds in the cabin had been closed shortly after take-off and the lights were low; perhaps they were hoping we would all go to sleep? Well, there was no chance of that; I wasn't going to waste a moment.

* * *

Lunch was served with a great deal of flourishing napkins, and I had proper cutlery and an actual glass. Perhaps they thought that having spent all this money, we were less likely to launch an unprovoked attack on each other?

I wasn't entirely sure what I was eating because it was a sort of fusion thing. Chunks of chicken and something Thai and some salad followed by an exquisite little cheesecake. I recognised that all right.

After a few hours, the cabin crew left us in peace. I stopped pressing all the buttons on my entertainment system and making my electric seat go up and down to find the most comfortable position and decided to investigate the loos. They were really nice and had drawers filled with stuff for the unprepared business traveller. Individually wrapped combs, cotton wool balls, eye masks, and even bottles of expensive perfume to use. Amazing.

Suitably refreshed and smelling gorgeous, I was about to go back to my seat when I heard laughter behind me and realised there was a bar. I mean an actual bar at the back of the plane and people were standing around chatting, eating snacks, and drinking cocktails. What sort of heaven was this?

The Elin of a year ago would probably have sloped off back to her seat. I would have probably made excuses for myself, questioned my right to be there. My years with Tom had somehow crushed a lot of my self-belief. Although crushed was probably the wrong word. It hadn't been as simple as that or as instant. Tom's campaign of making me feel unworthy, second-rate, was more a gentle but persistent squeeze over the years, so gradual that I hadn't really noticed.

Today, after hesitating halfway through the red curtain, I went and joined them. I had paid my fare, arranged my visa, done everything myself; I was entitled to enjoy the experience. And of course, from a health point of view, it was important to keep my circulation going on such a long flight.

There were a couple of keen looking chaps in striped shirts talking loudly about outsourcing the whole book and what were Gary and Patrick doing for God's sake? I moved past them to stand next to a chic, blonde woman draped in cream linen who was excavating the contents of her handbag over the rest of the seat. I ordered a Marmalade Martini. Well I asked Cream Linen Woman what she was drinking, and it looked suitably celebratory.

The steward behind the bar gave me a charming smile and flourished a paper coaster onto the counter in front of me.

'Does it actually have marmalade in it?' I asked. 'because I don't really like it.'

He gave me a fleeting look that said *then why have you ordered it?* and then patiently explained the ingredients.

Gin, Grand Marnier, lemon juice and orange zest plus a very small amount of marmalade. I decided to risk it. It looked really colourful.

I really should slow down a bit; at this rate I would need a lie down in a darkened room before I started dancing on the tables. Not that I ever had but I've often wondered what it would be like. I don't think I could get away with it now, not at my age. A teenage girl dancing on the tables in a night club is one thing. Me doing it on a plane would be quite another matter. Knowing my luck, we would hit turbulence and I would slip and fall off and – oh, never mind.

'Ah, there you are! Enjoying your flight?'

Oh good heavens! It was him again. Nice-looking Australian man with the laptop and the cable. He had lovely hazel eyes. Almost greenish.

Annoyingly, I felt my face grow hot. Perhaps it was the alcohol. Perhaps it wasn't.

'Hello! Yes, I am rather. It's the first time I've flown anything other than budget airlines in the small seats where nothing is included, and your legs go to sleep. Well, not *your* legs obviously, I meant my legs.'

Great. I was babbling again. He would think I was crazy. Or drunk or something. Perhaps I was? I thought about it for a moment. No, I wasn't. And I should know; I'd been the designated driver for decades and had never got anywhere near squiffy, never mind actually drunk. Not even when my divorce papers came through and my sister had sent me a bouquet and a bottle of pink champagne to celebrate. It didn't seem to hit the spot at the time and drinking a bottle of champagne on my own was a bit depressing.

'Yes, it's good isn't it?' he said, he jerked his head towards my cocktail, 'what's that you're drinking?'

I took a sip and coughed. 'Marmalade Martini.'

'Nice?'

'Strong,' I wiped my eyes a bit.

'I think I'll give it a miss,' he said with a grin.

With no apparent effort – funny that – he caught the attention of the stewardess who had dashed behind the bar to serve him and ordered a double espresso.

I sighed and wondered – as I have so many times in my life – if it might be possible to rewind the tapes at this moment and start again. And do things properly.

If it was, I would order a cappuccino and one of those nice-looking blueberry mini muffins in the basket on the bar. Apart from anything else, the cocktail was giving me a headache. Or perhaps it was the mixture of the champagne, wine, and this varied alcohol potion. And the steward hadn't used any measures, just slugged stuff into the cocktail shaker. Yes, that would explain it.

Hmm. I seemed to be making a lot of questionable choices with my new-found independence. Tom would have stopped me, I was sure of that. And Dan would have rolled his eyes at me and hissed 'Mum!' in the usual way.

But they weren't here and for once I didn't care, so instead – feeling rather glamorous – I sipped my Martini again and helped myself to some salted cashews from the porcelain bowl that the helpful steward had placed on the bar next to me.

I waved a vague hand around. 'So, you always travel with this airline? I mean, have you tried the others? I couldn't decide when I was booking.'

Cream Linen Woman finished her Martini, scooped all her clutter back into her bag, re-applied her crimson lipstick, and stood up.

The plane rocked slightly in a bit of turbulence (see, good job I hadn't climbed on to one of the tables), my companion gestured towards the comfortable looking bench she had vacated, and we sat down together.

It was rather exciting and totally unexpected. It was a long time since I had done this sort of thing. The longest meaningful conversations I had shared with men recently were with my solic-itor and the postman. This felt decidedly different. Was I flirting?

Was he? How could I tell? What were the rules these days? What should I say?

Up at the bar, the keen chaps were now talking in initials. Something about RFI's and SOW's, sneering at poor Gary and Patrick's parentage and intelligence and eating big slices of cake. I wondered where they had got those from? Did I need a slice of cake too? Probably not at this precise moment. But I'd remember it for later on. After all I was going to be here for a while.

'I've tried all the airlines over the years. I think this is the best one,' he said, 'certainly the most comfortable beds because I'm quite tall.'

He was too, probably over six feet and broad shouldered. Rather impressive.

I thought about asking a clumsy question about whether his wife agreed with him, but luckily thought better of it. I didn't want him to think I was flirting or potentially stalking. The thought was awful. Actually, I didn't quite know what I was doing. I wasn't the sort of woman to start engaging in personal conversations with strange men. But we were here now, and I couldn't exactly just walk off. He would have thought I was rude.

'And what business are you in?' I said.

I managed to spit out a crumb of cashew nut at this point. It landed on his chest. I froze in horror.

'Sorry—' I reached out a tentative hand.

'IT systems,' he said, brushing it off without comment, 'I focus on providing bespoke business solutions for the intermediary sector within the financial services industry.'

Hmm. I understood the individual words in this sentence but not the bigger picture.

I decided not to draw further attention to the cashew incident.

'That must be fascinating,' I said, trying to sound as though I had a clue what he was talking about.

His eyes twinkled. 'Well, it can be. My father started the company in the late eighties and when he died my brother and I inherited it. We have trebled the work force and it's doing well.'

'Good for you,' I said, 'it must have taken a lot of hard work. And a great deal of determination.'

'I suppose it did,' he said nodding thoughtfully, 'when I look back at it, which I don't very often, we've come a long way. Where we were and where we are now. Perhaps I've forgotten. I could do without the travel though, flights, and hotels; it's a terrible waste of time. I try to do Zoom calls as often as possible but some people in the industry are still pretty old school and insist on face to face meetings. And then I can't get out of it.'

'I think it sounds thrilling; to build something up like that. You must be doing a great job. But the travelling? Gosh, I love this plane. I've been so excited about this trip I haven't slept properly for weeks. I couldn't wait to get on board. Everyone is so nice, and the seats are so comfortable. And the food's good too. But I suppose if you do it all the time then the novelty soon wears off. Still I guess your brother can do it occasionally?'

My companion pulled a face that somehow made him look even more attractive.

'That would be nice,' he said at last, 'if it ever happened.'

It was a sort of 'closing down' statement. I felt I'd trampled onto dangerous territory. I sipped my rocket fuel drink and tried to think of something intelligent to say.

'By the way, what is an RFI?'

He blinked a bit. 'A Request for Information, why do you ask?'

'Just something I overheard. And what's a SOW? Apart from a female pig.'

'A Statement Of Work.'

At that moment the keen chaps on the far side of the bar roared with laughter and ordered more whisky.

'Ah, I see,' my companion grinned. He tilted his head towards them, 'when they start talking about an MBOC you know they are in trouble.'

I thought about it. 'My... um... Board Opposes Change?'

He laughed. 'Material Breach of Contract.'

'Ah yes, that makes more sense. That doesn't sound good.'

We discussed the weather in Australia. He told me a little about the meetings he'd had. We agreed how awful the traffic was in London and I confessed I hardly ever went there. On this trip he had visited the V&A and the Natural History Museum on his own and been taken to the theatre one evening by his business hosts. I felt a bit unsophisticated until he confessed he'd fallen asleep during the second act because he was so tired. And he laughed rather wistfully, and I felt a pang of sympathy for him. I'd felt a bit isolated already and this was the first and probably only time I would make this journey. What would it be like to do it every few months?

'It sounds lonely,' I said, 'I'm beginning to see that.'

'Yes,' he said rather quietly, 'it can be.'

'It doesn't sound much fun at all when I think about it.'

He looked thoughtful. 'It's not. Look would you like—'

He stopped suddenly and looked at his watch, an elegant, gold thing, not like the massive multi-dialled chunks of metal most men seemed to wear these days.

'No, no I mustn't get distracted. I don't want to, but I have a lot of work to do and I really must get on,' he said, 'no rest for the wicked.'

'Oh dear, poor you.'

He finished his coffee and stood up. 'Well, have fun, and make sure you get out and about. There are some lovely road trips you could take. See Queensland. The road to get there has been upgraded. And the Blue Mountains are just as wonderful as they ever were.'

'I will,' I said, wondering if I would.

He put his empty cup on the bar and went towards the red curtains that led to the cabin.

He hesitated as though he wanted to say more. 'Well... I hope you enjoy your trip,' he said, 'perhaps... well g'day.'

I was more than a little disappointed as I watched him go, because after all, I had been having an enjoyable chat with a handsome stranger. This made me feel unexpectedly optimistic. Apart from the cashew incident, I think I'd managed things really well.

I went back to my seat and started watching *Mission Impossible 4*. That cheered me up. I love that sort of thing; the more special effects and car chases, the better.

2

We had about an hour's stopover in Dubai and that was quite long enough for me. Definitely disorientated and feeling a bit weird, I had a walk around, following everyone who had got off my plane and hoping the person at the front of our flock knew where we were going. Everyone else seemed to have someone to talk to. Did they now realise I was travelling alone? Did they feel sorry for me or had I like many sensibly dressed, comfortably shod women of my age, just disappeared off the radar?

There were a lot of gorgeous waterfalls and gold decoration but there didn't seem to be many information boards. I found this very worrying. I'm the sort of person who thrives on information boards. The other concern was leaping to avoid the rather rude drivers who were beeping their horns and speeding in all directions through the terminal with electric carts filled with cross looking men and their many wives and children.

Eventually, I made my way through fresh rounds of security and men squinting at my passport and having my cabin bag X rayed again before we got back on another plane. Heaven knows what time it was, I had no idea, but when we got back onto the new plane ready to settle down for the next leg of my trip, I found an elegant pochette filled with goodies on my seat! I hadn't expected that! It was filled with all sorts of really great stuff. Creams and potions and socks and an eye mask and a toothbrush and hand mirror. I was like a kid with a party bag. You didn't get that sort of thing on budget airlines.

I had a go with a few of the wonderful smelling unguents, looking at myself curiously in the hand mirror to see if they'd had any effect. Then I spent a few minutes trying to work out the time difference. Did I need to take my cholesterol tablets? It might have been nine o'clock at night as far as my brain was concerned but a few minutes later, they brought us breakfast. And I found myself eating scrambled eggs with spinach and nutmeg. And some fried potatoes and salad. And some cheese. And a pot of apricot yogurt. And then a charming, smiling attendant came around with a basket of hot bread rolls and croissants. It was a meal that covered all the bases and I didn't have to prepare it or clear it away either.

After that, I went back to the bar, just to stretch my legs. Actually, I was wondering if he would be there. Several people were, still knocking back alcohol and the same intense looking chaps from the previous plane were still complaining about Gary and Patrick and drinking whisky. The barman was trying to persuade people to eat more cake too. It was surreal. I refused the cake again, although it did look good.

There was no sign of the handsome Australian businessman. Why hadn't I asked his name? Or said something casual like, 'well, let's meet up later and you can tell me more about providing bespoke business solutions for the – whatever it was – sector within the thingy industry because it's something I've always wanted to know more about.'

Maybe that would be pushing it a bit?

Perhaps we had exhausted our conversation and he didn't

have anything else to say to me. Maybe he had – awful thought – felt sorry for me to be travelling alone. Possibly he did this all the time on his travels, just to fill in the time. Perhaps it was a sort of game. Maybe it had been a sympathy flirt. A pity flirt. If it had been a flirt of any sort.

I went back to my seat and, after worrying if my luggage had followed me onto this plane, had a rather nice sleep on my electrically operated flat bed, wrapped up in a soft, grey blanket.

My God, Australia is a long way. I mean a really, *really* long way. How could I have forgotten? I slept quite satisfactorily and when I woke up there were still hours to go. I played around with the buttons on my seat again and took my earplugs out. Thank heavens I'd been given some in my goody bag because in the seat behind me a man was snoring. It put me in mind of the noise a cat might make if it was being forced through a trumpet.

Then I looked at the flight tracker on my entertainment screen to find out where we were. We were somewhere over the Indian Ocean with nothing below us or near us for thousands of miles. I could almost imagine the long, lonely plunge down into the sea. Perhaps Tom had a point.

Never wanting to leave us grubby, hungry, or thirsty, the cabin crew came around with more hot towels, food, and carts laden with drinks and snacks. I managed to show some maturity and just had iced water and then weakened and had a small cheese board. Which was lovely but not exactly small. Then I watched one and a half more films and had another snooze.

I peered out of my window several times but there was too much cloud cover to see anything. Until a couple of hours later it cleared and beneath us was a coastline.

I looked at the flight tracker again and it was true; it was my first glimpse of Australia for decades. I felt suddenly tearful, incredibly excited, and happy. The ocean was blue and rippled, a lone container ship ploughing along. I wondered if anyone on board would look up and wonder where this plane was going, anything about the people thirty-seven thousand feet above them as I often did. Probably not.

It was the first time since I met Tom that I'd travelled any distance on my own and I'd forgotten how it felt. There was nothing to distract me. No phone calls or text messages, no inter-ruptions from him or from anyone. I sat up a little straighter in my seat and felt brave and intrepid, which is not something I had felt for years. I could do this. Even at that moment I knew I had achieved something momentous. I didn't need help or praise or interference. My life was taking a different path, and this was the first step. Now I could just please myself. All the time.

Being on a journey that long was very odd. Sleep, wake up, doze a bit, eat something, watch a film. I went to the loo without someone hammering on the door asking for a clean shirt. While I was there, I looked at myself in the mirror. I looked solemn and tired but underneath it all, excited. I gave myself a broad smile. I liked feeling excited; there hadn't been that much excitement in my life for years.

I peered towards my reflection. Had I always had those wrin-kles? I spritzed myself with more free perfume and no one reeled back and complained I was gassing them.

* * *

We landed in Kingsford Smith airport exactly on schedule as the sun was rising out into a cloudless sky. It was nothing short of miraculous as far as I was concerned. How did they do that? I don't think I'd ever been on a bus that arrived on time. And don't get me started on trains.

Getting off the plane, I took a deep breath of Australian air for the first time in years. It seemed different somehow, although one airconditioned airport is probably much the same as any other. Then I reassured the immigration people I wasn't bringing any vegetables, fruit flies, or explosives into the country and went to reclaim my suitcases. Not long now and I'd meet up with Rowan again. I felt almost sick with excitement. I couldn't wait.

I watched as the bags trundled round on the conveyer belt. People leapt forwards and reclaimed all sorts of weird looking things. Massive cases wrapped in cling film. Golf clubs in huge plastic boxes, bags big, small, and in between. Cardboard boxes covered in tape and marked fragile (fat chance).

Across the concourse, I saw the handsome man from the plane grab a black case and wheel it off, peering at his phone as he did so. I gave a little wave but I don't think he saw me. Or perhaps he did but didn't have anything more to say to me. I don't suppose he wanted to be delayed by some random woman he didn't really know making idle conversation with him about her holiday. He probably had important things to do. Well so did I.

Eventually – after a very long time – I was left watching a single tartan holdall making its embarrassed progress around as the machinery under it clunked and thumped. I tutted, walked around the baggage carousel, and peered through the plastic flaps, hoping to see a helpful baggage handler. My sister is waiting out there in arrivals, I wanted to shout, hurry up!

Then suddenly with a flourish, my cases appeared. It looked as though someone had slung them contemptuously through the doors. Which was a cheek because they were new and certainly smarter than a lot of the others. I raced to grab them.

I hurried to the arrivals gate and there, twitching with excitement, was my sister Rowan, waiting for me with a big, home-made placard on a stick, covered in glitter and plastic flowers.

Which might have been nice, if she hadn't been standing right in front of the doors and if it hadn't read:

Welcome back from Re-Hab Elin!

Rowan dropped the placard which nearly clonked a passing pilot on the head, screamed, and swept me up into a big hug. We sobbed incoherently into each other's shoulders for a bit while other people arriving on the next flight read the placard and dodged round us.

'I can't believe you're here at last! Where on earth have you been?'

I wiped away my tears and explained about the problem with my suitcases. She didn't seem very bothered.

'Never mind that. You made it! You're back at last! I'm so happy!'

She bounced up and down a bit with excitement, and so did I. I felt young again. Like something had settled into place or a massive weight was being lifted.

'I'm here!' I agreed, feeling much better. 'I'm actually here!'

She leaned back and looked at me.

'Are you really shattered? Are you okay? You look almost grey you poor thing.'

'Do I? Well, I have been travelling for a long time. And I think I'm as jet lagged as it's possible to be.'

'Hmm, yes I guess that's it. So what did Tom say? Did he try and stop you?'

'I didn't tell him until I was at the airport and it was too late,' I said.

'Good for you.'

Rowan gave me another hug, grabbed one of my cases, and trundled it into people's ankles with unerring accuracy, talking all the way.

'Come on, the car's over here. At least I think it is. It might be over there. If we hurry it will only cost thirty dollars. It should have been ten but you took so long. I couldn't wait to see you! I've hardly slept a wink...'

She stopped in the middle of the road and hugged me again. We rocked back and forwards for a bit squeaking our excitement until someone tooted impatiently at us and we hurried on into the car park.

Rowan drove us carefully out of the airport and through a huge civic rebuilding plan. Everywhere there were massive yellow trucks, hundreds of traffic cones, and men in high viz jackets and hard hats staring into colossal holes propped up with steel girders. This was interspersed with stretches of new motorway that were equally as fast, crowded, and complicated as anything in England. I don't know what I had expected. Something smaller or simpler perhaps? Obviously I was way out of touch with my homeland. But then I hadn't been back for such a long time.

I felt a bit tearful again, and very annoyed with myself. How had I let that happen?

We'd had a comfortable home, enough money for a decent lifestyle, and yet my opinions, my preferences, my life hadn't seemed to be as important as his.

Why had I allowed Tom to be so controlling and not really noticed it?

Rowan had always had the ability to talk continuously and at speed, and nothing had changed. She chatted all the way as we left the motorway and onto smaller roads leading to a place I hadn't seen since for years. Kookaburra Bay.

I leaned forward in my seat, delighted by the advertising

hoardings, the road signs, the houses filled with Australians, thrilled to be back, longing to see the Pacific Ocean again. Remembering the summers I had spent there with a gaggle of school friends. It seemed another age.

I remembered us trying to bleach our hair with lemon juice, talking about boys and all of us absolutely desperate to leave Australia and see the world. And what had I done? Got my qualifications, gone to England, found a teaching job, and married my head of department. A man who increasingly stopped being easy going and fun. A man who was happiest controlling everything and who had feigned a strange and un-named illness every time I had tried to arrange a trip back home. Why had I let him get away with it? I suppose like the Australian man growing his business, it didn't seem quite so bad at the time, but thinking about it...

Well, my life now was different. I had new chances. The rest of my life was ahead of me. I should stop looking back.

'Maggie and Banjo can't wait to see you. Banjo phoned me this morning to tell you they will be back this afternoon. Maggie says she can't concentrate on anything with all the excitement,' Rowan said as we started the swerving descent towards the coast.

'They've been away? Where have they been?'

'Ballarat. For a wedding party yesterday otherwise they would have been at the airport with me. A couple of their friends have tied the knot after being together for forty-two years. And they wanted to find out more about the Eureka Rebellion. Well, you know them; always tempted by a bit of civil disobedience.'

'Are they okay?' I asked.

'Absolutely! Banjo's a stubbie short of a six pack from time to time but Maggie says it's just him being evasive. Seventy-three is nothing over here; they are both in fine form. Now then, don't forget to look!'

I looked, and there it was. That fabulous, wonderful view

down to the Pacific I remembered. I'd been on Google Earth many times over the years so I could see it. Every time, it had made me gasp. Just as it did today. A glorious undulating landscape of trees and then beyond it, mile upon mile of golden sand, turquoise sea, and creamy spray. A few surfers looking like black dots bobbing about on the water beyond the breaking waves.

'Brilliant!' I said, bursting into tears, 'absolutely brilliant.'

'Sorry you left now, are you?' Rowan grinned over at me and patted my arm.

Yes, in a way I was. But my life in England hadn't been that bad. Not at first. Not really. And if I was honest, a lot of the years had just been a blur. Although it was worrying to think that Dan might have turned into a younger version of his father if things hadn't changed. I hoped his new girlfriend would help sort that out too. Perhaps she would open his eyes to the world. Maybe she would...

I shook my head. I wasn't going to think about that now. I was just going to enjoy myself for once. Spread my cramped wings.

'So did you meet anyone nice on the plane in the posh seats? Any celebs?'

'There was one very pleasant man. He was incredibly handsome too. I saw him a couple of times, in the airport, and on the plane – we had a lovely chat – and I saw him at the baggage reclaim.'

'Neat! What does he do?'

'No idea. He did tell me, but I didn't understand. Something to do with bespoke something.'

'What was his name then?'

'I didn't ask.'

Rowan tutted. 'Strewth Elin, I know it's been a while but these days you need to do better than that if you're picking up men.'

I laughed at the very idea. 'I'm not picking up men; we just had a bit of a chat. I'm not looking for men at all, actually. I'm still not completely free of the last one. He keeps texting me.'

'Tom? What an arse. Why don't you block him? Well, doesn't mean you can't have a bit of fun now. You'll meet Shane when we get back. He's such a laugh. Younger than me too, which is a bonus.'

Rowan turned to wink at me which was perhaps a mistake as the car veered across the road. I grabbed the steering wheel.

'Sorry sorry sorry,' she gasped, 'God, I'm glad there are no cops about. You'd think I knew better!'

'How much younger than you is Shane?'

'Ten years. He's forty-six.'

'Ten years younger? Really? You don't look ten years older than him on Zoom!'

'Can you believe it? I didn't make a thing about it because I was sure you wouldn't approve. He's such fun. He owns a café on the beach called Wipe-Out. You should find a younger bloke too. They're up all hours, ready for anything. He's keeping me young. Having said that, I left him in bed this morning. He was up with his mates playing on the computer all night. Some shoot 'em up game.'

Wasn't he a bit old for that? I tried to imagine myself with a man ten years younger than me, spending all his free time on *Call Of Duty*. So Shane was forty-six and my ex-husband was sixty-one. Theoretically old enough to be Shane's father. How bizarre. I don't think my years with Tom had kept me young; the reverse was true if anything.

Rowan was dressed in a flowing tie-dye skirt, flip-flops, and a strappy top. Her shoulders were toned and tanned and gleaming with glittery body lotion that smelled of flowers. She had plaited several strands of her red hair, and each was tipped with a feather or a shell which flicked around her shoulders as she talked. She looked bright and engaging.

I looked down at myself. The contrast between us was stark. I was in my usual outfit of comfortable trousers and polo shirt. I even had Velcro fastenings on my shoes to add to the dull, middle aged look. In my defence, I had read that long haul flight could cause your feet to swell. But that was no excuse for dressing like an old woman who didn't make any sort of effort, who bought clothes because they fitted.

'Here we are. You haven't seen my place, have you? Except on WhatsApp. Home at last! Thank God for that. I got away with it,' Rowan sighed as we pulled into the drive of her house in a sweeping loop, narrowly missing the dustbins.

Rowan's house was a typical Queenslander bungalow. A single storey house set on stilts with a veranda across the front. Outside there was a battered 'Rat Look' VW camper van rusting gently in the sunshine, with surfboards on the roof and towels draped across the back seats.

'Shane's still home!' Rowan said rather accusingly, 'he should have gone to Wipe-Out by now. He told me he needed to be in early. Lazy sod. Come on, come and meet him properly.'

Shane was in the kitchen dressed in a salt-bleached t-shirt and board shorts, making himself some coffee. He was taller than I'd expected, tanned with greying, blond shaggy hair and his face lit up when he saw Rowan in a way that was rather lovely.

'Here she is! Here's my best girl,' he said, sweeping her up into a hug. He grinned at me over the top of her head and held out a freckled hand. 'And you're Elin! Here at last!'

'Well of course she is, isn't it brilliant? Can you see the family resemblance?' Rowan said.

She posed with her head next to mine and a silly grin on her face.

Shane took his time. 'Nah, not really.'

Well, that was nice, although looking at Rowan – gleaming with health and glowing with happiness – I wasn't surprised he couldn't see it. In comparison I probably looked a wreck. Crazy with jet lag, dull and pale from so many English winters.

'Cuppa?' he said cheerfully.

'Tea please,' I said.

'Do we have tea, Ro?' Shane said with a frown, 'I mean proper tea, not that silage stuff you like.'

Rowan pushed him aside. 'Of course we do. I got some in specially. Grown in Yorkshire. In that drawer. Aren't you supposed to be in work? You told me you were opening up, you mongrel.'

Shane sipped his coffee. 'I got Cheryl to do it. I'm on my way; there has to be some benefit to being the boss. I guess you ladies want to gossip?' He tipped his coffee into a tin mug. 'I'll take this with me then. And see you later?'

'Of course,' I said.

'Look forward to it! We're having a barbie, eh?'

He winked at me, gave Rowan's bottom a resounding slap as he passed her and left us to it.

'He does seem fun,' I said.

Rowan made my tea and then waved to him through the window as the throaty roar of the campervan heralded his departure.

'Yes, he's one of a kind,' she said. She didn't seem exactly pleased about something. 'I told you he was,' she said, 'Everyone loves Shane. Well everyone except someone who thinks he's a beach bum. I guess he is really. He spends all his time at the beach or in the café pretending to work. Maggie thinks he's a scream. She and Banjo are so excited you're back at last. They'll be over for the barbie later. I've got a load of shrimp in the fridge. And some steaks if you fancy one?'

'Sounds great,' I said, my mouth watering, 'I don't think I've eaten anything sensible for hours. Just snacks and airline food.'

'Bring your tea, I'll show you your room.' Rowan whisked away down the hallway, the feathers in her hair flicking around her neck. I caught sight of myself in a mirror; my hair was lank, badly brushed and in need of attention. My sister was only two years younger than me. I had an awful feeling I looked a lot more than fifty-eight. Perhaps I should make more of an effort?

'How do you do that to your hair?' I asked when I caught up with my sister.

Rowan looked blank. 'Oh this? Shane did it, sometimes I do. I just get the bits I can reach and off we go. Why, do you like it?'

She admired herself in the mirrored wardrobe door.

'Yes I think I do,' I said, yawning hugely, 'I think it's fun.'

Rowan came and give me a hug. 'You're going to have a lot of fun now you're back; I'm going to make sure you do. Now why don't you have a little nap? I've got some things to do and Shane won't be home until later. We've got plenty of time to catch up. Slip yourself under the Doona and grab some shut eye. Then you'll be bright-eyed later for your welcome home party.'

'Welcome home party! What a great idea! Thank you!'

She left me to it and I pulled off my clothes. Navy-blue trousers and shirt. They looked as limp as I felt. I bundled them up rather angrily and stuffed them into the wastepaper bin. I wanted excitement and colour back in my life. I wanted to buy something new, colourful, and frivolous. Just for a change.

3

I slept for a couple of hours and woke feeling much better. It was the first time for ages that I hadn't woken up stressed and angry.

I'd got into the habit of having ridiculous imaginary conversations with Tom. Calling him names, questioning his decisions, even – and this would have been the thing he would have hated the most – laughing at him. Saying all the things I wished I'd said about his negativity. Remembering his unkindness and his lies. It was a bad and very unhelpful way to start the day. Recently I'd even been waking up in the night to have the last, metaphorical word.

There's nothing worse than trying to forgive someone who's not sorry or hoping for an apology I'd never get.

Somehow now things were different. I felt new stirrings of confidence, I couldn't change the past, but I could be in control of my future.

I could hear Rowan moving around somewhere, the occasional rattle of cutlery or the closing of a cupboard door. There was the low murmur of a radio in the background.

I lay still for a bit, looking at the room. Painted turquoise with white units and woodwork and a multicoloured rag rug. It was so absolutely 'Rowan' that it made me smile. There were bird-patterned curtains at the window, although no birds I'd seen recently. Parrots, Galahs and some smaller ones with flashes of blue. What were they then? I dug around in my memory banks. Ah yes, Superb Fairywrens.

The sun was shining through the fabric, and there was the matching sound of birdsong outside. It was all so colourful and jolly.

I thought about things for a while, my life and my clothes. Even my hair, let's be honest. I suddenly wanted to do a bit better, show a bit of spark. I was at the start of an adventure, one I'd wanted for ages. I was so happy I felt almost giddy.

I got up and washed my face and then opened my suitcase, hoping to find something bright and cheerful to wear to match my mood. Of course, there wasn't anything.

I suddenly had the mad urge to put on a bright dress and weave feathers and ribbons in my hair too. Perhaps Rowan had something I could borrow. I opened the wardrobe; it was half full of clothes, but I guessed they were Shane's. A load of battered wire coat hangers with scruffy t-shirts and numerous pairs of jeans, plus half a dozen wetsuits hanging like limp bodies at one end.

I unpacked a few things from my case and pulled on a new, striped, grey cotton dress which was about the lightest garment I possessed. I brushed my hair and clipped it back off my neck. I peered at myself in the mirror. Rowan was right: I did look a bit pale, and a grey dress did nothing to improve that. I dabbed on a bit of make-up. Then I went to find another cup of tea.

'Nice sleep?' Rowan was standing at the sink with a colander full of prawns, 'Maggie phoned. They're almost home. When they get back they're going to freshen up and be straight over to see you. They are so excited.'

'Me too! I can't wait to see them. Now, can I do anything to help?'

'Just sit there and talk to me,' Rowan said, swooping down to kiss my cheek and give me a hug.

I cast an eye over the worktop next to her. There was a pile of cereal bowls stacked into a precarious pile and a metal jug filled with dirty cutlery. I couldn't help myself; I wanted to sort it out.

'Shall I do the washing up?' I said.

'No, you will not do the washing up!' Rowan said firmly, 'Shane's supposed to do it. That's his job. I've been waiting for three days and all he does it take a clean bowl. We'll run out soon and then he'll have to do it. He's not getting away with it.'

'But he will have been at work all day,' I said, my fingers itching to fill the sink with some hot soapy water.

'Work,' Rowan snorted, 'don't make me laugh. He knows the rules. Don't pander to him.'

This was an eye opener. Tom had never done the washing up in his life as far as I knew. But worse than that: I had probably never asked him to. I went and gave Rowan a hug. She might have been the annoying little sister who tagged along when I was growing up but now I was impressed by her attitude, maybe even in awe of her.

Instead, we went outside to the patio area and Rowan pulled out a table which she covered with a cotton, flamingo-patterned cloth. There were red plates and green glass tumblers and a pile of yellow paper napkins. Everything was mismatched and garish but here in the sunshine with the bluest of skies overhead, somehow it seemed to work.

At home I had a table and chairs in the garden under a water-proof cover and a plastic box of what I called 'picnic stuff', hangover from Tom's rare forays into al fresco dining; one of the few things he hadn't wanted to fight over when we got divorced, although he'd kept the barbecue of course. It suddenly seemed a bit unimaginative and boring. Perhaps when I got home I could do something like Rowan? Make more of my garden. After all, I used to like eating outdoors; my childhood memories were returning.

Barbeques in the back yard and picnics on the beach. I'd forgotten about that. But Tom – well he didn't. There was always a lot of fuss about wasps and a blank refusal to help once he stopped flourishing the barbeque tongs like a MasterChef contestant. So, we didn't. God, I had been an idiot, letting him get away with it.

I helped move all the cool boxes and chairs that had collected on the patio and did some thinking. Unpleasant as it was, I was beginning to realise I had been an accomplice to Tom's controlling behaviour. I had the growing feeling I was partly to blame too. What was it called these days? Being an enabler.

Perhaps it was being here, back with my family.

The years of his influence had already started to fade away. Since the divorce and the move into my first home with all my things around me and no Tom barging in complaining about something, I'd begun to see the light again. I felt even more liberated here. I was beginning to feel different inside.

* * *

Shane returned just before five o'clock, accompanied by several friends who piled out of the VW van, lugging cool boxes and bags with them. They were scruffy, absolutely delightful, and incredibly noisy. I certainly wasn't used to that. They did everything – from opening beers, tipping crisps into plastic bowls, or lighting the BBQ – with expansive gestures and whooping laughter. Someone put on some music and someone else turned it up. I asked Rowan if the neighbours would complain and she looked confused.

'I shouldn't think so; they're here too. Can't have a barbie without Will and Polly,' she pointed at a couple at the far end of the patio, nursing a baby in a sling and dancing around without a care in the world. They came over to welcome me and introduce me to little Nuala who slumbered obligingly throughout.

I thought of our neighbours in Cheltenham – a vicar and his wife – who would come around to complain at the drop of a hat. One evening, we had a small gathering of Tom's departmental staff round to celebrate the end of an Ofsted inspection and the vicar's wife had planted herself at the front door to complain after ten minutes because I had opened a window.

'How are you feeling?' Shane said to me in passing. He gave me a knockout grin and a friendly punch on the shoulder. 'A bit crook, eh? Always a bugger isn't it, travelling? You'll perk up.'

'Oh,' I said, wondering just how bad I looked in my dull dress and sandals. Rowan had changed into a floaty maxi dress in gorgeous shades of blue and green and was barefoot on the stone slabs. My first reaction had been to think she looked a bit like a hippy, but now I could see she looked comfortable and attractive. I, meanwhile, was already feeling hot, my feet sticking unpleasantly to the inside of my new shoes.

I was given a pint of lager in a plastic mug and introduced to Shane's friends: Elliot, Divvy, Trev the Tank, and Bazza. They were all rather lovely, asking me about my trip: how long I was staying, what did I think of being back in Australia.

'I'm having a great time,' I said.

'Course you are!' Bazza said, putting a muscly arm around my shoulder and enveloping me with the smell of coconut board wax, 'welcome home. Once a Joey always a Joey eh?'

'My family came out in the sixties from Wolverhampton. Ten-pound Poms they were. Name of Hutchins. Big family. Do you know of them?' Trev the Tank asked (so called because of his physique, which was impressive).

'No, I've never been there.'

'Shame, Wolverhampton looks a cool place, I keep meaning to go back. I've got cousins and everything.'

Not to be outdone, the others came over and told me about their relations in Scotland and Basingstoke. Then they got bored with that and tried to get me out surfing with them.

'Not a chance, you must be joking, not at my age. I tried when I was younger and I wasn't that good. And since then I've heard too much about shark attacks and box jellyfish,' I said.

'Aw, go on. You don't want to take any notice of that. That's just a bit of bad luck that is. And whadda you mean, at your age? You're never too old to have fun, are you? No age limit on that last time I looked. More likely to get run over that's what I say,' Divvy said, rubbing sand out of his grey hair into his beer, 'live a little.'

I boldly kicked off my sandals at that point, enjoying the gritty feel of the warm patio slabs under my feet.

'Yeah but be fair Div, I heard a bloke got bit by a shark up near Wollongong about a week ago.' Elliot added with a knowing shake of his head.

I gasped. 'How awful! What happened?'

Elliot shrugged and took a slurp on his beer.

'Dunno. I just know he got bit. His board was wrecked. I expect he's all right.'

How could he not know? I wanted to press him for dates and times but then they had a spirited, beer-fuelled debate about politics which continued in vehemence and volume as the sky above us suddenly changed into a fabulous, fuchsia-red sunset. Then

Shane came out with a washing up bowl full of prawns, and there was a loud cheer of approval.

'Hurry up Shane-o, I'm so hungry I could eat a horse and chase the jockey!' Divvy bellowed.

This seemed enormously funny to me in my slightly squiffy state, and I had to lean against the wall of the house for a moment so I didn't spill my beer. When I at last stopped laughing, it seemed there was a sudden lull in the noise levels and Shane gave a groan.

'Oh blimey, what now?'

I followed his gaze. Rowan was standing in the doorway to the kitchen looking nervous and apologetic.

'Visitor for you, Shane. He's been ringing the bell for ages he says. I didn't hear him. Anyway... sorry about this Elin...'

She moved to one side and a man followed her out on to the patio. Someone tall, wearing a respectable looking suit and tie. The contrast with the rest of us in our casual clothes, bare feet and party mood was extreme. Someone turned the music down.

'Shane, sorry to interrupt your evening but you never answer your phone. You know why I'm here.'

'Oh bloody hell Kit, can't you give it a rest?' Shane muttered.

It was the man from the plane!

I couldn't quite believe it and took another long look. My heart did a strange little skip of excitement.

Yes, it was definitely him.

I took a gulp of my drink rather hastily and of course it went down the wrong way. The newcomer looked at me coughing and spluttering, a wet stain of beer down the front of my new dress and a flicker of recognition crossed his face.

'Good God! What are you doing here? You're the last person I thought to see,' he said.

'You two know each other?' Bazza said, puzzled.

'No not really,' I said, my voice still rather croaky.

'Well this is my brother Kit,' Shane said with no enthusiasm, 'Fair go mate, your timing's immaculate.'

At that precise moment there was a cheerful call of, 'Yoo-hoo,' and 'G'day you bastards,' and my uncle and aunt came around the side of the house. I burst into tears.

Shane turned to greet them.

'Banjo! Maggie! Well aren't you two a sight for sore eyes! There she is, back safe and sound!'

My aunt in a citrus-yellow dress with a blue feather in her hair ran towards me with the speed and accuracy of a guided missile. My uncle came to embrace us both, laughing and crying at the same time. Then Rowan came to join in and we had the first proper, family hug we had shared for a long time.

'She's back! My girl's back!' Banjo shouted, 'I can't believe it. She's back!'

'Oh Banjo, I've missed you,' I sobbed, 'I've missed you both so much.'

'And we've missed you,' Maggie sniffled.

Eventually Banjo pulled away to wipe his eyes with a blue, spotty handkerchief and blow his nose.

He looked just as I remembered, older of course, perhaps a bit thinner, in some disreputable khaki shorts, a Grateful Dead t-shirt, and a joke bushman's hat with corks round the brim. Maggie was doing a little dance on the spot with excitement, her blue feather drooping over one eye. Perhaps they looked a bit crazy?

I realised everyone, Kit Pascoe included, was watching us. The boys smiling and pleased and raising their beer mugs to us, Kit expressionless and very still.

I felt slightly uneasy; it was as though two worlds had collided. Kit had been there at the start of this journey and now he was here again. I'd thought he was rather lovely when we chatted on the plane, but evidently Shane didn't and presumably he knew his brother better than I did.

Oh bloody hell Kit, can't you give it a rest?

Give what a rest? What was happening here?

That evening, as I reconnected with my family, he was suddenly there too.

I turned my back on him and the four of us stood and hugged each other a bit more and all of us talked at once. Very loudly. I'd forgotten about that too.

4

Kit Pascoe's arrival put a damper on the evening for a while. Which, considering we had all been looking forward to it for so long, was unforgiveable.

He and Shane went into the house where they started a very long, extremely loud argument which we all shamelessly listened in to until Trev the Tank tactfully turned the music up again and we carried on eating prawns and chucking the shells into a bucket. At one point I wanted to go inside and wash my hands, but I didn't dare.

Maggie and Banjo were in excellent form, thrilled to have me back and prepared to carry on into the small hours if at all possible. Which it wasn't really, when Rowan was looking so stressed and Shane only coming back outside occasionally with a face like thunder so he could grab another beer.

'What's happening with him?' Maggie hissed. 'Is that really Shane's brother? We haven't met him, have we? I think I would have remembered him. They aren't very alike.'

'No,' Rowan said furiously, 'I've met him once or twice before but he's not the sort to socialise. Kit's a miserable bastard with the manners of a... a bloody dingo.'

'I've heard dingoes can be quite nice,' Banjo said mildly, popping another prawn into his mouth, 'very sociable creatures. I was reading about them. D'you know a dingo pack largely consists of a mated pair, their current year's pups, and occasionally a previous year's offspring.'

Rowan rolled her eyes. 'Fascinating. He's been going on at Shane for months, endless emails and messages. Now he's back and come to rattle his bars in person. Poor Shane.'

This was so much at odds with my impression of Kit Pascoe that I was confused.

'What does he want?' I asked.

'No idea, Shane won't talk about it,' Rowan answered.

'But why not? What's the problem?'

Whatever his true nature, I was suddenly irritated that Kit Pascoe was hogging the conversation topic even though he wasn't even out here.

Evidently my aunt felt the same way.

'Oh come on Elin, forget about him. Tell me more about how you are, what you've been doing. And how's little Danny?' She hugged me again, 'I'm so pleased to see you back. I've been counting down the hours, honestly I have. And Banjo's been beside himself.'

I laughed. 'Dan's not little any more. He's six foot two, doing well, teaching of course and he has his own flat and still with his girlfriend Skye. She's a bit scary and gothic to look at but she's lovely. Once you get past the tattoos and the black eyeliner. She's good for Dan too I think. He was starting to get very introverted. She's been encouraging him to go out to events and the theatre these days in a way he never used to. He even went to Glastonbury which opened his eyes a bit.'

'Well good for him. That sort of thing is far more fun with company isn't it? Look at me and Banjo, in our seventies now, and we're having a new lease of life going off on our travels. You're never too old, that's my motto.'

Yes, that was true, and I'd relished my solo flight to Australia. I'd even enjoyed getting to Heathrow on my own. I was quite proud of being more independent these days, and it was much more fun without a disapproving presence at my elbow.

'And that miserable git you were married to? How is Tom coping with new fatherhood? I bet the baby isn't sleeping?' Maggie said with a naughty gleam in her eye.

'No, she's not, and apparently she's teething too.'

'Well good for her. I for one couldn't be more delighted,' Banjo said with a wink, refilling Maggie's beer glass from the plastic jug, 'not that I wish the little mite any harm. But there you go, marry a woman half your age and you're bound to stir up trouble of some sort. He must have been having a mid-life crisis or something. Isn't that what they say?'

'I don't know and I don't care,' I said, 'I was just glad to get away from him and his mid-life crisis.'

'Well you look very pale and you've lost weight, haven't you?' Maggie said, 'perhaps you should wear something a bit brighter? Cheer yourself up? You always used to when you were little. You liked purple and Rowan liked yellow. I remember those dresses I made for you when Noreen got married, do you? I've probably got a photo of you wearing them somewhere. You were outdoors all hours, getting into all sorts of trouble. Brown as a berry you were.'

I suddenly had a memory, sharp and almost tear-jerking. Rowan and me on the beach, perhaps I had been ten and she was eight. Our toes were buried in the sand, watching the waves roll in as we licked ice cream and planned our next adventure. There had been rockpools and kites and Maggie sitting in the shade of a parasol reading a magazine. Banjo had come to join us after work, bringing a flask of tea and a paper bag of sweets.

'Here they are, my three favourite ladies,' he'd said.

It had been a moment of pure joy. Why did I have to remember that now? It made me feel restless and angry. Almost weepy at the same time.

Maggie delved into her capacious bag.

'That reminds me, I brought this for you to look at.'

She pulled out a black, leather photo album which I recognised immediately. It was my wedding pictures.

'Oh God!'

'I know. I don't know what you want me to do with it but I thought you'd like to see it.'

'Not particularly—'

It was too late; she was already pulling her chair up next to mine and leafing through the pages. Pulling aside the tissue paper between the pictures.

'See this? How pretty you looked? And Rowan in that lovely dress. I don't know why she hated it so much.'

'Did she? She never told me,' I said.

'Well, she didn't want to hurt your feelings, did she. And look at this. Remember?'

I was young, bright eyed, my hair blowing in the fresh wind that cut across the churchyard. Tom looking pleased in a new suit, his mother Sylvia by his side in a dark maroon dress and jacket looking sour and disapproving. She was holding her rose and baby's breath corsage in her hand because she said it would spoil the fabric of her jacket if she pinned it on.

'And here, I found some pictures of you when you started school,' Maggie opened a packet of photographs, tucked into the back of the album, the colours starting to deteriorate with age.

There I was, grinning in my new school uniform, turning at

the front door as my parents waved me off. Me with some friends on the beach, all of us laughing, all skinny and brown after long summer days spent in the sunshine. Had I ever been that thin? That pretty?

Another one where I was dressed for a party in a bright-red maxi dress, my sister grinning next to me in bright blue. One at the beach in a purple and green striped kaftan over a yellow swimming costume. Rowan and I as teenagers looking excited in pink bridesmaid's dresses.

In every picture I was smiling or laughing. Arms around friends. I looked quite pretty and confident, eager to get out and see the world. Why and how had I changed?

Then forward to a formal picture of Tom and me with Dan at his graduation and everything was different. It was just a few years before we divorced. I was in a dull, navy-blue suit, proud and pale and still ignorant of what was going on in Tom's life. Tom, puffed up with self-importance, had told Dan that every spotty kid went to university those days and his new degree wasn't worth much in the real world. Dan's expression. Hurt, slightly bewildered.

Tom and I had a massive argument on the way home, the car filled with my anger and Tom's indignation. *God woman, calm down, I was only joking.* That's what Tom always said on the very few occasions when he was pulled up on something.

There was a pause in the conversation and for a moment we could hear the muffled sound of Shane and his brother in the house still arguing.

Banjo cleared his throat loudly and neatly changed the subject.

'Not much peace in there by the sounds of it. Anyway, never mind them Elin, let me tell you about Ballarat...'

We talked for a while about their latest trip away and they told me they had another 'meet up' planned soon near Cairns.

'Almost as far as you can go and not fall off,' Maggie said cheerfully, 'up the top of Queensland. It'll be the furthest we've even been. We promised to meet up with a gang of friends we know, The Silver Surfers. They're having an eightieth birthday party and it's going to be a belter.'

They were both in their seventies; was it wise for them to be meandering about the continent on their own? Everyone knew about the bushfires and the deadly snakes and spiders Australia had to offer the unwary traveller. I'd seen David Attenborough and Steve Irwin. I knew.

Rowan sidled up to the house, opened the patio door a crack, and listened for a moment, her face troubled. It had all gone quiet. I went and grabbed her and pulled her back to the table at the end of the garden.

'So, tell me some more about their travels?' I said, 'I mean is it safe?'

Rowan's face cleared. 'Safe? Of course it is! They are Silver Surfers, that's all; they haven't joined a Hell's Angels Chapter. I don't think they do much actual surfing, although with that lot you never know. They are just people like Maggie and Banjo who go off for weeks at a time, sometimes months, just driving around Australia and getting pissed up at regular intervals as far as I can tell.'

'Cultural trips,' Banjo said, one index finger held up, 'we're finding out about this beautiful country. Before us lot came over here and started building on it. Getting back in touch with nature, finding out about the indigenous tribes and their ways. They are great characters too. Always polite and welcoming. Lovely people, considering the way they were treated.'

'How long have you been doing that? I hope you are careful,' I said doubtfully.

'Well we don't go bungee jumping, or white-water rafting,'

Maggie chuckled, 'Norm did that once and lost his false teeth. We're not daft.'

'I'm glad to hear it,' I muttered, 'but what if you break down?'

Rowan put her arm around my shoulder and hugged me.

'Always the worrier, aren't you? They've been doing it for ages, ever since Banjo retired and Maggie started to have cabin fever with him under her feet all day. You know they bought a motorhome. Well, it's changed their lives. They're hardly ever here for long; you should be flattered they came home early especially for you and didn't stay on for the wedding weekend party too.' She threw a nervous look at the house. 'It's no good; I'd better go and see what's going on in there. Bloody man coming here uninvited and spoiling your party.'

I stayed chatting with the others. Maggie had lost the blue feather somewhere. Banjo put his bushman's hat on Divvy's head and both of them roared with laughter. It was very different from what I was used to. It was fun, pure and simple, and I suddenly realised I really could relax and enjoy it.

* * *

Sometime after that the jetlag started to get the better of me and the party started to break up. The neighbours took their baby home. Nuala was still sleeping very peacefully in her sling so evidently was used to this sort of occasion. Had I ever taken Dan to a party when he was that small? Were we ever invited to one? Tom had always had good and clear reasons for not doing something he didn't want to.

At last Shane came outside looking thunderous and grabbed a beer, which he downed very quickly. Kit had gone without any farewells. Why was that man so angry? He'd seemed completely different on the plane, but why? Which was the real Kit?

Trev and Bazza started talking to Shane about the surf conditions for the following day, and gradually Shane recovered his
cheerful mood and they had a good-natured argument about
what time to meet the following morning 'before work'. Which
made Rowan laugh.

'Before work, you're having a joke, aren't you?'

'I'll be out there at seven, see if I'm not,' Shane said, looking
around for confirmation from his friends, 'and then I'll open up
the Wipe-Out and everything will be fair. You wait and see. When
did I ever not?'

'Many times, Shane. Many times,' Divvy said with a snort, 'but
then it's not as though you need the money you idle bastard.'

This made me think. Now what had Kit said about his brother
on the plane? About sharing the workload.

That would be nice if it ever happened.

Perhaps that was a clue.

* * *

The following morning, I was up and about very early thanks to
my jetlag, waiting impatiently for Rowan and Shane to stir. Now
that I was here, I didn't want to waste a minute; I wanted to be
with my family as much as possible, I wanted to catch up on the
time together and find out what else I'd missed.

I had a shower and looked in my suitcase for something to
wear that matched my new enthusiasm for the day ahead. There
didn't seem to be anything that did the trick. Just the usual
matching skirts and cardigans, some rather baggy jeans that did
nothing for me, and a few jersey dresses that had seemed a good
idea because they wouldn't crease. Not because they flattered me
or made me feel good wearing them. I pulled one on over my
head and looked at my reflection. I could have been a police iden-

tikit for a middle aged, middle height, middle sized woman. How
dull.

I remembered Maggie's photographs from the previous night.
How my life had been filled with colour and laughter, or at least
that's how it seemed. I had changed into someone far less confident, more cautious. What should I do about that? Should I do
anything? Did it even matter? I rifled through my make-up bag,
looking for mascara. I could at least start to make an effort.
Perhaps I needed some blusher.

* * *

Good as his word, Shane was shambling around at six thirty
looking for coffee. He picked out a wet suit from the wardrobe,
took whatever else he needed, and was ready to leave by quarter
to seven.

'See,' he said with a wink as he left, 'told you I'd be out on
time.'

'Are you okay?' I said, 'I mean after last night and all that... you
know.'

Shane looked a bit blank for a moment. 'What, Kit? Aw don't
take any notice of him, he's all mouth and trousers. Nothing to
worry about.'

The roar of his VW van starting up woke Rowan and she came
out still in her dressing gown. She ran over to give me a hug.

'I'm so excited! I woke up and I thought, did I just dream that
or is Elin really here? I can't believe you're actually standing in my
kitchen! Did you sleep okay?' she said.

'Well, no, not really,' I said, 'and I've been waiting for you to
wake up for ages!'

'Good old jetlag eh? Oh well, you'll get over it. Anything you'd
like to do today?'

'I want to go shopping. I haven't anything nice to wear,' I looked down at my dress and shrugged, 'nothing flattering anyway. I want something bright and cheerful that goes with all this sunshine.'

Rowan's face lit up. 'Excellent, I know just the place to take you in Kookaburra; a friend of mine runs it. She sells a lot of different things and if you don't find anything you like, I'll be very surprised. We'll think outside the box, and you can try on everything. Jilly won't mind. She loves a challenge.'

I wasn't quite sure how to take this.

'I'll even buy lunch if you don't find something you like. There's a brill place on the sea front, I take Maggie there sometimes.'

'She is in good form, isn't she? Very lively,' I had memories of my ex-mother in law and her many ailments, her constant complaints, her drawer full of pills. 'No health problems?'

'No, don't think so.'

'Haven't you asked?'

Rowan looked puzzled. 'I suppose they'd tell me if they did.'

She made me a mug of tea and passed it across the table.

'You should see Maggie and Banjo when they are off on their trips. They are so funny. They have a routine; everything goes in the right place in the right order, nothing like they are at home where they hang everything on the chairs and never put anything away.'

I suddenly felt all fuzzy with warmth and happiness. Being back with my family. Being a proper part of their lives again. Even if bits of it did seem chaotic.

'Oh, it's so good to see them. I've missed them such a lot. Zoom calls are all very well but it's not the same—'

I stopped. That's what Kit had said wasn't it? Which reminded me.

'So what happened with Shane and his brother last night?'

Rowan shrugged. 'I didn't ask. I've learned not to get too involved where Kit is concerned. But you actually knew him? That's what I can't get over.'

'I told you, we met at Heathrow and later on the plane. We don't exactly know each other.'

'You said you'd met an Australian businessman and he was pleasant. Really?'

'Yes, he was, he was lovely. Easy to talk to and funny. But perhaps he was just being sociable on a long trip. So you've no idea what he wanted?'

'Nope. Only that it was something to do with the family business. Something that provoked a massive row. There's a company their father set up. Something to do with IT. Kit runs it and Shane is a partner. A sleeping partner. I expect that's what the problem is; too much sleeping. Shane's a great sleeper.' Rowan smiled.

What was it Kit had said on the plane?

That would be nice if it ever happened.

Perhaps Kit had been left to do all the work and Shane hadn't pulled his weight? Yes, that would annoy anyone.

I thought about it. 'Bespoke business systems for the – something or other. He told me a bit about that on the plane. How he'd been travelling all over the world, building up business. So that's what Divvy meant last night when he said Shane didn't need to worry about money?'

She shrugged. 'Suppose so.'

I frowned, exasperated. 'Rowan, don't you know?'

I knew practically to the last penny how much was in my bank account before we divorced. Well apart from Tom's secret account that paid for various hotel trips and jewellery for Ashley. I didn't find out about that until our finances were sorted out and he'd had to own up. And he had been commenting on my over-spending at the time. Bloody lying, deceitful, hypocritical sod.

'No, not really. It's not important anyway. And it's none of my business. He makes enough from the Wipe-Out to keep him happy, anything else... well, I don't know. He has a house by the beach he rents out now he's moved in with me. And there's a big surfing championship coming up soon in the Bay, Shane says he'll make enough from that to keep him going for the rest of the year. I'm going to be helping him out, you could too if you fancy it?'

I had the distinct impression my sister was changing the subject.

'Yes, why not? And you've been together for a year?' I asked, trying to get her back on the topic.

Rowan thought. 'Eighteen months... no, nearly two years, give or take.'

'And you were teaching? But Maggie said you've given that up.'

'Well, I was but then I realised I'd done it for nearly thirty years and I didn't want to any longer.'

'Why didn't you tell me?'

'I didn't want you to worry. I'd got to the point where I couldn't stand it. You didn't need to listen to me droning on about the paperwork and the school parents evenings. You know what it's like. Heck, you took early retirement, why can't I? These days I work in the café sometimes and occasionally I help a couple of friends out in their shops. It pays the bills, and it's much less stressful.'

'Do you get a good pension? What about when you're old?'

Rowan was rummaging about in the fridge for some eggs. She paused and looked thoughtful for a moment. Then shrugged.

'Dunno, okay I guess. Anyway, something will crop up.'

* * *

I thought about this for a long time while I showered. My aunt and uncle had been travelling all over the place. My sister had started a relationship with someone ten years younger and given up teaching. I hadn't known any of this. Why hadn't they told me? What else didn't I know? Was it because they didn't want to worry me, they didn't remember to tell me, or because I was so far away that my opinion didn't count anyway? But then had I told them every detail about Tom, each step of Dan's life? No, I hadn't.

I suppose I wanted to feel that even if I had been going through my own instability, that they were carrying on as they always had. That nothing had changed. And that wasn't the case.

It was unrealistic of me, I could see that, but it was also worrying and a bit upsetting. I'd worked all my life, I had my little house, a reasonable pension pot, and some savings, but I still had a lot of life to live.

Didn't people worry about pensions and retirement nest eggs like we did in England? Jugs of cold beer and buckets of giant prawns were all very well but you couldn't live on sunshine and blue skies, could you?

5

We went shopping in the nearby village of Kookaburra, although it wasn't really a village any more. There was a new shopping mall and a massive supermarket where there used to be a small boat repair yard. And unexpectedly, Rowan insisted we went on the bus.

The shops she liked were nothing like the places I remembered or would have chosen. All of them were run by cheerful, enthusiastic women like her, all of the clothes were what I would have called cruise or beach wear. Bright prints, vibrant colours, and a fair amount of sparkle; Rowan was on a mission.

We went to Rowan's friend's shop, and I gave up the struggle to find something sane, remembered my dreary identikit reflection that morning, and tried on all the stuff Jilly chucked at me. She was so positive, so keen to help, and so determined, it was easier not to object. Some of her clothes made me look ridiculous, some of it was okay, and all of it was like something from another planet.

In the end I was persuaded to try on loads of things: maxi-dresses (something I hadn't picked off the rails or even considered since I was a teenager), floaty skirts, t-shirts, and even some knee length shorts. Shorts?

'I think this is a challenge too far,' I said as I looked doubtfully at my reflection, 'I shouldn't be wearing shorts at my age.'

'The only thing you shouldn't wear at your age is the weight of other people's opinions,' Rowan said, 'they look fine. Your legs are great, they just need a bit of a tan.'

Then I bought some flat, strappy sandals and leather flip-flops. Neither were shoes I was familiar with because Tom didn't approve of them. He used to pull a face and used to say I would look like a stall holder in the local market. Which, looking at myself in the shop mirror, was probably slightly true. I looked a bit strange actually, wearing those colourful clothes when I was so pale. Perhaps they went better with a tan too.

One thing I did realise: I felt a lot sunnier walking out of that shop than I had walking into it. Even peeking into the carrier bags where Jilly had wrapped my new things in sparkly tissue paper made me feel happier. Slightly surprised but definitely happier.

Then I bought some toiletries and some new makeup. And a big wide-brimmed Kooringal sunhat with a flowery lining. It was great fun. I hadn't splurged on myself like that for ages; I wondered why and then remembered Tom's tightening hand on the financial reins over the years we had been married and the way he steered me into clothes that were probably more suited to my mother-in-law. I wondered if his new wife Ashley was quite as acquiescent as I had been. I hoped she wasn't.

'We're having lunch and you're buying,' Rowan said at last when we had got to the point where we couldn't carry any more bags.

I plonked on my new sunhat and, feeling slightly exotic and carefree, we walked along the row of shops that were separated from the coast by a small road and a patch of sand dunes. It was absolutely beautiful.

People were sitting on tables outside cafés under the shade of parasols, chatting and clinking glasses of wine in a very jolly way. Didn't anyone do any work here? Perhaps they saved so much on their heating bills that they could afford to take long lunch hours?

'Want to sit outside?' Rowan asked, 'not too chilly for you?'

'Rowan, it's twenty-five degrees. The sun is shining. How can you possibly think it's cold?'

She pulled a face. 'You should have been here in February; it was forty degrees. I think the roads were probably melting.'

We went into a little wine bar called Loaves and Fishes and were shown to a seat on the edge of the veranda. White ironwork table and chairs with yellow cushions under a blue parasol. Beyond us a view of the Pacific Ocean, the sweeping bay, the sea sparkling in the sunshine. It all looked wonderful.

We ordered a glass of wine each to raise a toast to my old neighbour Joyce who had made this trip possible, and I sat back to drink in the perfect view spread out before us. The red and yellow flags of the lifeguards, surfers astride their boards bobbing about beyond the breaking waves.

'How's the jet-lag?' Rowan asked, taking a sip of her wine.

'I'm doing my best to ignore it,' I said, with a careless wave of one hand, 'I have no idea what time it is or what I should be doing.'

'Best advice is not even try to work it out; go with the flow.' Rowan said wisely. 'Not that it worked for me the last time I came to visit you. I never quite got my head sorted.'

'I remember,' I grinned, 'particularly that morning when you didn't wake up until lunchtime? Tom thought you were just being lazy.'

'I thought so,' Rowan said, 'I know it must have been awful for you, but I was never so relieved as when you told me you had split up. How you stood him for so long is anyone's guess. How's Dan coping?'

'Fine I think, after the initial shock of hearing his father had been having an affair with a woman young enough to be his daughter and then horror of horrors, that Ashley was pregnant. You know what the younger generation are like? They don't believe their parents have a life, never mind a sex life.'

'Do you miss him now he's moved out?' she asked.

I thought of my son twelve thousand miles away and felt a bit sad and guilty for a moment; the last time he'd contacted me, he'd wanted to come over and do his washing and I'd changed the locks.

Oh God. Bad mother alert.

'I see far more of him now Tom and I have split up. He's got Skye and they seem well matched. Which is odd really; the maths teacher who still has all his boyhood comics and would like to build a train set in the spare bedroom, matched with a crazy girl who wears black all the time, has a new tattoo each time she wants to make a political statement – do you know she had the words "Brexit My Ass" tattooed on her bottom? She told me, I didn't actually see it – and last time I heard she was sourcing skull and crossbones fabric for curtains. I'm just letting them get on with it. Perhaps I'm a rotten mother?'

Rowan was reassuringly vehement. 'No way! You have your own life to lead. A second lease of life. Let them make their own mistakes. We all had to. And what about men? Have you had a go at dating?'

'Good God no!'

'So, this thing with Kit?'

'Rowan! Kit Pascoe and I shared a little bit of a chat in the airport and on the plane and trust me, that's all. There is no "thing".'

'Probably just as well. From what Shane tells me, he's almost permanently angry.'

This didn't sit well with me.

'Well he wasn't then. He was smiley, polite, and charming. And just because you're all loved up doesn't mean it's going to happen for me, Rowan. I've only just got out of one disastrous relationship; I'm not going to risk it again. I'm older and wiser now.'

'Well at least you could have some fun. While you're thinking about it. You know?' she gave me a wicked smile and a wink.

'You mean sex?'

'Well yes, why not?'

'I'm happy as I am.'

If I was honest, that sort of possibility had been off my radar for a long time. The thought of having a relationship with a new man was frightening. The prospect of sex was terrifying.

'Then you're happy in the wrong way and that's the same as being unhappy,' she said, finishing her ice cream and letting the spoon fall into the dish with a clatter.

'You do talk rubbish sometimes, Rowan. Where did you meet Shane? At the beach?'

'In the supermarket. We were both buying fruit and Shane was juggling with some apples to make some toddler in a stroller stop screaming. And the security guard came over and told Shane to stop messing about and Shane wouldn't, and he threatened to arrest him. And I stepped in and advised him not to make any sudden movements because Shane was with me and he was on day release.'

'Rowan!'

'You've never seen anyone vamoose as fast as that guard. We

were in stitches. And then the next day, I saw Shane at the beach. I mean it wasn't a co-incidence; he dropped some pretty heavy hints.'

I laughed. 'That sounds like Shane. Does the age difference ever bother you?' I asked.

Rowan looked a bit surprised. 'No. Should it?'

'Well, I mean he is ten years younger than you.'

'So what? It doesn't bother him.'

I thought about it. What would I know, after all?

'No, I suppose you're right.'

We talked about Maggie and Banjo and their travels. They had been all over New South Wales since they had bought the motorhome and made dozens of new friends. They were even members of closed social media groups advising on road closures, free sites and places to avoid, plus notifications of meet-ups, of which the party in Cairns was the latest.

'They have a little group of seriously crazy people; you'll probably meet some of them if you hang around long enough. The Silver Surfers might be old, but they make us look very sensible and respectable,' Rowan said.

I thought of Tom's parents who, despite their financial security, had lived lives bounded by an addiction to constant health checks, meagre diets, and complaints about everything. I know which sounded more fun and it wasn't living in Uxbridge with the curtains closed to stop the carpet from fading.

But what would happen if they got ill or even worse died? Or they were stranded in the outback with no water and no help? Would this be something else they kept from me because I was back in England and unable to do anything?

I was on the point of saying as much when I realised I was completely contradicting my previous decision to be more spontaneous. Instead I was thinking like the old me, and it didn't seem to go with the sunshine, the brilliance of the sea, or my enjoyment of being here with my sister. At last.

'Right let's go home. The bus stop is just over there, no distance.'

'So when did you start being a bus fan?' I said, picking up my carrier bags. 'That's not like you.'

Rowan looked vague. 'Oh I don't know, just easier sometimes. No problems parking. And it's more ecologically thingy. Isn't it?'

The jet lag and the miles we had walked had taken it out of me so we sat in the garden with a glass of cold white wine, examined our new purchases, and watched the birds in the trees at the end of the garden wheeling around and fluttering their wings.

'I'd forgotten about the birds here,' I said, 'how noisy they are. And how huge. We have tiny birds in comparison. Robins and blackbirds, that sort of thing. And all sorts of tits.'

Rowan snorted into her wine. 'Shane would love to think there were tits in the back yard.'

I laughed. 'You know what I mean! When are you expecting him back? Would it be okay if I went and had a nap? So I can be a bit more awake this evening.'

'Of course. Shane's working until seven. Or later if there's a crowd. I've got load of things to do, some laundry and some general tidying up. I thought we could walk down to the Wipe-Out later,' Rowan said, 'have some food there.'

'Great,' I said, 'that would be brilliant.'

I took my pile of swag into my room and briefly thought about hanging it all up. I even got as far as opening the wardrobe door and looked at the empty hangers that Shane had cleared for me. And then I didn't bother, and just dumped it on a chair. Perhaps Australia was rubbing off on me in more ways than one?

* * *

I woke just after six and found Rowan asleep on the sofa with a magazine over her face.

'Oh hello,' she said, completely unabashed, 'had a nice nap?'

'Great thanks, finished your chores?'

I looked around. There didn't seem to have been much tidying up done as far as I could tell.

Rowan stood up, pushing her hair off her face.

'Nah, I'll do it later. Or tomorrow. I had a call from Maggie earlier; they have been busy unpacking the motorhome and cleaning everything, but they're meeting us for a drink at the Wipe-Out. I'm going to have a quick shower. Then shall we walk down to the beach?'

'Great.'

'Go and put one of your new dresses on! And Elin, please just for me, don't take this the wrong way but put that one you're wearing in the bin.'

'Well that's nice!'

I went and changed into a new outfit: a loose-fitting, pink and white, linen dress that was rather lower-cut and shorter than I'd realised when I tried it on in the shop. It was many years since I'd worn anything so daring. I fidgeted with the straps and tried to stretch it down over my knees without effect. Then I fastened my hair back with a raffia pineapple hair tie I'd bought and slipped my feet into my new gold sandals. I stood in front of the mirror, rather pleased with my reflection. I could hear Rowan singing in the shower. Either that or she was in pain.

There was a loud knock on the front door, and I went to open it.

Standing there was the last person I had expected to see. It was Kit Pascoe, dressed in jeans and a white t-shirt. He looked a lot less intimidating than he had in the suit and tie. And unnervingly, a lot more attractive.

'You again,' I said rather foolishly.

Rowan might think he was a bad-tempered bully with the social skills of a dingo, but he was very easy on the eye.

We stood looking at each other for a moment. He had the sort of face that belongs on an advertising hoarding for something manly and outdoorsy. Perhaps dogfood.

I meant the sort of 'my devoted, rugged looking dog and I are out for a healthy ten-mile hike before we go and renovate an old barn' rather than 'I have a face that makes you think of dogfood.' Well, I knew what I meant anyway.

He gave me a long, sweeping look and it was suddenly very hard to concentrate on what he was saying. Then I realised he was holding out a bulky Manilla envelope towards me.

'...make sure he signs it. I'm sick of all this ridiculous delay.'

I came to my senses and tried to forget about the rugged dog and the hearty beef chunks in nourishing gravy and the check shirt scenario I had imagined.

'I'm awfully sorry, I was thinking about dogfood for some reason. Would you mind repeating what you just said?'

Kit gave an exasperated sigh and his brows knitted together in a frown.

'Dogfood? For heaven's... I said give this to Shane. I've sent him three copies of this and chased him up with emails God know how many times. He needs to sign it and return it to me as soon as possible.'

'I'm sorry. I think he's at the beach – at the Wipe-Out...'

I really did need to stop apologising; this wasn't anything to do with me.

Kit made an irritated noise. 'Yes, I know that. I went looking for him but apparently he's catching a few waves. Well, we all know what that means; he'll be out there for hours, lazy bloody toad. And I have an evening Zoom call to dial in to. I'm late as it is. We can't all slope off to the beach when it suits us. Here's my business card; you can contact me on these numbers anytime if there is any problem. Look, I'm entrusting you with this, it's extremely important, and I expect you to give it to him when you see him. Immediately, do you understand?'

This sparked something inside me. The memory of being spoken to like that. Of being given orders. I wasn't going to put up with it again.

'Don't you dare take that tone with me!' I said suddenly angry, stuffing his card into the front of my dress, 'I'm not one of your office minions.'

He rolled his eyes and huffed a bit. 'I'm not suggesting you are an office minion. I just politely asked you if you would—'

'Politely? I don't remember any please or thank you or the faintest suggestion of politeness,' I said furiously, 'just you turning up here uninvited and unannounced barking out orders.'

'I seldom bark,' he said through gritted teeth, his expression darkening.

'Well, you did today.' Perhaps the 'dog advertisement' thing had got to me. I reached out and grabbed the envelope. 'However, in the interests of peace and quiet I will take this and give it to Shane when I see him later.'

'Right.'

'Right.'

We glared at each other for a moment and then he turned away.

I hesitated for a moment then shouted after him, 'Mr Pascoe, I think you meant to say thank you!'

He took a couple of steps back towards me and I slammed the door with a dramatic flourish before I really lost my temper.

I stood looking at the door, my thoughts whirling. I wondered if he had gone.

God, what had I told him on the plane? All that stuff about being newly single and having an adventure. Why couldn't I just make pleasant small talk without embarrassing myself and spewing up my life story?

I closed my eyes, inwardly cringing.

And had I just seen Kit's true nature? That was a blow, I'd been quite prepared to stick up for him, but I wouldn't forget that encounter in a hurry.

'What's going on? Who was that?' Rowan came into the hall, still in her dressing gown and rubbing at her wet hair with a towel. 'Sorry I took so long, I had to get all the feathers out. Wow Elin, what's the matter?'

'Kit bloody Pascoe,' I said, holding out the envelope, 'turning up here with some documents for Shane. Ordered me to give them to him and to make sure he signs them. Honestly that man has the manners of a... a...'

'How about a Tasmanian Devil?' Rowan suggested this time. 'I get the feeling they don't even like each other. Tasmanian Devils have no manners at all.'

'Well nor has he. I shouted at him. And I slammed the door in his face.'

'Good,' Rowan said, 'it's hard to believe he and Shane are related, never mind brothers.'

I turned the envelope over in my hands. It felt like quite a substantial document.

'What is this anyway?'

Rowan pulled a face. 'No idea.'

I shook my head. 'Honestly! You have no natural curiosity Rowan, do you? It must be really significant.'

'It's none of my business. Right, I'll get dressed and we can go and find Shane.'

'Apparently he's surfing, that's what Kit said.'

Rowan rolled her eyes and huffed a bit. 'Is he? Surfing? He's supposed to be working at the café, not messing about with his mates. Lazy bloody toad.'

'Funny, that's exactly what Kit called him,' I said.

6

Down at the beach, people were arriving in SUVs and vans with surf boards attached. I guessed they were calling in after work for a few hours in the sea. Most of them were young and lithe and good-looking and they all looked cheerful and carefree. How wonderful to feel like that. My memories of going home after work in England seemed to be of overcrowded buses, rain, and being cold.

I'm sure they can't all have been blissfully happy and I'm sure some of them must have had homework to do but that warm evening seemed to be sort of glowing and the whole world was gilded in a wonderful, perfect light. It was refreshing to see it.

No one was sitting in a beach chair reading the *Daily Telegraph* and checking their watch every five minutes as Tom had been known to do. No one was shouting angrily about being late for something. Perhaps I would try surfing again after all?

How pedestrian and restricted my outlook had become. Was that the English climate? The endless cold, foggy winter days? The unpredictable summers of torrential rain and unexpected heatwaves? Was it Tom's fault for being a control freak? Was it partly my fault too, for being prepared to put up with it? Probably.

Rowan and I made our way to the Wipe-Out, which hadn't been built when I left Australia. It was quite a large, single-storey building overlooking the beach, the lights glowing, the patio busy with customers. It was bigger than I had imagined it would be, a stone white-painted structure with red shutters faded by the sun and the sea spray. Outside on the patch of concrete were half a dozen plastic tables with matching chairs, and parasols with beer logos printed on them and straw fringes around the edge. It looked basic but inviting and was doing a fair trade with a line of people queueing up for drinks and snacks. I went to sit at an empty table and Rowen went inside to try and find Shane. She came out a few minutes later with two glasses of iced water and some menus. From her expression, she wasn't entirely happy.

'That dopey girl Cheryl, who appears to have had a personality and intelligence bypass, said he disappeared at about two o'clock after the lunchtime rush and he hasn't been seen since. He was with Trev, and he's never a good influence,' She stood up to look at the darkening waves, shading her eyes with her hand against the last of the afternoon light. 'That could be him over by Nobby's Point. Or I suppose it might be Trev. I hope not, the rocks there are dangerous.'

I followed her anxious gaze. 'I hope he's all right. Should we go and look for him? Should we tell someone? The lifeguards or something.'

Rowan came and sat down and sipped her water. 'Good God no! Don't fuss. He'll turn up.'

Once again, I was surprised by my sister's laid-back attitude. But then I could distantly remember feeling like that when I was younger. The Australian phrase *she'll be right* that covered every problem or challenge. Stop panicking, calm down. Perhaps I should try it?

Rowan passed me a menu. 'I'm not waiting for him, I'm starving. Now what do you fancy eating?'

She passed me a menu. It was typical café fast-food, but it all sounded good, and the walk to the beach and the fresh sea breeze had given me an appetite. We ordered some chips and some barramundi goujons which were posh fish fingers and they were delicious. Then we had a glass of wine which came in paper cups. Something to do with Shane's dislike of glasses on the beach and his occasional attempts at ecological awareness.

Just as we finished our food, Shane trotted out of the surf and up the beach with his surfboard under his arm. He stopped in front of us and stuck his board in the sand like a monolith and then posed against it so we could admire him.

'Hiya lovely ladies,' he called, 'having fun?'

'Shane, where have you been? We've been here for ages,' Rowan pouted.

'Aw you know how it is, Ro. I was just doing some bits and pieces in the office and then I looked out of the window. Sun was shining. Surf was looking too good to miss. I thought bugger this for a game of soldiers!'

'What about that paperwork you keep putting off?'

'Well, I was doing that earlier,' Shane said, shaking his wet hair like a dog. 'There's no reason to get tetchy. Get us a beer, there's a good girl?'

'Ha! Get it yourself you lazy sod,' Rowan said, 'it's the maid's day off.'

How would Tom have reacted if I'd spoken like that to him? I should have tried it.

Elin, my suit is still at the cleaners, you haven't picked it up, I need it for Monday.

Ha! Get it yourself you lazy sod.

Elin freshen up this whiskey, will you? Three ice cubes.

It's the maid's day off.

I snorted with laughter at the prospect and almost wished I had the opportunity to try it out.

Shane came towards us, peeling down the top half of his wetsuit. I think he was still what young people call 'buff'. He certainly had impressive muscles.

Rowan watched him for a few seconds and then crumpled. 'See? That's what he does. It gets me every time.'

Then she went to get him a beer.

'So have you had a good day, Elin?' he said sitting down on the chair next to me.

'Marvellous,' I said and held out the Manilla envelope, 'until your brother called at the house to have a bit of a rant and give me this. I was told in no uncertain terms to give it to you as soon as I saw you, so that's what I'm doing.'

Shane took it and stared at it. 'Even his handwriting is furious. What else did he say?'

'I've told you as much as I know. You need to sign it and give it back to him as soon as possible.'

Shane didn't even open the envelope but tossed it onto the chair next to him.

'If he comes back tell him he's dreaming.'

'Wouldn't it be easier to just sign it? Get it out of the way?'

'Oh it's all right, I'll look at it later. Hey there, beautiful! Here she is! What better sight than your gorgeous lady bringing you a cold beer?' He rubbed his hand over his wet curls, flicking water onto my sister and the table. Rowan protested but not very convincingly. As she put his beer down, he pulled her onto his knee and kissed her.

'Shane! You're soaking wet!' Rowan squeaked.

He kissed her again and she gave me a rueful look.

'See what I have to put up with?'

'She can't resist me,' Shane said, beaming at her.

I felt a lump in my throat to see how clearly he adored her. Why hadn't it been like that with me and Tom? Fun and uncomplicated with genuine affection between us. Tom had hardly ever kissed me with that sort of passion after a few years, and only then when he wanted something.

Shane took a long pull at his beer and wiped his mouth on the back of his hand.

'Jeez that's good. Blooming salty you know? The sea?'

'Yes we know, Shane. Did Elin tell you Kit's been round again? Whatever it is, you're going to have to sort this out,' Rowan said, moving onto her chair.

Shane pulled a face. 'I will sweetheart, I promise I will.'

'So what is it about anyway?' Rowan said, shaking out her damp skirts.

'Aw it's just Kit nagging, you've seen what he's like.'

'It must be important,' I said, 'he says it's the third copy he's sent you. Or was it the fourth?'

Shane looked amused. 'Is it? Well that will teach him not to be such a prat, won't it? I'm significant enough when it counts apparently. Now then, what have you two been up to? You're looking very pretty Elin, I must say. That dress makes your eyes sparkle somehow. Being back in Australia suits you, wouldn't you say?'

Rowan was right; his charm was almost irresistible. It was a pity his brother didn't share it.

'Well it's nice of you to say so but Kit said…'

'Here they come,' Rowan said, and started waving at someone.

Banjo and Maggie were coming down the slipway from the car park, carrying a cool bag between them. Maggie started waving back and almost dropped her side of the bag.

'I'll go and help,' Shane said, and jumped up, trotting across the sand towards them.

'Saved by the bell,' I said, watching as he embraced Maggie, exchanged a back-slapping man hug with Banjo and took the cool bag from both of them after a brief and good-natured tussle.

'Cooeee,' Maggie said when she was close enough, 'my stars, it's busy here.'

'Good for business, Maggie. And looks like the weather is set fair for the surfing tournament according to the forecast. Let's hope it lasts. You say one for me, eh? The man upstairs will listen to you,' Shane said.

Maggie gave him an affectionate look and came to give me a big hug. Then she sat down next to me, covering my hand with hers.

'Sorry we're late. We had to sort out the van. Banjo's been having some trouble with the wastewater hose. All sorted now. So how are you getting on, you and Rowan enjoying catching up?' she said. She clasped her hands together with excitement. 'It's so lovely to see you girls together again. And what a pretty dress! That's more like the Elin I remember. You look five years younger already!'

'We're having a great time,' I said, smoothing down my new dress with childish pleasure, 'it almost feels like I never left.'

'I wouldn't go that far,' Rowan said, 'you need a bit more sun on your bones and if you want to see just how much time has passed, you should meet up with some people from school.'

'Are there any left around here?' I said.

'A few, although you wouldn't recognise some of them. Do you remember Simon Bateman? Bald as a coot and the size of a small house now. And June Webster? On her third husband and fourth facelift by the look of her.'

'Now who's having a drink to celebrate us all being back

together?' Banjo said, unfastening the cool box and pulling out some cans of beer.

'Now naughty naughty, you're doing me out of business, Banjo,' Shane said, taking one and holding it to his forehead. 'Nice and cold though. You might have eaten but I'm ravishing! I'll get a basket of fries shall I?'

'That would be nice,' Maggie said.

'Well don't forget about this,' I said tapping the manila envelope.

'Yeah, right.' Shane laughed and went off to the Wipe-Out at a brisk trot.

Charming he might be but he was also exasperating. Even though it was none of my business, I did feel a pang of sympathy for Kit. All that travelling and business meetings he'd had to do over the years while Shane spent all his time on the beach.

Banjo was looking tanned and well underneath his cork-brimmed hat. He certainly didn't look his age.

'So what have you girls been up to today?'

'Shopping. Rowan made me buy lots of things.'

Maggie clapped her hands. 'Excellent! Well done Ro!'

'Shopping? Well that sounds like... fun?' Banjo said with a grimace.

'It was great fun. I had a lovely time,' I said, standing up to give him a hug.

'Well I think you look smashing,' Maggie said, 'just like the old days. You're getting your sparkle back. It does my heart good to see it.'

'I bet when you unpack your case properly you take one look and bin the lot,' Rowan said, swigging at her drink.

'Well, we'll see,' I said, trying hard to remember what I had actually packed. Even after a few days the thought of pulling on some of those dull clothes was ghastly.

'Your uncle and I will be over tomorrow for breakfast and you can show us your new things.'

Shane returned with a huge paper basket of fries and we all dived even though I wasn't at all hungry.

Almost immediately a gull of some sort swooped in on hopeful wings.

'Shoo it away, Shane!' Rowan screamed, her arms over her head. 'Shoo it, Shane!'

I'd forgotten Rowan had always had a thing about gulls, ever since she was six and one had plunged down and swiped her ice cream cone mid lick.

Shane obligingly stood up and capered about like a mad thing, all arms and legs and flying curls and the sight seemed to me one of the funniest things I'd seen for a long time. I laughed until my ribs were sore.

We caught up with each other's news as the light faded from the sky and the last surfers came into shore. Shane went inside to get changed and turn up the music coming from the café. A young couple got up from their table and started dancing. Someone switched on the fairy lights that surrounded the Wipe-Out. They were like white stars against the dark, sea-scented sky and the whole evening was suddenly unforgettable.

I looked at my aunt and uncle, laughing together across the table, Banjo trying and failing to flip and catch six beer mats at once. Maggie mopping up his spilled beer with a paper napkin and slapping his arm for his clumsiness. Next to me, Rowan and Shane were singing along to a Beatles song, Shane with his arm around her and tapping out the beat with his feet. It was lovely to see how relaxed and carefree they were.

The tears prickled my eyes. How and why had I stayed away from my lovely family for so long? I'd left Australia filled with optimism and excitement. I'd returned having learned a hard lesson, one that had changed me from a confident, extroverted young woman into someone who had settled for so little when life had so much to offer. And Dan, what about him? He had been brought up by one parent who had allowed herself to be dominated and another who had asserted his superiority into every aspect of our lives.

Things were going to change; they had to. I was nearly sixty, I had my freedom and my independence again. Now was the time to help Dan find his enthusiasm for life too. And I could do it. He deserved my help, my attention. Something more than phone calls and emails and the occasional visit.

I felt more positive than I had for a very long time. I needed to grab this feeling and keep it close to my heart, so that when I went back home...

Home, what did that mean to me? How did I feel about going back to my little house in England? It was a place filled with many memories already. It had seen the first stirrings of my renewed enthusiasm for life and my relief at being single again.

Over the last months, I had taken tentative steps in cooking the food I wanted, decorating and furnishing my home, dealing with the bills, budgeting, organising my life. And yet I knew then that there had always been something missing. There was a part of me that needed to be back in Australia with my family, in the sunshine, the wide spaces, the humour, the energy of the people that was so invigorating. The longer I was here, the stronger the feeling was becoming.

* * *

A few days later, Maggie invited us over to their house for a barbeque. They were very excited and their house was in chaos because they were packing up their motorhome for their immi-

nent trip to Cairns. I poked about for a while, happily remembering the house from when I had lived there. Revelling in the
feeling of coming home. Of being a proper part of something
again.

The kitchen had been remodelled and a bedroom turned into
a dining room but basically it hadn't changed much at all. The
same books in the bookcase, a collection of china plates on the
wall, a little clock ticking on the sideboard.

We went out into the warmth of the afternoon and sat round
the table underneath the trees. Maggie fussed about with plates
and bread rolls and bowls of salad before she sat down. And then
she got up again to fetch a plastic box of condiments from the
fridge. Banjo took his place at the barbeque, dodging the smoke
as he put things onto the grill. Tweaking at them with some tongs
as he always had.

'We're only going to be a week or so, perhaps ten days. I wish
in a way we could get out of it because you've only been here five
minutes. You really don't mind?' Maggie asked.

'Of course I don't mind; it's an eightieth birthday party, it must
have been organised for ages, hasn't it? Rowan and I have a lot of
catching up to do and Shane has asked us both to do some shifts
in the Wipe-Out. I'm rather looking forward to it. This surfing
championship starts soon, they are expecting loads of people.
Honestly, I will be fine.'

'Well, we are setting off tomorrow morning. Early if I get my
way. As soon as the party is over, we'll come straight back. We are
joining up with Malc and Patty in Coffs Harbour, and Jim and
Dinkie are bringing Norm over from Perth. And Frank should be
there too. By the way, have you heard from Dan recently? You
haven't mentioned him much.'

I held up my phone. 'I've sent Dan a few emails, telling him
all about the flight. The time difference makes it a bit difficult,

but I spoke to him yesterday; he seems okay, looking forward to the school holidays. He and Skye were thinking of going off together for a break. They both send their love. I've been thinking about him a lot. It wasn't only me who was damaged by my marriage; he was too. I don't think Tom can quite believe what I've done. Going off to Australia and leaving him behind with his needy second wife and a six-month-old screaming baby.'

'Well what are you supposed to do about that?' Banjo said, depositing a plate of cremated burgers onto the table in between us. I wondered briefly about my cholesterol medication.

I shrugged. 'Show sympathy for Tom? I think it's a bit late for that.'

Maggie nudged me. 'Go on, turn your phone on, see if he's sent anything. I could do with a laugh.'

I did so and six text messages from Tom appeared.

Maggie took my phone from me and chuckled as she read them out loud in a rather pompous tone that was reminiscent of Tom.

Elin, I'm asking you to return my messages.

I began to feel rather uncomfortable and reached out to take my phone back but she swerved away.

Elin we need to talk. I'm only human. I made one mistake. Do you have no Christian compassion?

'Oh, I like that one, that's great coming from him!'
'Oh... don't.'

Elin, are you really in Australia? How can you possibly afford that? I

went on to the website and the cost of a business class flight is astro-
nomical. Have you lost your mind?

'I think that's a case of MYOB,' Maggie snorted.

Daniel's just told me he's got a girlfriend and she's moved into his flat.
Did you know about that? She's called Skye and I've seen a picture;
she looks like a witch. She wears black all the time. And black lipstick.

'Sounds interesting,' Rowan said through a mouthful of
burger.

I nodded. 'But she's really nice, she's bringing Dan out of
himself, and having fun...'

Maggie was on to the next message.

It's two-thirty in the morning and Josie is still crying. Ashley is crying. I
feel like bloody crying. I don't know why I am telling you this. You've
become a hard-hearted, unsympathetic woman. It's very unattractive.

'That poor baby, she gets my sympathy vote every time.'

I can't find our wedding album. Have you got it?

Maggie turned to me. 'Well, have you?'

'The wedding album? I did have a copy but it's in the landfill
site somewhere. Why Tom wants to look at it is beyond me.' I
reached out and took my phone back before she could read out
anything else. Bringing Tom, even if it was just his words, into the
mix made me feel uncomfortable. He had no place here.

I sent him a quick reply.

Stop texting me. I will not be reading any more of them.

'Perhaps he's getting sentimental? I'm sorry to say it because he is Dan's father but crikey, he's made a dog's breakfast of things, hasn't he?' Banjo said as he helped himself to some mustard. 'Still, perhaps he'll learn his lesson?'

'Where's Shane this evening then?' Maggie said, looking around as though Shane might be hiding somewhere. 'Isn't he joining us?'

'He's at work,' Rowan said, 'or he should be.'

'Has he signed that document yet?' I said.

Rowan held up her hands. 'No idea. I told you, I'm not getting involved. Anyway, Shane never deals well with pressure.'

'What document?' Maggie asked, wedging a burger into a bread roll and slathering it in some unidentifiable sauce.

'Don't go there,' Rowan said, 'it's something to do with his brother and the family business.'

'Shane has a brother?' Banjo said, perking up, 'well, you should introduce him to Elin. They might get on.'

'You've already met him. Don't you remember? He's the one who interrupted the barbeque the day I arrived and took Shane off for a loud argument,' I said.

'Oh yes, of course I remember him. Tall man in a suit, he had an expression like a badger chewing a wasp. Ha!' Banjo nodded, 'Still, as I remember, you thought Tom was Prince Charming when you met him and look how that turned out.'

Maggie looked smug. 'I knew everything I needed to know about your uncle within six weeks of meeting him.'

'And look how that turned out,' Banjo said.

Maggie flicked half a tomato at him and he ducked, howling with laughter.

7

They set off the following morning for Cairns. Maggie sent Rowan a text, triumphant that she had managed to get them behind the wheel before six thirty, and by the end of the day they were hoping to be in Port Macquarie.

Later that afternoon, Rowan got out a map so we could follow their route.

'They're making excellent progress,' I said, 'are they sharing the driving?'

Rowan scoffed. 'No chance. Maggie doesn't drive any more, she says her distance vision isn't what it was, and she kept missing road signs and getting lost.'

'Oh yes, I keep forgetting they are in their seventies. They don't look it. Poor Banjo. I hope he doesn't mind?'

I pushed away the vision of my aunt peering hopelessly out of the windscreen and stabbing a finger at an out-of-date road map.

'Aw he's fine. He likes being in charge, and Maggie's better at navigation than he is. Now, let's have a glass of wine. We can eat outside when Shane gets back.'

'Can I help with dinner?'

'Nah, I'm just doing steak and salad, Shane can sling them on the barbie. The steaks I mean, not the salad.'

We sat outside in the gathering dusk drinking red wine and watching the fruit bats flying overhead. I'd forgotten about them; the way they all suddenly appeared in the evening, like a giant, silent flock of crows. Rowan did a bit of sketchy food preparation and brought out some plates and cutlery.

After a while she started fidgeting and looking at her watch.

'It's nearly eight o'clock, Shane should be home by now. What's keeping him?'

She tried ringing him a couple of times but his phone went unanswered.

'You could always drive us down to the beach and meet him?' I suggested.

'No,' Rowan said quickly, 'he wouldn't like that. Perhaps he's closing up late?'

'Or doing a stock take?' I suggested.

Rowan made a dismissive sound. 'That would be a first.' She looked at her watch again and then topped up our wine glasses. 'Anyway, we can't drive now, the police round here are pretty hot on traffic violations and we'll both be over the limit. I'm sure he will be home soon.'

Half an hour later, even Rowan was really starting to worry and so was I. She phoned the café and everyone else she could think of but no one answered.

'Who else can I ring?' she said, tapping her fingers against the table. 'And before you even say the words, I don't know Kit's phone number. Not that Shane would go there.'

'Kit gave me his business card,' I said, trying to remember where it was.

'Well you ring him then, I'm not going to!'

We hummed and haahed for a bit longer and then suddenly

we heard the familiar sound of Shane's camper van pulling into the driveway.

Rowan blew a sigh of relief. 'Oh thank heavens for that. Don't tell him I was worried; he'll think I'm pathetic.'

After a few minutes we heard Shane's familiar laugh and someone with him, both of them coming around the side of the house. Rowan arranged herself to look casual, even slightly annoyed, and then we saw him.

Shane was holding some crutches and his right leg was splinted and bandaged from above his knee to his ankle. He was hobbling, one arm around Trev's broad shoulders.

Rowan screamed and pushed back her chair so hard that it fell over.

'Don't make a fuss Ro, I'm fine. Honest to dingoes, I'm fine,' Shane said.

Hands outstretched, Rowan hovered around him, not daring to touch him.

'He is, he's okay,' Trev said, fussing around him, pulling out a chair and encouraging him to sit down.

Shane wobbled a bit.

'My god, what happened? Were you in an accident? Why didn't you ring me? Will someone tell me what happened?' Rowan cried.

Shane sat down and propped his foot up on an empty beer crate Then he balanced his crutches against the table rather inexpertly and they both clattered onto the ground. I went to pick them up.

Rowan pulled up a chair next to him and he patted her hand.

'Look stop fussing Ro. Trev drove me back. There was no need to ring you. I'm fine,' Shane said again.

Rowan took a deep breath. 'Okay, I'm not fussing. I'm perfectly calm. What happened?'

'Had a bit of a nibble didn't he? Out by Nobby's Point,' Trev said, helping himself to a beer from the cool box.

'Nibble?' I said blankly. What did that mean?

There was a moment's silence and then Rowan screamed again.

'Oh my god! You mean a shark bite? God almighty, Shane! You've been bitten by a shark?'

'Aw, it's nothing, more of a nibble, like Trev said,' Shane said, holding out his hand for a beer.

'Now then, the Doc said you weren't to have any,' Trev said, his jaw sticking out stubbornly, 'the antibiotics and the painkillers? Remember?'

'Tell your story walking, Trev. The Doc was having a laugh,' Shane said, taking Trev's beer from him.

'And he said you might have a concussion, from when you banged your head on your board,' Trev added.

'Concussion? Rubbish, I don't remember any concussion,' Shane scoffed.

'Well no, big wow. You wouldn't, would you, you moron?' Trev said looking peeved.

Rowan dropped her face into her hands and then looked up at him.

'Shane Pascoe, tell me what happened. Before I kick your good leg.'

Shane took a swig of his beer. 'We were just shooting a few out by the Point and I felt a shove on my leg. That's all. Just a little nudge. And when I got to shore I was bleeding.'

'So it might not have been a shark bite?' I said hopefully.

'Aw yeah, it was deffo a bite all right,' Trev said happily, 'you could see the tooth marks and everything. And there was a big...' He saw Rowan's expression and changed his tone to a more serious one. 'But only a little bite. Just a nip actually, like a tiny, baby sharky kiss. Perhaps it didn't like the taste? You can't blame it. I wouldn't want to bite Shane's leg either.'

'Trev, shut up,' Rowan said through gritted teeth, 'Shane, are you going to be okay?'

'I'm fine Ro, honestly. Got just a few stitches and some tablets. They said a day or so and I'll be good as new.'

Trev shook his head slowly and then butted in. 'No, that's no right. Doc said two weeks actually and you have to go back and have the stiches out after a week and the dressings changed before...'

'Ro, don't listen to him, I'm in great shape,' Shane said, 'No damage done. Bit of a bruise.'

'You could have lost your leg. Or died!' Rowan cried.

She threw her arms round him and pressed her cheek to his chest.

Shane patted her shoulder and winked at me over the top of her head. 'Yeah but I didn't. I'm fine. All great surfers have scars; it's part of their sex appeal. Like a rite of passage. Remember that bloke from Darwin used to come in Trev? Hopping Joe Dixon? Tall bloke with red hair. The girls were all over him.'

'He was called Hopping Joe for a bloody good reason Shane! He lost a foot!' Rowan shouted.

'Yeah but it didn't stop him did it? Not once he got his metal one. If you don't do it you're not in the races are you? Now give us another beer and we'll say no more about it. Anyway, I have to be right by next week for the surfing championships.'

Trev butted in again. 'Aw now Shane-o, Doc said you weren't to...'

Shane silenced him with a glare. 'It'll be right. Just don't tell Maggie or Banjo, okay? They'll only worry.'

I wondered if they would have told me if I hadn't been in the country. Or would they have kept it from me? What would I have done if I had suffered some sort of accident? Did I have the sort of support network that Rowan did? I felt quite worried for a moment. Yes, I had friends, but this close-knit group was something different.

Rowan leaned back and gave Shane a hard stare. 'We'll see about that. And once the painkillers wear off you might change your tune.'

* * *

Shane soon stopped trying to be the hip surfer dude with the cool shark bite and morphed into the patient from hell. He had numerous grumbles: the stiches were painful, his leg wouldn't bend properly, and for the first few days he lay on the sofa eating biscuits and binge watching terrible American box sets that seemed to involve various bad-tempered detectives, shouting, and family disagreements. Like EastEnders with a lot of guns.

Rowan did tell Maggie about his accident, much to his annoyance. Added to this, Rowan refused to drive him to the beach and he had to reply on Trev or Bazza to give him a lift. On the third day, Rowan agreed I should be put onto her insurance, and I drove him to work, although what actual work he was able to do with one leg strapped up and propped on a chair I couldn't imagine.

He got very snippy with the girls who served behind the counter, and one eventually threw her apron at him and walked out. This left Rowan, me, and the two girls to do all the work. It didn't take us long to realise Cheryl (blonde and dense as sea fog) and Lyn (slightly punk) were only there for the packs of hunky looking young men – who really were very eye catching – and not for clearing tables. But I did perfect my toasted sandwich making. And as far as a work place went, it couldn't be bettered.

Outside, the sea shone and sparkled and the customers all

seemed to be young, cheerful, and attractive. After they got used to my accent and stopped asking me if I knew their relatives in Leicester or Cardiff, a few of the chaps even started flirting with me. Which was totally unexpected and rather lovely. I even bought a new swimming costume. Red with white stars.

The first time I wore it, Bazza gave a piercing wolf whistle. 'Look at you sexy momma!' he shouted, alerting half the beach, 'let's get you out on a board!'

And unbelievably I did. Not with any degree of success, and only when there were no reports of sharks in the area, but as I came up for the umpteenth time, spitting out seawater, I realised I was having fun. Muscles I didn't know I had ached from the exercise the next day.

Tom would have had a fit. The thought of this made doing it even more enjoyable.

* * *

Over the next few days, the weather gradually became cooler, and people were huddling into hoodies and coats on their trips to the beach and grumbling about the onset of autumn. Which was weird; as far as I was concerned, it should be the start of summer and the weather should have been getting warmer. Over here people were shivering and complaining because it was only twenty-two degrees, which seemed almost ungrateful. In England there would warnings on the news about using factor fifty and pictures of girls in bikinis on Brighton beach. But then lots of things that I'd forgotten about were different here in the southern hemisphere.

The first thing I checked was that the water still did go down the plughole the other way, something I found oddly pleasing. But on top of that, the sun seemed to rise and set in the wrong place, the moon looked different, and the stars were unfamiliar. Apart from the famous Southern Cross constellation which Shane proudly pointed out to me on several occasions, presumably forgetting that I was after all Australian and had been looking at it before he was born.

Rowan and I, assisted by the two airhead girls, managed to keep the Wipe-Out going as the days passed and the surf championship came ever closer. I gave the kitchen area a thorough cleaning, much to Rowan's amusement. I wondered about food hygiene rules and when I realised all the most vital paperwork was just stuffed into an empty crisp box, I sorted it all out.

Shane generally sat on a chair in the shade of a parasol, drinking beer, criticising and complaining about how unfair it all was, and fidgeting and scratching when he got sand under his dressings.

'I wonder how Maggie's getting on,' I asked when we had a five-minute breather. Rowan was re-loading the coffee machine and I had been clearing tables of dirty crockery and cutlery.

'Oh yes, I forgot to say, I had a text from her first thing this morning. They met up with their friends and should be in Cairns by now,' she said, 'I bet its hotter there.'

'How can you think it's cold?' I asked, 'it's boiling.'

'Not by Australian standards it's not,' Rowan said, 'you've seen the adverts on TV; everyone is ordering wood and getting their boilers serviced. Someone said there had been snow further south.'

'Really?'

Rowan pulled out her phone to show me the forecast.

'Look it's only going to be thirteen degrees tonight.'

Suddenly her phone lit up and began playing 'Waltzing Matilda'. Which meant it was Maggie.

Rowan answered it and in seconds, she looked shocked.

'What is it? Put her on speaker,' I said.

Rowan flapped a hand at me and turned away.

'Bad line, can you say that again? No. No. Elin's here, we're working in the café. Yes. Oh God! How? What was he doing?'

There was a long pause while Rowan listened. I could just hear Maggie's voice, talking quickly, obviously upset.

After a few minutes, Rowan turned tragic eyes towards me and began crying.

I felt a plunge of fear. This was exactly the sort of thing I had dreaded.

'Okay, we'll sort something out. Yes, of course. Yes, ring me in an hour when you've seen him and I'll tell you what we're going to do. Don't worry. No, don't worry. Oh sod the surfing championships. Yes. Take care. Speak later.'

Rowan ended the call

Then she wiped her eyes on a tea towel and took a deep breath before she turned to me.

'It's Banjo.'

* * *

We left Shane at the café, hopping around on his crutches and encouraging Cheryl and Lyn to ramp up their work rate and we headed home in the van, Rowan bringing me up to speed with what had happened.

Banjo had been standing on a picnic chair on top of a picnic table attempting to free part of the electric awning on the side of the motorhome which had jammed when he tried to open it. Both table and chair had collapsed underneath him, and he had fallen, knocking himself out, injuring his wrist, cracking a couple of ribs, and frightening my aunt into an asthma attack. What on earth were they doing, taking risks like that at their age? It beggared belief.

'You're sure it's not serious?' I said for the tenth time. 'He's not seriously hurt?'

'I don't know. I don't know,' Rowan wailed. 'Oh God, what if it's really bad?'

I hugged her.

'I'm sure they are being well looked after. And they have their friends there, the Silver Surfers. I'm sure they will be okay. Just take a deep breath and calm down.'

Rowan did as she was told.

'Oh crickey, Elin. I'm so glad you're here.'

Five minutes after we got home we had a call from one of their friends, Patty. She sounded capable and comforting which was something we really needed. She even seemed casual about the whole thing which was not reassuring.

'We called an ambulance which took both of them to the emergency room at Cairns hospital. Malc and I followed them. Banjo came round pretty quickly but he needs something doing to sort out his wrist. The nurse looking after him said he should make a full recovery. Mind you, he needs time to recover from the concussion,' she chuckled, 'not that we'll know the difference, silly old thing.'

'Oh Patty, thank you so much for helping,' Rowan said, tearfully, 'my sister Elin is here with me. We've both been so worried; are you sure he's going to be okay?'

'Well I'm sure he will be, once he starts acting his age.'

'And Maggie? How is she?' I said.

'Maggie was put on a nebuliser in the next room. She's fine now. Furious with Banjo of course. Once she got over the shock. She thought he'd killed himself. Daft old buzzard.'

All these years I had been away and now this had happened. I think it brought home to me with horrible clarity how much worse I would have felt if I had still been in England. And what if this had happened and they hadn't told me anything about it?

'Maggie's staying with him as long as she can. She's going to book into a nearby motel when she's discharged. We told her we'd come and fetch her back to the site but she won't leave him. You know what she's like,' Patty said.

'Poor thing,' I said, 'of course she won't. How long will he be in?'

'A few days, maybe more depending on how the concussion pans out. He's in the best place. You're not to worry. But there is a problem.'

'Oh God. What?' Rowan said, a fresh burst of tears streaming down her face.

We exchanged a look. Rowan grabbed hold of my arm and hung on to it.

'It's okay, it's just logistics. The van. Someone has to come and get it. Maggie won't drive all that way and Banjo won't be able to. Not with his wrist crocked up.'

'No of course he can't,' Rowan said.

'Go on, Patty. How can we help?'

'When Banjo's discharged from hospital, he and Maggie are going to fly back to Sydney from Cairns. Malc and I have tried to think if one of us or one of the others could help out, perhaps bring it part of the way, but...' Patty tailed off. 'They contacted their insurance people and they could send someone, but it would mean their premiums would rocket. And Maggie's not happy having someone else rummaging through their stuff. I mean I'm sure they are trustworthy but, well, she doesn't like the idea.'

'No, of course not. We'll sort something out, Patty,' I said, 'please don't worry.'

We chatted for a few minutes and then Patty rang off,

promising to keep an eye on the motorhome and visit Maggie and Banjo to make sure they were comfortable.

Rowan and I looked at each other for a moment, both of us trying to come up with a solution to this problem. What could we do? We needed to think clearly. We needed a plan.

'Okay. It's fine, we'll go to Cairns, find the site they are on, and get the motorhome back here, you and I can do that,' I said. 'We could share the driving. If they can do it at their age, we can manage it.'

'Well...'

She didn't sound too keen.

'Come on Rowan, we'd have each other. We can do it.'

Rowan blushed and sipped her water, muttering.

'Well of course we could. But, well you see. It's not quite that simple.'

'Why not?'

Rowan blew her nose and mopped her tears again before she spoke.

'I've lost my license.'

'You've lost your driving license? What do you mean, lost? You can't find it? Well it must be here somewhere. Or perhaps you could get a replacement?'

Rowan picked at a fingernail, her face as shifty as the time when she stole my first lipstick, smeared it around her face, and then denied everything.

'No, I mean I've been banned for three months...'

'What?'

'It was a few weeks before you arrived. I can't believe I was so stupid; I know the police watch that stretch of road, I've been caught before. That time it was just a fine, but it was Anzac Day, and the demerit points are doubled. I was lucky they didn't take the car away.'

I blinked hard. My thoughts spinning. 'But hang on Rowan, you came to collect me from the airport.'

'I know. I was terrified I'd be caught.'

'Rowan! Are you mad? How could you?'

She put her hands over her face. 'I know, I know. I couldn't think what else to do, Shane had to work because – oh, I can't remember. That's why I was cross when I found him still at the house when we got back. I was so keen to see you. I just took the risk.'

'You nitwit! That's so irresponsible! For heaven's sake! I could have got a bus or something!'

'I didn't think. Look, they didn't catch me, so let's not keep going over this. The problem is, how are we going to get the motorhome back here?'

We went outside and sat down, both of us trying to think of a solution.

'I could come with you?' Rowan said. 'I could navigate.'

'Yes that's true. I'd prefer someone who could share the driving though,' I answered, 'what about Shane's friends?'

Rowan counted off the options on her fingers. 'Divvy doesn't drive. Trev's just started a new job at Tents, Tents, Tents selling tents, Shane can't drive until his leg is better. You want to be cooped up with Elliot or Baz?'

'It's not ideal,' I admitted.

'Maggie's going to ring later so we need to come up with an answer.'

'Well we haven't! Unless you have any more bright ideas?'

'Okay, don't snap at me,' Rowan said, her eyes filling with tears.

I looked at my sister crying, and my annoyance faded away. Irresponsible she might be but me pointing it out wouldn't help. I hugged her.

'I'm sorry, Ro. I'm not snapping I'm just worried,' I said.

'Okay,' Rowan sniffed, 'be worried in a less snappy way.'

She blew her nose and took a few deep breaths.

'But you could fly to Cairns with someone? Once we find someone? I'll ask some of my friends. But I'd be better than no one.'

The prospect of the trip was very daunting, and my thoughts ping-ponged backwards and forwards over the various issues I'd have to face.

But foremost in my mind was this was an opportunity to seize those chances I'd been looking for, to step outside my comfort zone and give life a go. I'd never driven anything bigger than a family car. But I knew I would do it. Of course I would, come what may. I was back with my family after such a long time, I'd missed out on so much; now was my chance to do something for them. To be actively involved instead of left in the dark. And how hard could it be? A car was a car wasn't it? But driving on my own? All that way? Was there a sat-nav? Could I work one without someone grabbing it from me and shouting *for God's sake, give it to me.*

I went inside to get my laptop and find out how far it was on Google maps and then I researched a route. Nearly three thousand kilometres. It would take three hours to fly there and twenty-seven hours to drive back, and that was if I drove non-stop, day and night and didn't stop for petrol or break down. And that was the most direct way. The coastal route would take even longer. The inland route longer still.

'What do you think?' Rowan said, coming indoors to sit next to me. From her face I could tell she had been crying again. I put an arm around her and hugged her.

'No sweat,' I said cheerfully, 'it'll be fine, it just might take me a while. Women can do anything these days. They just need to add me to the insurance for the motorhome before I go anywhere.'

'Oh Elin!' Rowan burst into fresh tears and laid her head down on the table, 'I'm so sorry. I could kick myself. Bloody police!'

It didn't seem the right moment to remind Rowan it was her own fault. Instead, I went and poured us both a glass of wine and we sat trying to make plans until Maggie phoned. Rowan put her on speaker, and we crouched over it listening to her voice, which suddenly seemed small and frightened and not like her at all.

Banjo was okay, he was going to have his wrist sorted out and he was sleeping like a baby thanks to the painkillers and sedatives he'd been given.

'We're sorting it,' Rowan said, 'Elin is going to fly up to Cairns to see you and then she'll get the keys to the motorhome and drive it back here.'

'On her own?' Maggie said, 'really? Are you sure she's up to that?'

I swallowed her implied lack of confidence in my abilities. 'No, hopefully with someone else to share the driving. You're not to worry. Don't give it another thought. I've got this.'

'But who – does Elin know you lost your license, Rowan?'

Rowan and I exchanged a look and Rowan's bottom lip wobbled.

I patted her arm reassuringly. 'Don't worry, just look after yourself and keep in touch, right? Have you had something nice to eat?'

'Well, I had a sanga from the hospital shop,' Maggie said, 'I'm not sure if it was nice or not. I couldn't work out what it was; cheese and something. And the bread was stale.'

'That's the way, keep your strength up. And don't worry, I'll be with you in no time.'

We chatted for a few more minutes and then my aunt admitted she was shattered and needed to go to bed.

Half an hour later, sunburned and pissed, Shane came home.

8

I'll give him his due: Shane was a pleasant drunk. He was still charming, affectionate to Rowan, and genuinely concerned about what had happened.

And then he asked how it had happened again so perhaps he wasn't really taking it all on board.

After half an hour, Rowan encouraged him off to bed and we sat trying to finalise our master plan. Rowan even suggested she might get in touch with the police to ask if her driving ban could be postponed. Then we realised the idiocy of this and Googled 'people prepared to help drive a motorhome from Cairns to Sydney.'

Unsurprisingly, we didn't come up with any satisfactory answers. Just a load of sites that probably meant my Facebook page would be filled with adverts for maps, sat-navs and discount van hire for the rest of my life.

* * *

In the morning I got up, having hardly slept because of the worry, to find Shane leaning against the sink with a glass of water.

'Tiny bit of a headache,' he said, pulling the blind down a little to block out the sunlight.

'I'm not surprised,' I said, switching on the kettle and finding the teabags. For some reason they were kept in a drawer along with a bottle opener, three dozen discarded beer caps, some string, and a couple of plastic bags.

'So any news of poor old Banjo?' Shane said.

'He's being looked at again today. Maggie's bearing up but you can tell she's worried sick.'

'Poor old Maggie,' he said, his mouth turned down in sympathy. Then his expression brightened. 'Anyway I've been thinking about it and I've had a great idea.'

'You have?'

'I have. It came to me in the middle of the night. I often have good ideas when I'm asleep, you just ask Ro. She'll tell you. But just in case my brilliant idea doesn't work, I'll tell you about it later,' he said, tapping the side of his sunburned nose.

'Well that's no good, I need to pack a bag, find a flight to Cairns, get a book of maps that have actual roads on them instead of pencil scribbles. At least I won't have to worry about losing my suitcase.'

'Not unless the pilot chucks it out the window,' Shane said cheerfully, 'then you might.'

'Thanks Shane.'

He fished his phone out of his pocket and checked the time.

'Righty ho, I'll do this. Leave it to me and the irresistible Shane Pascoe charm.'

He went out into the back yard and closed the door behind him. I sat at the kitchen table and drank my tea.

Ten minutes later he came limping back, looking a bit solemn.

'I've sorted it,' he said at last, his face lighting up with a proud smile, 'the trip to rescue the motorhome. At great personal cost I don't mind telling you. It took all my powers of persuasion. I know someone who can help.'

I felt my shoulders relax with the relief.

'You do? Shane that's brilliant! Thank you so much! Who?'

He looked a bit wary. 'You won't hit me? Or kick my good leg? Rowan keeps threatening to do that and it's very worrying.'

'No, of course not,' I said cautiously. I began to feel rather uneasy.

'I rang him up and he agreed. He said it's okay with him. He'd be happy to help you bring Banjo's van back.'

'Shane, what have you done?'

'It's an emergency isn't it? Desperate measures for desperate times. I couldn't just sit back and do nothing with poor Maggie in a state. She's like my own mum. It's Kit. I asked Kit and he said yes. He'd be thrilled.'

'Kit? Your brother Kit?' I said.

Shane flinched and held his glass of water in front of him as though I was going to hit him. He nodded. 'He would be thrilled and very pleased to help out. He'll arrange the flights to Cairns and everything.'

My jaw dropped in astonishment. 'I don't believe you!'

'Honest to dingoes, Elin. It'll be easy peasey. He'll get his PA to book you some flights and as long as you both get onto their insurance; it shouldn't be a problem. Can you get that sorted?' Shane said.

I thought about it for a moment. Shane was looking decidedly shifty.

'He didn't say anything of the sort, did he? All that rubbish about being pleased and thrilled and happy?'

Shane looked at me, all wide-eyed innocence. 'He certainly

did! He's happy to help. We had a long chat. I told him what had happened.'

'So I have to spend days driving with your brother in a bloody motorhome! Are you insane?'

'I'm just trying to help,' Shane said with a hang-dog puppy face, 'I thought you'd be pleased.'

'You presumably tried other people? Look, I don't mind paying someone for their time.'

'Nah, no can do, I've asked everyone I can think of. All my mates are going to be held up with the surfing championship. Either that or they're at work. Or they don't drive. Or in Trev's case putting up tents. Or busy.'

'Oh God, what am I going to do?'

'Honest El, it'll be fine. I'm sure it will.'

I gave him a hard look. 'Would you be so positive if it was you having to do it?'

'You can Google him if you like. He's a fine upstanding citizen. No arrests or misdemeanours. Just a lot of boring stuff about how marvellous he is in the business world.'

'I might just do that,' I said furiously.

I went to get my laptop and logged on. Kit Pascoe.

There were pages and pages on the man. Pictures of him looking stern in a business suit. Photos of him at various conferences. Even a picture of him at some gala event in a tuxedo.

Hmm, look at that bad boy. He certainly scrubbed up well. Not that there was much scrubbing needed.

'This is fascinating stuff. Have you ever Googled yourself, Shane?' I asked.

He scratched at the dressings on his leg.

'Not for a while. I don't have to. Not now I've got Rowan,' he said absently.

'Shane!'

He grinned. 'Only kidding.'

I tried to get my head around what lay ahead.

Flying to Cairns, finding the motorhome, planning the route, having overnight stops, eating meals, driving back to Sydney, and all with Kit Pascoe in the seat next to me. It would be like having Tom back in my life. There had to be an alternative. There must be.

There wasn't.

* * *

The following morning – so I didn't even have time to think about it too much – Kit Pascoe, dressed in jeans and a cotton shirt with a pattern of tiny palm trees, arrived at the house to pick me up.

His car was as unlike Shane's van as it was possible to be. It was dark, sleek, spotless, and airconditioned. And Kit wasn't even driving it. Some impossibly glamorous woman was in the driving seat, her eyes shaded behind mirrored dark glasses She was dressed in an impeccably tailored dark suit and her hair was a glossy, blonde swirl pinned up in a tight pleat. She looked like an FBI agent, or at least like the FBI agents who appeared in the box-sets Shane had become addicted to over the last weeks. I wondered if she had a gun.

Kit barely addressed a word to me other than a brisk 'good morning' as he raised the boot so I could put my case in. He opened the car door so I could get into the back seat and he went into the front next to the FBI agent, tapping away on his laptop during the hour's drive to the airport. He made some short, snappy phone calls to people called Jane and Sukie. I wondered if Jane or Sukie was a significant other. Not judging by his tone of voice. If they were, he was equally bad tempered with them as he was with me.

I watched his broad shoulders moving under the palm tree shirt, the way he ran one hand through his silvering hair or pointed a finger when he was being emphatic about something. He was used to doing all the talking and getting his own way, that much was obvious. I shrank down into the seat. It was going to be awful spending so much time with someone who didn't like me very much.

Although what right he had not to like me was a mystery. After all, he was the one who had been unpredictable and tetchy when he delivered that envelope, not me. Although perhaps slamming the door in his face hadn't helped. When we had been chatting on the plane, he seemed okay. Perhaps he really had just been putting it on? Perhaps it had just been an amusing diversion to him? I bristled with indignation at the thought.

As we neared the airport, he snapped his laptop shut and packed it away into a leather bag. I wondered if he was going to be typing all the way to Cairns and back to Sydney? That would make for a fun time.

Perhaps he would just bark out directions to me when I was driving? Maybe when he was at the wheel, he would ignore my advice about traffic delays and short cuts and then I would panic and feel even worse, and we would spend hours not talking. It really would be like being back with Tom.

And – oh my god – where would we sleep? I couldn't sleep in the motorhome with him for heaven's sake. I'd have to insist on motels or something, with very separate rooms.

'Right, here we are. Thanks Sam.' Ah, so he could actually bring himself to say thank you occasionally. 'You phone Les and tell Jane I'll be in touch later and see what Crosby says to the new developments.'

Sam nodded, her face expressionless behind the dark glasses.

She waited until Kit had got our cases from the boot and then drove smoothly off.

We stood in silence for a few seconds. I hate long, uncomfortable silences. I've sat through quite a few over the years and I'm incapable of letting one stretch on.

'Well,' I said brightly, 'this is it.'

'Is what?' he said, without looking at me.

Good grief.

'This is where the rescue mission begins,' I said, trying to sound upbeat, 'off to Cairns.'

'Yes, I suppose so,' he said, and started to wheel his bag towards the entrance door.

I hurried after him. This was ridiculous. We would have to talk to each other sometime.

'I wanted to thank you,' I said, 'I'm really very grateful for your help. Getting my aunt and uncle back safely. I know how busy you must be. I'm sure you have plenty of other things you would rather be doing.'

'Well, I have plenty of things I could be doing,' he said, 'but sometimes things happen to force the issue.'

'What do you mean?' I said, confused.

'Nothing. I'm here, aren't I?'

This wasn't reassuring.

We went through security and into a lounge where he found a seat next to a power point, so he could recharge his phone and laptop.

'You were doing that when I met you,' I said, 'charging your laptop, do you remember?'

'Of course I remember,' he said still not looking at me, and then he started typing very fast.

Oh.

* * *

I left him typing and making more terse phone calls and wandered off to look at the planes. Then I found a café and had a cup of tea and a massive cranberry muffin. For some reason, I didn't want to be seen stuffing my face in front of him, or have the discussion with him about how he liked his coffee, would he like a muffin? It seemed too intimate. Too personal.

I suppose that's one of the things about a long marriage. You gradually get to know everything about someone. Well, most things anyway.

I bet Kit barely told his wife (if he had one) when he would be home or what he wanted for breakfast. I bet the poor woman spent most of her life on the edge of a nervous breakdown. Would he want scrambled or poached eggs? Or toast and Vegemite? Or would he leave the house with just black coffee and a snarl so that his wife went to find the gin bottle and collapsed crying on the sofa?

I made my way back to the lounge and found him looking out of the window at the runway. He'd put his laptop away and his expression was thoughtful.

'I love planes,' he said, when he realised I was there, 'I never get tired of watching them.'

'Me too,' I said.

He pointed at something.

'Have you noticed there is always one man in a high-viz jacket and ear defenders who doesn't ever seem to be doing anything? '

'Yes!' I said, rather surprised, 'I have, how amazing that you have too.'

'I could do that job. I'd love that job,' he said. He sounded a bit wistful.

'You'd get bored,' I said, 'you wouldn't find that much of a challenge.'

'No, probably not. Although it would be nice to just do something so uncomplicated for once.'

'We don't know; he might actually be responsible for the most important part of the airport's smooth running. Hundreds of jobs might depend on whatever it is he's doing.'

Kit didn't answer for a moment and I wondered if we were back into the silent treatment again. What else could I talk to him about?

He glanced at his watch and then looked at me. 'Look, I didn't get any breakfast and there's just time for coffee and a muffin. Would you like that?'

He was actually talking to me; he wasn't snapping or growling at me. And although I didn't really want either, I didn't want to spoil things.

'Great idea,' I said, 'although to be honest, I'd prefer tea. Lead the way.'

9

The flight to Cairns was uneventful mainly because the plane was full, and Kit and I weren't actually sitting next to each other. In fact, we were three rows apart and all I could occasionally see of him was the back of his head as he turned and spoke to the cabin crew. There was one particularly attractive stewardess who seemed to think it was her life's work to sashay up to him at every opportunity to bring him something or ask if he needed anything. She certainly didn't spend as much time with anyone else. Perhaps Kit did have the same sort of charm as his brother, but chose to use it more selectively?

At Cairns, we got off the plane and collected our baggage in no time.

'Shall we get a taxi to the hospital?' I said as we made our way out of the airport.

'I've sorted it,' Kit said. He was pulling his case along behind him, checking his phone and looking for someone at the same time. Multi-tasking at its finest.

Shortly after that, a man with mirrored glasses approached

him, took his case, and without a word put it into the back of another sleek, dark car. And then he took mine too. Either this was another FBI agent look-alike, or we were being politely kidnapped. Or perhaps Kit needed a lot of security because he was so important. Or perhaps like Rowan he had lost his license?

It turned out he was a driver called Les, who took us smoothly in air-conditioned, leather-seated comfort to the hospital. Having opened the door for me, he then escorted us into the building and stood in classic FBI mode; legs slightly apart, hands clasped in front of him, the light glinting off his mirrored sunglasses. It was like having a bodyguard. I was almost expecting Les to start muttering up his cuff, communicating with Langley, Virginia. Telling someone that The Subject was on the move. That's what they usually do.

Kit and I went to find the right ward, and found Banjo in bed, in a room with a wonderful view over the ocean. Maggie was dozing in a chair next to him.

She woke up with a start, got to her feet and came over to greet us, slightly tearful.

'Oh Elin! You got here! I'm so relieved. I was wondering what we would do if your plane had crashed or been diverted or something.'

'Ever the optimist, Maggie,' I said hugging her.

She suddenly seemed tiny, older, a bit battered.

'How are you both? Are you okay? How are you feeling? We've been so worried.'

'Oh, we're indestructible, or so it seems,' she said, wiping her eyes.

I passed her a box of tissues, and she blew her nose and straightened her shoulders. At last she calmed down, went towards Kit and he held out a hand, which she shook.

'You're Kit, aren't you?' she said. 'We've met before.'

'Under happier circumstances I think,' Kit said smoothly.

Maggie pondered on this. She'd never been one to let a thought go unaired.

'Well, I don't think that's quite right, as I recall you were the one having a very loud argument at Rowan's special party to welcome Elin back. You wrecked the whole thing. And you were tearing a strip off Shane. I mean dear old Shane! His poor leg! Is he recovering?'

I reassured her that Shane was going to be fine. Maggie turned a steely gaze onto Kit as though he'd bitten Shane, not the shark.

'Are you really brothers?'

'Yes we are. And I'd like to apologise for my behaviour that evening. It was unforgiveable.'

'Hmm. I see. You're very different from Shane, aren't you? Well anyway, I'm very grateful to you for helping Elin do this,' Maggie said, 'but I'm terribly sorry it had to be you who was dragged in. I wish Rowan could have found someone nice who was free.'

Tactful Maggie, really tactful.

'It's perfectly okay,' Kit said, and he twinkled his eyes at her.

My aunt blushed! I couldn't believe my eyes. Handsome comes with a get out of jail free card it seems.

I stared at her for a minute before Banjo distracted everyone with a loud stage cough.

'I'm over here, you remember me? I'm the star of this show.'

I went over to hug him. He looked older and frailer too, the hospital gown gaping at the neck, and I felt like crying.

'You're sure you are going to be okay?'

Banjo squeezed my hand. 'It was just a silly tumble that's all, love. No need for all this fuss. It takes more than that to knock off an old cobber like me.'

Kit went over to the patient.

'Good to meet you again, sir.'

'Don't be daft. Call me Banjo, and she's Maggie. We don't answer to anything else,' he said.

Kit held out a hand to shake and Banjo wrestled with his injured wrist for a moment before holding out his left hand. Then they nodded and grinned at each other in a manly sort of way and Kit spent a few minutes turning on the charm gamma rays. Asking if he was comfortable, how he was feeling, if there was anything he needed.

Banjo seemed to fall for it like a house of playing cards in a fracking area.

Maggie handed over the keys to the motorhome and gave us a little hand drawn map on the back of an envelope to show us where the camp site was. There was a plan worked out already. We should unpack and fill our empty cases with their clothes. Then Malc and Patty would take them into my aunt and uncle at the hospital before they returned for the main event: Storming Norman's eightieth party. Apparently, Norman knew about the party but had not yet been informed about Banjo's accident in case it triggered another heart attack. I wondered if this was the same Norm who had lost his dentures when he went white water rafting. And was it really wise to do so if he had a heart condition.

I then had a mental image of a field full of pensioners staggering around on Zimmer frames, listening to big band music and comparing prescription regimes.

'Malc and Patty will be sorry we're not there. I hope they won't be too upset. But Malc's desperate to hear Vince and the Deadbeat Rockers – he was at school with Vince – and Patty was bringing some of her special brownies to help the party go with a swing,' Maggie said.

How special? I didn't think I needed to know that.

At that point a doctor – who looked about fifteen and slightly terrified – came into the room asking if it was convenient to check them out and Kit tactfully suggested we went to find some tea and biscuits.

'Thank you for this,' I said as we queued up at the café to pay.

'You're welcome. I bet they are sorry to be missing this birthday party. It sounds like it's going to be a blast.'

I sneaked a look at him to see if he was joking, but I don't think he was.

He smiled at me.

A proper smile.

And it was as though the sun had come out.

'I know you think I have no sense of humour or fun, but you might be wrong you know,' he said.

'You seemed all right on the plane, when we met,' I admitted, 'but ever since then, you've been completely different. Each time I've seen you you've been… in a mood.'

'Well,' he picked up the tea tray and stood looking at me for a moment, 'have you ever thought there might be a reason for that?'

For a brief second our eyes locked and a startling little fizz of something went through me. I don't think I'd had a fizz of anything for many years.

Flipping heck, he was handsome. Even the sour looking woman behind the till had cracked her face into a smile for him as she handed him his change. He had put it into the charity collection box next to her and she had almost melted. Not a good look in a woman.

By the time we got back to Banjo's room, the doctor had gone – off to Scouts maybe – and Maggie was standing looking out of the window, watching the sea rolling in from the vastness of the Pacific.

'It's okay, you don't need to look so worried. He's told us we're fine. Both of us,' she said as we came in. She was smiling and looked better than when we had left her. 'Banjo needs a couple more investigations, but he should be discharged in a few days, and I'm fit as a flea.'

'I've been thinking. Perhaps we could just come home with you. In the RV,' my uncle said from his bed behind her.

Maggie rounded on him. 'Don't even think about it. You heard the doctor; there's no way we are doing that.'

'Oh all right, woman, just an idea for heaven's sake. Who's the boss around here anyway?'

'After all these years, you shouldn't need to ask,' Maggie said tartly and came forward to clear a space on the table for the tea tray.

Back downstairs, Les was still standing in the hospital foyer, looking as though he hadn't moved since we left him. I wondered if he had? I bet once we disappeared upstairs to the ward, he had gone off to slump on one of the plastic armchairs with a copy of *Who* magazine, reading about Kylie Minogue and her pert *derrière*.

We followed him back out into the heat of the afternoon and into the car. After a long, silent stare at Maggie's envelope map, Les managed to log the Happy Surfer Campsite into the sat-nav and we were off.

I sat in the back of the car, looking out of the window while Kit rested his head back and closed his eyes. I sneaked a couple of glances at him. He looked tired, strangely vulnerable, and I wondered again if I had been wrong about him.

* * *

When we arrived, our limo stuck out like a Chieftain tank in a
shopping mall, creeping around the one-way system of the campsite. Les drove cautiously over the numerous speed bumps, round
the huge trampoline park, and past the pool where about a
hundred children were splashing and screaming. I opened the car
window and looked out, letting in the wonderful smell of barbeques and suntan oil and the sounds of people having fun.

Then we slowed even further, following a dreadlocked surfer
dude pedalling a large two-seater go-cart. He had a child in the
seat next to him, a toddler hanging onto his back and a baby in a
white plastic bucket between his knees. Eventually they veered off
towards a massive blue canvas tent covered in bunting and flags
where a dreadlocked girl was lying on a sunbed reading a book.
Delighted, I craned to watch them as we inched past. The two
children tumbled off the go-cart and ran to leap on their mother
with screams of excitement so that her sunbed collapsed and the
three of them rolled around on the grass laughing. They looked
utterly adorable, young and happy and loving life. A family
enjoying each other's company, absolutely nothing like the family
life I had been a part of.

Had Dan ever leapt on me with a delighted scream? I couldn't
remember him ever doing it. If he had I could almost hear Tom's
rebuke. *Don't do that, what will people think?* I shouldn't have let
him get away with it.

We went past the open-sided camp kitchen block where
people were cooking or washing up. There was a huge television
on the wall showing some sporting event and several people were
standing watching, beer cans in their hands. As we passed,
everyone turned to look and two broke away from the group and
trotted towards us.

Les had to stop rather abruptly or he would have run them
over and they waved delightedly.

The woman came around to talk through my open window, her hands resting on the car door. Les would have a fit when he saw the sun cream handprints she left on the glossy paintwork.

'You must be Elin! It's us: Patty and Malc!' she said, 'I'm so glad to see you! How's Banjo? And Maggie?'

'He's doing well,' I smiled, 'disappointed he's not here.'

'Daft old buzzard, he could have killed himself. Or landed on Maggie and then where would we be? Pull over up there by the van with the stripy awning and we'll catch you up.'

They made us tea and Patty, dressed almost identically to Malc in grey combat shorts and a blue polo shirt, brought out some brownies.

'Are these safe?' I said, 'I've been warned about your baking skills.'

She laughed. 'Perfectly safe; you don't want to believe everything you hear. Times have changed, you know.'

With a lot of persistent twittering and nagging, she even managed to get Les out of the car, made him sit in a canvas chair, and pressed a cup of tea and a brownie on him. He sat, still with his sunglasses on looking distinctly uncomfortable, the brownie held out in front of him like an unexploded grenade.

Meanwhile Malc was showing Kit how the motorhome worked, how to connect it to the electricity and water if we parked up. How to empty the toilet cassette (I looked away at this point and vowed never to use it) and deal with something called grey water which involved drains. There seemed to be a lot of pipes and reels of cables involved and something about a battery; I hoped Kit was paying proper attention. He and Malc were even sharing a joke and laughing about something. Kit looked about ten years younger than he had at our previous meetings, his hair a bit ruffled, his face relaxed out of its usual stern expression. It was rather surprising. And nice.

'I've folded up all Maggie and Banjo's clothes, so if you and your friend want to get unpacked, we can take their stuff away in your cases. Clever idea of mine wasn't it?' Patty said proudly, 'I mean it's a big old van but you don't need all their things in there, do you? There's a bit of their washing needs doing so I'll get that done tomorrow too.'

I felt a bit tearful at their simple thoughtfulness. This was what good friends did for one another; it was rather humbling.

'Thank you so much,' I said, 'are you sure? You're so kind.'

Patty flapped a hand. 'Nah! It's only what they would do for us. Although I'll give Banjo a lend of me step next time. Silly old fool. Anyway, sounds like he'll be fine and that's what matters.'

Kit and Malc came across and sat down with us. I noticed Les was sipping his tea as thought it might be poisoned and the brownie remained untouched.

'Nice of you to help out with this rescue mission, Kit,' Patty said encouragingly, 'really kind.'

'I didn't really have much of a say in the matter,' Kit said. He gave a brief, tight smile, 'but here we are.'

Didn't have much of a say? What did that mean?

Patty took me into the motorhome to show me how various aspects of the kitchen worked, although why she would think I was going to be doing anything other than boiling a kettle I had no idea.

She lowered her tone. 'I must say your boyfriend is a bit tasty isn't he? Known each other long?'

'Not long at all, and he certainly isn't my boyfriend,' I muttered back.

Patty favoured me with an incredulous look and then gave me a dig in the ribs with her elbow for good measure. 'Well shame on you! I'd get his stamp on the back of my hand if I was you!'

'Patty!'

'Don't mind me, I speak as I find and he's nice.' Patty gave me another sly dig and winked.

Nice? Was Kit nice? Perhaps he was. When it suited him.

* * *

'So why don't you come over and join in the camp barbie once you're settled?' Malc said a bit later. 'The birthday boy Norm will be arriving later and the other Cairns group. You'll love 'em. The Silver Surfers are a whole heap of fun and we've got far too much food. You'd be doing us a favour, really you would.'

Oh good heavens, once we were settled. That means once we had sorted out the motorhome for sleeping.

Inside the van I had been relieved to see there was more space than I had expected. Two big driving seats in the front which could be turned round to face the inside of the van and seating at the back which would turn into a large double bed. There was a dinky little sink, fridge freezer, toilet and shower cubicles, and a single bed space in the roof over the driver's seat that had used to store towels and bed linen. One of us would have to sleep in there. I guessed it would be me and my heart sank a bit. Oh well, we could look for motels tomorrow it would only be one night; we would manage. As long as neither of us snored too much.

It didn't take us long to unpack and put our clothes away. Every possible space had been designed for storage. There were cupboards everywhere. The fridge freezer was full of food, there were pots and pans and cutlery, a small television on one wall, and even an air-conditioning unit on the ceiling.

By this point Les was starting to get a bit edgy as a crowd of small children had collected around his car and were asking if they could have a ride.

'Perhaps you'd better get going, Les,' Kit said with a grin.

Les nodded and gently shooed the kids away before handing his mug and the brownie back. I don't think he entirely trusted Patty or her baking.

He had a muttered conversation with Kit and then got into the limo and set off, hotly pursued by half a dozen yelling boys and a scraggy looking terrier.

I watched rather wistfully as Les disappeared back to civilisation and places where toilet cassettes didn't exist or need attention. It was a bit of a solemn moment. Kit and I were on our own.

I felt a bit like a pioneer about to set off into the outback, albeit one with an airconditioned van instead of a horse drawn wagon. Perhaps I was being a bit dramatic? This sort of experience must be enjoyable on some level otherwise people wouldn't do it. But then they would be doing it with people they knew, people they'd chosen.

'Hey you two, great news! Dusty Jack is playing later,' Malc called through the open door as we explored the van, opening and closing doors and drawers, playing with the special catches that meant they wouldn't burst open when we were driving. I was very concerned about that; I didn't want my new, holiday knickers flying out when we went round a corner.

'Dusty Jack?' I said.

'Dusty Jack and his Ditties and Jokes from the Outback. He's a scream,' Malc said, 'you can't miss him. He's only here for one night and he's Norm's favourite.'

I looked at Kit to see what his reaction was and he raised one eyebrow.

'Well we can't miss that, can we,' he said, much to my surprise, 'a barbie and Dusty Jack all in one go. Sounds like our evening's entertainment is all set to me.'

'I guess it is,' I said uncertainly, and Malc beamed.

'Come over to the cook house when you're ready. I'll get the beers lined up and save us all some seats. Don't hang about, he's very popular.'

10

I enjoyed Dusty Jack (grey ponytail, battered bushman's hat, and jeans held up with red braces) and his 'Ditties and Jokes from the Outback' far more than I thought I would. It wasn't 'Waltzing Matilda' for once, but some rather sweet sad songs and poems, plus some terrible jokes and monologues that anywhere else would have got him heckled off the stage or pelted with fruit.

Some of the other Silver Surfers had arrived, including the four who had come across country from Perth. Frank, Norm, Jim, and Dinkie were all travelling together in a huge RV which was like a removal van, and they were as noisy and excited as a flock of starlings. Sitting in the midst of them was hilarious. They all seemed so full of life, so enthusiastic.

Norm took his seat about ten minutes late and received some good-natured heckling from the stage, which he batted back with style.

'Okay you wombat, I'm eighty tomorrow and so's me prostate, so put a sock in it!'

Of course, this meant the whole audience took it upon themselves to sing 'Happy Birthday' to Norm, and he squirmed in his seat, embarrassed but secretly looking rather pleased.

Kit, sitting next to me, seemed to enjoy the evening too, laughing in all the right places and applauding enthusiastically after a rather touching rendition of 'My Country' by Dorothea MacKellar. She'd written it in England, homesick for Australia.

I hadn't thought about that poem since I left school, and it was wonderful to hear it again. I could understand it now, that love of 'the wide brown land.'

Thanks to all the beer, I made several trips to the loo block during the evening, and it was spotless, with shower cubicles and next door a room filled with coin operated washing machines and driers. I was impressed, I don't mind admitting. Maybe I could understand why Maggie and Banjo were so keen on their lifestyle and the camaraderie of the Silver Surfers.

After the show had finished, they all congregated, bringing their folding chairs and beer with them, around Jim and Dinkie's RV, which was the size of a small house, had been towing a small car behind it, and even had electric panels on the side which opened out to make more room.

Proper introductions were made, although I knew I wouldn't remember their names. They were all cheerful, friendly people, who liked to laugh a lot. They discussed routes and campsites, and someone put candles in jam jars on the table and we sat in the dark, warm evening talking for hours. And then Jim said he was hungry again, so Dinkie went inside and brought out snacks and a bowl of sweets and Patty went to fetch a box of biscuits.

Just after ten, Frank brought out a guitar and at the sight of it they all cheered. Except Dinkie who rolled her eyes.

'I knew you'd bring the tone down,' she said.

'Go on Frankie, give us "Click go the Shears",' Malc shouted.

'And "The Wild Colonial Boy",' Patty added, 'that's me favourite. A terror to Australia. I liked the sound of him.'

'I tell you who is a terror to Australia and that's Dinkie when she gets behind the wheel of that van,' Jim shouted, and everyone laughed as though this was a very old joke.

Frank did some perfunctory tuning of his guitar, and the other Silver Surfers gave good natured groans.

'Aw put a sock in it you lot, you know what I'm going to play and you mongrels better sing along.'

Of course, this time it was 'Waltzing Matilda' and of course we all joined in.

It was a song that had been so familiar to me as I was growing up. I hadn't sung it for years; it had become a cliché, something teenagers discounted as too sentimental but suddenly I found I was crying. I hadn't realised how much I had missed this wide brown land; how wonderful it was to be back again. I grabbed a paper napkin off the table and blew my nose.

I felt a hand on my arm.

'You okay?' Kit said.

I took a deep breath. 'I'm fine.'

We were there for a long time, singing all the old, traditional songs, drinking beer, listening to stories. And then it got to midnight, and it actually was Norm's birthday, so we sang to him as well.

Before we went back to the van, which took a long time because we had to say goodnight to all the Silver Surfers and they were in no mood to end the evening, I went to the loo again for luck. I was pleasantly tipsy from all the beers I'd swigged back, and full of barbeque food we had enjoyed. I think they were beef burgers; they might have been kangaroo for all I knew.

When we were children, we hadn't been to sites like this one, with proper paved roads, swimming pools and even a shop.

Perhaps they hadn't existed. But I still remembered those holidays with affection; they had been simple but such fun. I'd enjoyed my childhood; I didn't think Dan had ever had much fun with us.

With few exceptions, Tom had liked to go to the same place every year: an unexciting cottage in an unremarkable town in Wales, where there was nothing much for a child to do except go for walks, visit museums, and listen to his father talk about the importance of exams. What a shame; so many opportunities missed.

I had to think about the sleeping bit, that was the thing. Did Kit wear pyjamas? Did he have a dressing gown? I wasn't going to use the motorhome loo, but would he? God, I hope he didn't, if he did, I'd have to sing or stick my fingers in my ears. What would he think when he saw me in the morning with no make-up and bed hair? Did that actually matter? No of course it didn't; he'd have to take me as he found me.

But where and how would we both get undressed?

I'd never been one to wander around with no clothes on; in fact I'd become quite the opposite. I had been a lights-out sort of wife who changed into her pyjamas in the bathroom.

When I got back, Kit was looking concerned.

'You can have the bed and I'll go up there,' he said, pointing at the bunk.

'No don't be daft, I'll go up there, I'm smaller than you, it would be too cramped,' I said, folding my arms.

'I honestly don't mind,' he said.

'Nor do I.' I gave a small hiccup.

'Flip a coin?' he suggested with a grin.

'Rock, paper, scissors,' I said.

We stood straight-faced, watching each other and actually did rock, paper, scissors. Then we disagreed on what won (I said the rock smashed the scissors and he said the scissors could be sharpened on the rock) so we set some ground rules and did it three times because I lost and Kit insisted best of three.

I ended up in the bunk, leaving the bed for Kit.

'This doesn't feel right at all. You should be in the proper bed,' he said.

'Too late, you won fair and square,' I replied, 'anyway I don't need the bed just because I'm a woman.'

'Well I'll go out for a walk and leave you to get sorted,' he said picking up his wash bag. I guessed he was going to the loo. That was a relief.

I was undressed and in my pyjamas in less than a minute. Then I remembered my contact lenses and took them out. At which point Kit could have paraded around the van wearing just his socks and I wouldn't have been able to see him. Of course, that set me unexpectedly wondering what that scenario would look like and by the time he came back, knocking on the door and calling out, 'are you decent?', I was feeling rather hot and bothered.

He had already changed into something that might have been a t-shirt and pyjama shorts combination although I shut my eyes and didn't look for too long. He seemed even taller in the van and he padded about for a few minutes getting himself settled.

'All right if I turn the lights out?' he said at last.

I pulled the covers up to my chin.

'Fine,' I said. And he did.

Wow, it was dark. I mean really dark. We were at the far end of the site away from the lighted areas but once my eyes got used to it, it was rather lovely.

'Are you okay up there?' he said.

'Yes fine,' I replied, although I was rather hot and if I sat up suddenly in the night I would probably knock myself out. I wriggled a bit and stuck my feet out from under the covers. I always do that.

'It was a good night, wasn't it?' he said.

'Excellent. The Silver Surfers are a lot of fun. I hope I'm as energetic when I'm their age.'

'They've got plans for tomorrow. Norm wants to go to the beach; he did mention surfing. After all, it's his eightieth birthday, he gets to call the shots.'

'Good grief! He's certainly game for a laugh,' I said.

Kit chuckled. 'He certainly is. And he asked if we would stay on and join them all.'

I didn't know what to say to this. I was surprised and a little shocked at the suggestion. I certainly hadn't expected it.

'I mean, it might be fun,' Kit said.

'I'm sure it would be,' I replied.

There was a long pause before Kit spoke again.

'So shall we?'

'What about work,' I said, 'I thought you were busy?'

'I'm always busy. It doesn't mean I can't take a few days off. People do, you know?'

I considered all the options. Not rushing off at first light to find a motel somewhere along our route. Instead staying here, joining in with all the Silver Surfers and Norm's birthday celebrations.

'I suppose we could,' I said.

'Great, I'll tell Patty in the morning. If you're sure.'

Yes, the more I thought about it, the more I liked the idea. I'd spent a lot of time on my own over the last few years. Tom being out of the picture, and even when we were still together, he had been sort of absent. Or telling me lies about education confer-ences and meetings he had to attend. And Dan away at university and then moving out altogether. It might be good to have some company, and even if the Silver Surfers were all in their seventies or over, they were still full of life. I think I had laughed more that evening than I had for a long time.

'By the way, what did you mean when you said you had no say about coming here with me?' I said.

He didn't reply for a moment and I wondered if he had gone to sleep. But then he answered.

'Oh I don't know. It seemed the right thing to do,' he said.

'Well I'm very grateful, thank you.'

'You've thanked me already,' he said.

So, day one was over and nothing awful had happened. I thought of all the positive things. We had got from Sydney to Cairns, seen that my aunt and uncle were being well looked after, and made it to the campsite. We had made new friends and enjoyed a great evening. Nothing bad had happened and it was all thanks to Kit.

There was a long silence while I listened to the trees rustling outside. Somewhere in the distance I heard country music playing, the occasional sound of a door closing or a child complaining about something and then I fell asleep.

* * *

The following morning, I woke to find Kit had already gone out. That answered the loo question. I clambered inelegantly down from my bunk, put my dressing gown on, and put in my contact lenses. Not only had he gone out but he had tidied away the bed and put two mugs ready with coffee in one and a tea bag in another. He'd remembered; that was rather sweet. Goodness, he must have been quiet. Either that or I had been in an alcohol induced semi-coma.

A moment later the door opened a little.

'Are you decent?' he said.

'Reasonably,' I replied wondering what my hair was doing this morning. I wasn't in the mood for much conversation; I was desperate for the loo.

He came in, dressed in jeans and a sweatshirt, and already showered; his wet hair slicked back. He looked very presentable. Blast. How do men do that? I'd probably have to apply a full face of make-up. Oh for heaven's sake, of course I wouldn't. Why on earth should I have to?

'I'll make you some tea,' he said, 'I've been to the shop for some milk. The stuff in the fridge was a bit off.'

'Thanks,' I said, 'I'll just go and...'

I made a grab for my wash bag and some clothes and made my way to the shower block.

* * *

When I got there, I could hear a couple of kids in the family shower cubicle making a heck of a racket and doing a lot of giggling. I wondered what they were up to. I soon found out.

I went into an empty cubicle and tidily put my towel and bag of clean clothes on the hooks behind the door. Then I reached forward and turned the shower on.

A blast of cold water shot out straight towards me and in a second I was soaked from the neck down. I gave a startled yelp and did a bit of undignified dancing on the spot, the kids shot out hooting with laughter. Well, that was one way to get rid of a hangover.

'You little mongrels!' I shouted after them. It seemed my grasp of the Aussie lingo was returning.

It was a really impressive shower too, terrific water pressure but more acceptable once I had adjusted the water temperature and tilted the showerhead down. I squelched about for a bit in wet trainers; my dressing gown and pyjamas were soaked. I'd have to use the driers, otherwise I'd face an embarrassing time later this evening. I had another pair of new pj's, but they had cartoon characters all over them. Nothing less alluring than a woman who thought Roadrunner and Tweety Pie made acceptable leisure wear. I hadn't thought this through. If Kit saw me in those he would think I was completely round the bend.

After my shower, I caught sight of myself in the mirror and did a bit of rapid repair with some mascara. I don't think for one moment it made me look any better. As I'd suspected, I certainly didn't look as good this morning as Kit did. Rats.

Why is that? Some men didn't even have to put on smart clothes or shave in the morning to look presentable. Life's very unfair sometimes.

By the time I got back into the motorhome, Kit was sitting at the table with his laptop open and poring over my father's book of road maps at the same time. As I'd anticipated, the maps were years out of date and several pages were ripped and some were almost unreadable with coffee stains. He didn't look up.

'The kettle has boiled. By the looks of these maps it's a good job I brought my sat nav,' Kit said, pulling it out of a bag and firing it up. 'Make yourself some tea and come and sit next to me, see what you think. The Wi-Fi is a bit slow but there are several options.'

I slid into the seat next to him.

'Options for what?' I said rather confused.

'Which way we should go when we eventually leave here,' Kit said.

He pushed the map book over to me and outlined his ideas.

'We could go the fast way which would take us this way, straight down the A1.'

'Yes,' I said, 'I thought that's what we were going to do?'

He looked up from his sat-nav and smiled and suddenly I was blushing and a bit flustered. For heaven's sake.

'Well, I've been thinking. We don't have to do that, you know. There are other options and opportunities.'

'Like what?'

My mind was spinning. What the heck did he mean?

He showed me the Google maps page on his laptop. A long, blue line squiggled along the east coast, dodging backwards and forwards all over the place.

'That route would take much longer,' I said.

'So?' he shrugged.

'So I thought you wanted to get back as soon as possible.'

He pushed out his lower lip thoughtfully. 'Do you?'

'Do I what?'

I was getting a bit muddled and overheated here. We were rather close together too and the faint whiff of his lovely after-shave was distracting me. How can a middle-aged, perfectly sensible woman who has a generally low opinion of men in general, be distracted by aftershave?

He looked at me again. It was suddenly a bit difficult to look into those beautiful eyes that were sometimes hazel and sometimes greenish.

'Like I said, I've just been thinking about things. About what you said on the plane from London actually, and it really struck a chord—'

I'd said something meaningful on the plane? What would that be then? I just remembered being my usual garrulous self.

'—About how hard I have been working. I haven't had much of a break from work for a very long time, I slept better last night than I have for years, and this is a trip I always wanted to take and never got around to doing. I mean I've flown to Brisbane but never been to the koala sanctuary for example. Or Straddie Island. I've flown over lighthouses but never been able to enjoy the view of the sea from there. I've never had the chance to see pods of whales or dolphins surfing and this is the time of year they migrate. I've been to Coffs Harbour and Port Macquarie on business but never actually explored them properly. Every time I go there, I glimpse nice-looking wine bars and cafés and never get to go in to them. I just go from one conference room to another. The same with places like Byron Bay. I haven't been there for years. These days I fly there or I'm driven there and then I come home, but never had a chance to look around. I like drinking Australian wine, but I've never been to the place where the vines grow. The Hunter valley. I've always wanted to revisit the Three Sisters, the Glasshouse mountains. I know you haven't been back to Australia for a long time, but this would only take a few extra days. This country is beautiful and worth seeing, don't you think? So I'll ask you again. Do you really want to get back as soon as possible?'

This was the longest speech I had heard from him and when he finished I took a breath, ready to say yes of course I did. And then I realised that actually...

He finished his coffee and went to make himself another. 'Perhaps I've got it wrong? I just thought it might be fun to go on a road trip.'

A road trip?

I felt a burst of excitement.

All my life I'd wanted to do a road trip.

I'd imagined one around New England, calling in to see cute country stores and stopping at diners and viewing areas. Places that Tom would have whizzed past if we'd ever got across the Atlantic in the first place. This was a chance to do it in my own country. We would be like a younger chapter of the Silver Surfers.

What could we call ourselves? The Flying Foxes. The Fruit Bats. The Kookaburra Two.

God, it sounded exciting.

Kit gave me a crooked smile, almost apologetic.

'This is a bit sudden for you, isn't it? I know you're someone who likes to plan things properly. But it would only be a few extra days. And if we don't really get on then we can change our minds. It might be fun, you know.'

Would it? Yes, I supposed it could be. Unbelievably, I was considering it. This wasn't like me at all. And what did he mean by 'get on'?

For some reason, driving with him suddenly didn't seem such a bad prospect. Instead of thundering down the motorway towards Sydney as fast as the speed limit allowed, I imagined myself sitting beside him as we went the pretty way.

It wouldn't be the same as driving with Tom, I knew that already. Kit and I would watch the scenery change, visit new places, travel down the Great Pacific Highway, stopping off where the fancy took us. Perhaps we would eat seafood at cute water-front cafés, maybe we would walk together along endless golden beaches.

The idea seemed both rather appealing and vaguely unnerving. Both emotions swirled around my brain; he was right, I wasn't used to this sort of spontaneity. I clutched my mug in front of me with both hands and considered the prospect.

Why was I feeling this change between us? Was I attracted to him? Of course I wasn't. That sort of thing hadn't entered my mind for a long time. And if I was, so what? It didn't mean anything, did it? Could I think for one second that he – a man with business to attend to, who flew all over the place, had personal drivers and glossy cars to call upon – enjoyed my company? Maybe even liked me?

Well I could only assume he wasn't repulsed or indifferent to me. But all that business with Shane? That side of his nature.

What about that? And would anyone worry about me if I disappeared off the radar for a few days?

Should I?

He made me another cup of tea and pushed it across the table.

'So? What do you think?'

I looked up at him and I couldn't help myself; the possibilities won me over. I nodded.

'I think it might be okay.'

'Excellent!' he smiled back, and he was almost boyish in his delight. 'Now we'd better sort out some breakfast if we are going to the beach with Norm and the gang. I hope you've brought your bathers?'

What was going on here? One minute he was a surly, bad-tempered man with the charm of a warthog. When it suited him he could turn the charisma on faster than a dog eats its dinner. And I'd fallen for it. Yet again.

And wear a swimming costume in front of him? I don't think so! Yes, I had packed it, although I hadn't thought about where I might wear it. I suppose I'd assumed there might be a motel with a pool.

I wasn't expecting this. And I hadn't expected to feel quite so excited at the prospect. What the hell was I doing?

11

We went to the camp café for breakfast as I didn't feel entirely confident about cooking in the van yet. Stoked up on a Full Australian Banging Breakfast, which consisted of one of everything the chef had on his hotplate, we went back, both of us I think with indigestion, and began to pack up the van.

Then we were distracted by a loud cheer from outside and went to see Norm sitting in front of Patty's motorhome while she presented him with a plateful of Lamington cakes, a lit candle stuck in each one.

'Great news you're sticking around for a bit,' Malc said, 'Vince and the Deadbeat Rockers are going to be playing this evening. I went to school with Vince. When he takes his false teeth out, he can put two snooker balls in his mouth at once.'

Well that wasn't a sentence I'd ever expected to hear.

After a lot of discussion and some good-tempered wrangling, it was decided that we would go with Malc and Patty in their van, following the others in their little car. Getting everyone organised and ready to leave at the same time was how I imagine rounding up sheep must be. Without the dog. Just as we were ready to go, someone would get out of the car, remembering something they had forgotten to pack or want to go to the loo.

'Always take the opportunity, that's what I say,' Norm shouted across as he wedged himself into Ken's hatchback, 'you never know when you might find the next one.'

At last, just before ten, we set off in convoy following Frank, Norm, Jim, and Dinkie jammed into their car. We sat behind them on opposite sides of a fixed table, our knees bumping underneath it.

It was one of the most beautiful roads I'd ever seen. We drove along by the side of the ocean, under trees where the sunlight flickered through the branches.

'I didn't see anyone pack surfboards,' I said.

'I don't think the surf's up to much on this part of the coast,' Malc said laughing, 'but all things considered perhaps it's just as well. Sometimes Norm forgets he's an old bloke and thinks he's twenty-five again. Remember that time we went to Alice Springs, Patty? Norm wanted to do the walk around Ayres Rock because of course you can't climb it now. And it was ten kilometres, thirty-five degrees, and Norm just had a hip operation.'

Patty swivelled round in her seat and offered me a sherbet lemon.

'I think you mean Uluru. Norm wanted to come here because he visited years ago. When his wife was still alive. I think he'll find it's changed a lot though. There's a proper esplanade and beach houses and cafés. We'll find somewhere nice for lunch if we can ever get everyone to agree. With this lot it's like herding kittens.'

We drove along the esplanade, shaded by tall palm trees. The ocean to the left of us, and shops and wine bars on our right. It looked fantastic.

Dinkie parked on the seafront outside a very attractive café with a veranda and Patty pulled up next to her.

'Norm says here,' Dinkie said as she got out of her car, 'he wants the loo and then he says he wants a steak.'

'Will his dentures cope with it?' Malc wondered.

'Well, no worries! We've got some superglue in the RV if they don't,' Dinkie said happily.

* * *

We had such a lovely time there. The food was great, the staff were cheerful and made a great fuss of Norm, even bringing him a big slab of chocolate brownie with a candle stuck in the top when they found out it was his birthday. Far from being the quiet, older people in the place, the Silver Surfers were enthusiastic, swapping seats until everyone was content, and very noisy.

Sitting next to Kit, chatting with him, discussing which would be better, one of the massive beef burgers or spaghetti marinara (Kit suggested we order both and I could choose which one I wanted), I felt so happy. And surprisingly relaxed with where this trip had taken me. Yes, it was out of my usual comfort zone, but suddenly it didn't matter. After all, my usual comfort zone had been pretty dull.

This was better, partly because it was so unexpected. It was good to be spontaneous. It reminded me of my younger days when I had always been up for a party or a spur-of-the-moment adventure. I wasn't going to lose this determination again in a hurry.

We left the restaurant and Dinkie and Norm went to sit under the trees in the shade, talking about maybe getting an ice cream while the rest of us went down onto the beach.

'Are you enjoying yourself? You look as though you are.' Kit said after a few minutes.

I pushed my hair, tousled by the onshore breeze, out of my eyes.

'So much. Are you?'

'It certainly beats sitting in an office,' he said, and he grinned, 'and the company is better too.'

I shaded my eyes against the sun and looked out across the ocean to hide my pleasure at this statement.

'Do you think there are any sharks out there?'

'Maybe. I read recently that more people are killed by a champagne cork or coconut every year, than sharks. It's the jellyfish that are the problem, that's why there are some nets around the beach.'

'So mind yourself,' Malc called over, and he laughed, 'you don't want us peeing on your leg, do you?'

'You know that doesn't work,' Patty tutted, 'it makes it worse.'

'I bow to your superior knowledge,' Malc said.

I thought about Shane and his injured leg with its tiny baby sharky kiss; it was on the tip of my tongue to mention it. I had seen in the past how the mention of Shane had caused Kit's face to close, for that little frown line to reappear and I didn't want anything to spoil that afternoon.

'So, no surfing?' I said.

Malc waved a dismissive hand at the ocean, which was unusually calm, the waves no more than a couple of inches high.

'Nah, just a load of ankle biters out there, not worth getting wet.'

Well, in a way that was a relief. I wouldn't have to expose my new swimming costume. But there was also some disappointment; I wouldn't get the chance to check out Kit either.

* * *

When we got back to the campsite, Norm went off for a nap, but by six o'clock he was banging on our door with the end of his walking stick, telling us to hurry up if we wanted seats near the front of the concert.

'Vince and the Deadbeat Rockers. They're all in their seventies now, they'll be starting soon. They never go on much past nine these days,' he said encouragingly, 'and I've just heard there's a barbie too. Get a wiggle on. Me, Jim, and Dinkie are off to save some seats.'

Kit had been writing some emails and I had phoned up Rowan to tell her what we were doing, then Maggie to have a chat with her and reassure myself they were both improving.

Then I sent a long email and some pictures to Dan. Looking at them made me feel unexpectedly pleased at what I was doing: the lovely views over the ocean that afternoon, a couple of pictures of the Silver Surfers, who all seemed to be holding up beer bottles as they cheered. Then I'd been reading for a bit and trying not to snooze. All that fresh air and a big lunch had made me feel very sleepy.

I looked over at Kit.

'I don't think I need anything to eat; I'm still stuffed from lunch,' I said.

'Me too, but the smell of hot dogs and onions frying always works for me.'

'With mustard.'

He shook his head. 'Ketchup.'

'You savage,' I said.

He laughed, did a bit more typing, and closed his laptop.

'Anyway, I'm all done. Perhaps we could find a cold beer?'

'Excellent idea.'

* * *

By the look of it, the whole campsite came out that evening to watch Vince and the Deadbeat Rockers. All the seats were taken, and people had brought their own chairs and some just spread a blanket out on the ground.

'He was meek as milk when we were in school,' Malc said, 'never a peep out of him. A bit older than me, he used to spend all his time round the back of the gym, smoking as far as I remember. And then one Christmas his dad bought him a guitar, and the rest, as they say, is history. He found a couple of mates who wanted to form a group and went to rehearse in someone's shed. And then he and his brother saw Johnny O'Keefe in concert, and they was off. All the girls screaming like maniacs.'

'I think I remember him,' I said.

'Vince's done it ever since. Never had a hit record but made a living. He's good too.'

'Well we're looking forward to it,' I said.

'Patty had a right old crush on him. Back in the day.'

'I never did,' Patty said heatedly, 'anyway it's six thirty, time he was on. Some of this lot will be wanting their Horlicks.'

Malc folded his arms and sat back in his canvas chair.

'Well don't you go chucking your knickers on the stage, you'll put him right off.'

Up on the makeshift stage, a grey-haired man was plugging things in and tweaking the equipment.

'That's his brother, Lance,' Malc said, 'he was in my year. A right sort. Cheek of the devil.'

Someone at the back started a slow handclap and a few minutes later an elderly man, a little stooped with age, came on holding a guitar and the audience started cheering.

'Crickey, he looks old,' Patty said.

'He is old you daft bat,' Malc said, 'we all are.'

'Will he do the thing with the two billiard balls, do you think?' Dinkie said.

* * *

'Well, that was better than I thought it would be,' Kit said later as we walked back to the van, 'and Norm enjoyed it which is all that really matters.'

'It's been a great day,' I said, 'I've really enjoyed it.'

'Me too,' Kit said, 'thanks for your company.'

I fumbled in my bag for the keys.

I realised Kit was watching me, and for some reason his gaze made me blush. Which was rather annoying.

'So, we are off tomorrow,' he said.

'Yes, I hope you have decided which way we are going?'

'I've got a fair idea.'

For one moment as we stood in front of the open door, just looking at each other, I had the crazy feeling that he was going to kiss me.

I almost fell up the step in my haste to get inside. This was not what we should be doing at all. And certainly not as we were about to set off on our road trip. Alone.

'I'll pop to the shower block,' I said, grabbing my sponge bag.

Typical me, I hadn't fastened it properly and things started to fall out of it. I scrabbled around on the floor, grabbing for my toothpaste and lip balm, thanking god it was nothing more embarrassing.

'If I didn't know better, I would think I'm making you nervous,' Kit said.

'Of course not!'

I gave a slightly wild laugh and darted off to the right, heading towards the lights shining out into the warm night. Then I realised I was going the wrong way, and skittered off to the left, nearly tripping over a small dog, meandering about, his nose to the ground.

'Sorry, sorry, sorry!' I called to him.

The dog raised its head and gave me a look.

* * *

The following morning, we packed up our remaining belongings and Kit disconnected all the hoses and cables. Then we had to say our farewells to all the Silver Surfers, who had called in to see us off.

I felt rather sad to think we would probably never see them again. They had plans to visit the Skyrail Rainforest Cableway which would take them over some stunning scenery and there was also the prospect of yet another barbie, which cheered Norm up no end. That man must have had the constitution of a lion.

Eventually we set off and called into the campsite office on our way out to return the keys to the shower block and pay the bill. This took longer than it should because the women behind the counter – identified by their name badges as Bev and Mo – wanted to hear all about the accident.

'Such a shame. I mean, he was daft to try it but still, such a shame,' Bev said, her features pinched together in sympathy, 'we could have leant him a stepladder if he'd asked.'

'Could have broken his neck,' Mo added, 'although we've never had anyone die here have we, Bev? One man did his best to drown himself a few years ago. Mixing alcohol and swimming pools never works, does it? And then there was that French woman with the broken leg, which really was her own fault. She had no business being on the cookhouse roof in the first place.

Just because there was no actual official signage telling her not to climb up there and start dancing. I mean, how dumb are people?'

'So can I pay their site fees before we go?' I said.

'If it was up to me, I wouldn't charge you,' Bev said.

'But it's not up to us,' Mo said, 'it's policy.'

'I'm more than happy to pay,' I said, 'just let me know how much.'

Bev did a bit of rapid typing on her computer and some hum-humming and then Mo pointed at something on the screen and Bev did some more typing. Crumbs, how much did these places charge anyway? I braced myself.

'I'm afraid it's quite a lot. Our prices had to go up this year.'

'It's fine,' I said firmly.

'One hundred and sixty dollars I'm afraid,' Bev said her eyebrows creased into a new expression of sympathy.

'Per night?' I said, a bit shocked.

Bev and Mo laughed uproariously until Mo started coughing and had to go into the office to get herself a drink of water.

'No, dear, for the whole stay; we're not the Ritz you know!'

I paid up and eventually got back to the motorhome where Kit was studying his map again.

He looked up as I hauled myself awkwardly up into the cab. He smiled at me and for some reason my heart did a funny little jump.

'Problems? I can pay if there's a problem?'

'No, it's fine, really,' I said, fussing with my seatbelt so I didn't have to look at him, 'everything's fine. Anyway, I still owe you for the cost of my flight. I'm happy to pay for yours too...'

'Everything's fine,' Kit said, 'no worries. Let's ride!'

* * *

The countryside whizzed past: trees and towns and petrol stations. A range of hills to our right.

'What's it like to drive?' I asked after a while.

'Fine, no different from any other truck,' Kit said.

'I've never driven a truck of any size.'

'Well you don't have to drive this one if you don't want to,' he said, 'I like driving. I don't do it as much as I used to. But if you want to, you can.'

'Well, you have drivers,' I said, 'who look like FBI agents.'

He tilted his head to one side and thought about this. 'Yes I suppose they do. Les was in the SAS so he does have an air of menace about him.'

'I kept watching him to see if he whispered up his sleeve.'

He laughed. 'I've never seen him do that but perhaps he does when no one's looking. So what do you do, Elin?'

'Do?'

'Work? Hobbies? Home? We don't seem to have had much time on our own to get to know each other.'

Crumbs, how could I answer that without gabbling on indefinitely?

'I went to England when I was twenty-two to do a teaching job. I live in a little village in Gloucestershire now. I didn't mean to stay more than a couple of years when I came over to England but – well then, I married Tom. He taught at the same school, we had Dan, and I just stayed. I don't have any interesting hobbies worth discussing, just the usual ones: reading, gardening, cooking.'

'And your ex? You don't have to tell me, but I'm interested.'

'My ex-husband couldn't keep his trousers on. He's now remarried to a much younger wife and has a new baby daughter who is teething.'

Kit grimaced. 'That can't have been much fun for you. And tell me about your son?'

'Dan. He's twenty-eight and a maths teacher in Bristol. He has a Goth girlfriend called Skye and they share a flat with each other and a rapidly increasing colony of mice. It would help if they took the rubbish out occasionally. My son and his girlfriend I mean, not the mice. I keep telling them to get some mousetraps, but Skye says they have an equal right to be there. She won't think that in the winter when the mice start wandering over the break-fast table to help themselves to Cheerios.'

He laughed again. It was a nice sound.

'No indeed. And what's brought you back to Australia now? After such a long time?'

'A dear friend left me some money when she died, with the strict instructions I should use some of it for travelling. She had been all over the world: China, Africa, South America, the Far East; you name it, she'd been there. My ex-husband hated flying, so we hardly travelled anywhere. And you're right: I do like to plan things. I haven't come back to Australia once in all those years and if I'm honest, I really don't know why. I don't know where the time's gone.'

'Just whizzes past, doesn't it?'

'So what about you then? Work? Hobbies? Home?'

Kit sighed and thought for a few minutes.

'That's a hard question. Work you already know about. IT business solutions.'

'Oh, the bespoke whatsit?'

'That's it.'

'I still don't have a clue what you do. I just pretended to under-stand when you told me on the plane.'

He chuckled. 'I thought so. I'll explain it properly one day.'

I looked out of the window hoping he couldn't see my confu-sion. Did he mean there was going to be another time in the future when we would talk about this sort of thing?

'So what about hobbies?' I said.

'Oh good heavens. I don't have time for hobbies. Going to work. Coming home from work. Home is a house near the beach where I can watch the ocean and worry about work. That about sums it up really.'

'That sounds absolutely terrible; even worse than my hobbies,' I said. 'Are you married? Any children?'

Surely a man like him – successful, attractive – would have a significant someone?

'Not now,' he said rather abruptly.

My heart gave a funny little thump. What did that mean? Don't ask me now or I used to have someone but I don't now?

'Ah,' I said to fill the silence.

'What I mean is I had a wife. But I don't now.'

What did that mean? He had carelessly mislaid her somewhere on a shopping trip? She was dead? He was divorced? He'd murdered her?

'Oh well. It was a very long time ago,' he said, 'I'm older and wiser now.'

'So am I,' I said in case he was thinking I was completely taken in my all this charm and easy conversation.

'I'm sure you are.'

He didn't speak for a few minutes as he negotiated a slip road and then he sighed.

'Let's talk about something else. What's it like to be home after all this time?'

We chatted about England and Gloucestershire and the things I'd noticed that had changed in my absence from Australia. Gradually the conversation became a bit easier.

'Your family visited you in Gloucestershire though?'

'Banjo and Maggie came over every few years and Rowan too three times. But it's a long way, you know that better than I do.

Still, things are easier nowadays; we have Zoom and WhatsApp. We speak most weeks.'

'But like I said before, it's not the same,' he said.

I chewed my lip and thought about it.

'No. It wasn't the same. I almost booked flights a few times, but Tom always seemed to have a reason not to go. Once he feigned appendicitis. I even took him to hospital. Of course, they said his symptoms were inconclusive. He kept it up for weeks.'

Why was I telling Kit these things? He couldn't possibly be interested in the murky details of my dead marriage. I really needed a mute button sometimes.

But Kit chuckled and shook his head. 'Unbelievable.'

Yes it was, thinking about it. I felt far more confident that in the future I would be able to deal with a man being deceitful, two faced. Mucking me about as Tom had.

'On another occasion Tom claimed someone had rear-ended him at the traffic lights and he had whiplash, although I never saw any damage to his car.'

Kit laughed again.

'As you say, let's talk about something else,' I said, 'like where you want to stop for lunch.'

'You choose,' he said.

'I don't mind, just somewhere near the sea?'

He gestured with his left hand. 'Well, the ocean's over there so I'll see what I can find.'

We eventually turned off the Bruce Highway and onto a single-track road which got more and more sandy as we headed closer to the ocean. When we stopped there was a boat ramp, empty of any boats that day, and the path was covered in fragments of palm fronds blown by the wind from the sea. As we had hoped, there was a café and a wine bar there too, with a fabulous view over the bay. It was midweek, so both were practically empty.

After we'd eaten our toasted sandwiches, we walked down to look at the beach. I was delighted to see a sign warning that the beach was a turtle nesting area. Not so pleased to read other notices about there being no lifeguards and the possibility of vermin and snakes in the undergrowth.

Above us the skies were grey and loaded with clouds, buffeting in from the Pacific. The beach itself was huge and deserted apart from a couple in the far distance walking their big, brown dog. He was having a lovely time too, running in and out of the waves.

Kit shaded his eyes and watched him. 'D'you know, I think I would like a dog.'

'Why don't you get one then?' I asked, trying not to remember the whole dog, dogfood, barn renovation thing I'd imagined all those weeks ago.

He shrugged. 'I'm away too much; it wouldn't be fair on the animal. They need company and walks and all that stuff.'

'That's a shame. You could change your lifestyle. Do something to suit yourself?'

'Well we'll see, perhaps. I had a great dog when I was a kid. An Aussie – an Australian Shepherd – called Blue. He was a brilliant dog. Great fun.' he said. And then he sighed. 'Oh well, we'd better move; it's definitely going to rain.'

After a few minutes, we returned to the van and Kit turned his sat nav on. As he did so, a few huge spots of rain fell, clattering like pebbles onto the windscreen. Thirty seconds later the heavens opened, and torrential rain sluiced across the car park; the noise on the roof was thunderous. Within moments the road was running with water; sand and palm fronds washed into the gutters and down towards the beach.

'Well this impressive. I think we'd better wait a few minutes,' Kit said.

Marooned in the van, the screen began to mist up and the heat in there was stifling. The neon open sign of the wine bar was gleaming out into the dark afternoon.

'We should have gone in there,' I said, wiping the windscreen with a chamois leather pad.

'You're right. We could make a run for it though, couldn't we?' Kit said, 'have a cold drink?'

I grinned. 'I'm game if you are? Rock, paper, scissors?'

He laughed. 'Nah, just let's do it.'

We exchanged a look and I shouted 'Three, two, one, go!'

By the time we got to the door of the bar, we were both soaking. My hair was plastered to my head, any traces of make-up gone.

Kit held the door open for me and we fell into the room laughing. Standing there dripping, it somehow seemed the funniest thing ever. We looked at each other, still laughing. I think we might have been slightly hysterical for a few seconds.

'You're mad!' Kit said, wiping the rain out of his eyes.

Suddenly, shockingly he slung his arm around my shoulders and hugged me. I could feel the warmth of his hard body through our wet shirts, and I was unexpectedly a bit giddy. And yet I'd known that at some point, some time, something like this would happen.

At the end of the room was a countertop with half a dozen bar stools and a bored looking girl sitting filing her green nails.

'Come on, let's have a drink,' he said, drying his face with a paper napkin, 'my shout, what do you fancy?'

Bloody hell, I rather fancied him if I was honest. I mean yes, he was attractive but the more time we spent together, the more I liked him. I wasn't expecting that. I suppose at the start of all this, I'd imagined myself with the angry version of Kit Pascoe, struggling for things to talk about, steering carefully around his bad moods. But it wasn't like that at all.

He had a beer in a frosted tankard, and I had a glass of wine and we sat side by side, steaming gently as our clothes dried out. He clinked my glass with his and our eyes met.

'Thanks, Kit,' I said.

'My pleasure,' he said, with a wide, white grin.

God, he had a lovely smile.

Stop it. I really needed to get a grip on myself. I'd already got suspicions about him, about why he was sometimes charming and at other times not. I was not going to be seduced by his smile and his lovely eyes. Oh shut up, woman.

I'd been really uncertain about this trip, and in just a couple of days I had started enjoying myself. There was another side to him that I was just beginning to see.

Perhaps he wasn't just a miserable, bad-tempered git as I had first thought; it was also possible he was a kind, very attractive man. And from the flirtatious glances he was receiving from the girl behind the bar, I wasn't the only one who thought so.

12

After the storm had cleared, we drove back to the Bruce Highway and continued south towards Brisbane. As quickly as they had come, the clouds cleared, and we pressed on for a couple of hours. We were just chatting about nothing in particular, stopping at a drive-in where Kit made some phone calls and I logged on to their Wi-Fi and sent some texts to Rowan and Dan to tell them I was okay.

Within minutes Kit booked us into a site nearby which turned out to be possibly the closest I had even been to heaven. Neither of us had even mentioned finding a motel. Should I have said something? Was I okay with my bunk for yet another night? I suppose I'd have to be.

But my doubts were swept away by the view from our new pitch, which was utterly breath-taking. There was a beautiful strand of golden sand in front of me and then a blue, wave-streaked sea under a clear cobalt sky. There were flocks of para-keets and cockatoos rattling about in the trees above us and brush turkeys strutting their stuff between the motorhomes.

I stepped down from the cab and jammed my sassy Kooringal hat on my head against the brightness of the sun.

'This is fabulous,' I said.

'Out there is part of the Great Barrier Reef,' Kit said, 'isn't it wonderful? Have you ever visited it?'

'I think we went when I was about six, but I can't remember much about it. I'd love to go again,' I said.

He hesitated. 'You should see it properly. Maybe next time,' he said, 'take a couple of weeks. Maybe go snorkelling. The water is so clear and warm, and the sea life is fantastic. It's like paradise.'

There was going to be a next time? Did he mean I should go, take a couple of weeks and all that stuff?

Or that we should go? Together? Surely not.

Of course not. We hardly knew each other. I was getting swept up into all this ridiculous enforced companionship and stuff. Like cabin fever. Van virus. I needed to take a step back.

'I haven't done snorkelling since I was a teenager,' I said.

'It's a great thing, you should take it up again. Didn't they do it in the UK?'

I remembered the time when Tom had agreed to take Dan to the beach so he could try surfing. Tom had gone dressed in a suit and tie. We'd driven two hours to get there, stayed for about forty-five minutes and then gone home again. It had not been a success.

'The climate isn't quite so warm. Or the water.'

'Are you sure you don't mind sleeping in the van again?' he said, 'I don't know... I just assumed... I can easily find a motel or something if it makes you feel uncomfortable?'

I looked around again. This was my chance to change things.

I hesitated for a moment.

'No,' I said, 'this is fine.'

And it did feel fine at the time. He wasn't creepy, he didn't make inappropriate comments, I felt quite relaxed. In fact I was having fun.

We set up camp.

Kit did the necessary things with lengths of cable and hose pipes, and I investigated our food stores. We seemed to have a lot of salad stuff in the fridge that was definitely past its sell by date, the rest of the space taken up with beer and white wine. I wandered off to the camp shop for some supplies and found a café next door, which was doing a buzzing trade in hot pies. I took a sneaky look at someone's plate as the waitress whizzed past me. Those pies really did look good, and they were huge. Like big, golden hat boxes, bolstered up with salad and chunky chips. Whatever I might think of producing from the van kitchen, it wouldn't beat that.

Then I turned my phone on and rang Rowan.

'Where are you?' she said without preamble.

'On the East coast on the way to Brisbane. We've stopped for the night in the most fantastic place right by the sea. How are the rellies?'

'Fine. They are going to be on a plane back to Sydney in a few days and Maggie is going to stay at a motel near the hospital until he's ready to travel. Are you getting on okay with Mr Grumpy?'

'Kit? He's fine. Better than I realised. He's been very thoughtful and is doing all the driving so far. How's Shane?'

'Shane would be perfectly okay if he wasn't such a bloody wuss. He had his dressings off yesterday with a great deal of whimpering and fuss. I almost told him he could have a lolly if he was brave. He's not going to have much of a scar as far as I can see, just a bit of a dent. I mean it isn't exactly *Jaws 4*, more like he walked into a fence or something. I think he's a bit disappointed. So, tell me more about Kit. Have you found out any juicy gossip? Shane never tells me anything.'

I thought about the story of the disappearing wife and decided not to tell her.

'Nothing much to tell really. He hasn't been particularly grumpy at all. At the moment he's getting the van set up. There are things to be done with electricity and water every time we stop. There's a loo but I think both of us have decided not to use it, thank heavens.'

'What? What the hell are you doing sleeping with him in the van?'

'I'm not sleeping with him in the van, Rowan. Both of us are sleeping in the van. There's a difference.'

Rowan snorted. 'I think you're splitting hairs there.'

'He's taking the bed and I'm in the bunk.'

'Typical man! Selfish—'

'No, we did rock, paper, scissors and I lost. Perfectly fair. And it's quite comfortable, actually. Although I wish it was a bit wider.'

'Oh for goodness sake! So when will you be home? Any idea?'

Suddenly I didn't want to tell Rowan about our road trip, that we weren't shooting down the motorway as fast as we could. I'd been feeling rather buoyant that day. I was having an unanticipated adventure; all sorts of great things might be ahead of us. Landmarks and funny little towns. Beautiful vistas and unexpected detours. The road twisting through the hills and the forests. At that moment I wanted to keep it to myself and not allow anyone to dissuade me.

'I'll keep you up to speed. I'm not exactly sure at the moment. All depends on the traffic of course.'

When I got back to our pitch, Kit had connected up whatever needed to be done, had sorted out the awning without accident, and was sitting in the shade with the table and chairs set out and two glasses. It looked rather civilised. It felt very pleasant.

I opened the red wine I'd bought and poured out a couple of hefty measures.

'Well this is rather lovely,' I said. We clinked glasses at each other.

'Very welcome. Any sign of Dusty Jack? I wondered if we might be following him down the coast,' Kit said.

'Not that I could see,' I said, grinning.

'He was entertaining,' Kit said. He sipped his wine and closed his eyes. 'That's better, just what I need.'

His face was peaceful for a moment as we enjoyed the sunshine.

I watched the sea, the waves foaming far out against the reef. There were boats and gulls and people. The distant sounds of children playing. It was fabulous. I closed my eyes too and felt myself relax.

When I opened them, I realised Kit was looking at me. Not in a worrying way, just sort of watching.

'Okay?' I said.

'Yes,' he said, 'I'm fine. What are we eating tonight? I can cook if you want? I enjoy cooking. Especially Italian food; I make a mean lasagne. Or curry, that's another favourite. But maybe I'd need a bit more space and a lot of ingredients we don't have.'

He could cook?

'That would be wonderful. But I've spotted a great café on the site, which would be a lot easier. We could go there? You're not a vegetarian or a faddy eater are you?'

He raised a quizzical eyebrow at me. 'I think you know I'm not, not after the Great Australian Banging Breakfast.'

I laughed. 'No of course not; I wonder what was in those sausages? They do pies at the café, huge ones. With salad and chips. I looked.'

'There's absolutely nothing about that sentence I don't like,' he said.

We drank our wine and he topped up our glasses and I began to feel very mellow and calm. Which I hadn't felt for days. Well, months if I was honest.

Was it being independent again, being back in Australia where the climate was kinder, the lifestyle familiar and yet for so many years forgotten? Or was it Kit?

'But there is one thing I'm not happy about,' he said after a while.

I was immediately on high alert. What?

'And what's that?'

'Our sleeping arrangements. I don't like you being up in that bunk. It looks cramped and uncomfortable.'

'Oh, it's okay.' I said.

'And it must be hot. And stuffy,' he said firmly.

'It's not that bad,' I said, unconvincingly. 'Anyway you're far too tall to go up there. Your feet would be hanging over the edge.'

'So we could always adopt Plan C,' he said, 'or Plan D.'

'What's Plan C?' I asked, hardly daring to breathe.

What was he about to suggest?

'Don't look so startled. There's really no need. Well, Plan C: we can stay at hotels when we feel like it, every night if you prefer, of course,' he said, 'or then there's Plan D: we can both sleep on the bed.'

'Um,' I said intelligently, 'I'm really not sure about that.'

Plan D sounded very worrying.

'We can sleep head to toe, it's very comfortable and you don't need to worry about any funny business,' he said, 'I'm very trustworthy—'

Bloody hell. What counted as funny business?

'—and we seem to be getting on reasonably okay.'

'I suppose we are,' I said.

'You don't sound very sure. Which is quite understandable. Under the circumstances.'

I slugged back some wine and looked at the sea.

I tried to imagine myself lying on that bed, in my cartoon pj's, with him a fingertip away. It wasn't very romantic. Not that I was expecting anything romantic, of course I wasn't. He was just being considerate. He was just thinking of my comfort. And if I was honest, my dodgy hip had been a bit creaky. It took a bit of time to get everything moving in the mornings.

'And I would hate to think of you falling out of that bunk,' he added.

And see? That seemed to make the idea a bit more reasonable. He was just thinking of health and safety issues. It wasn't impossible that one night I would roll over and crash down on to the steering wheel.

'Well, I suppose...'

'Let's go and find something to eat,' he said, 'and you can think about it.'

Not that I've had a great deal of experience in these matters but that surely was the strangest way that anyone had ever suggested sleeping with me. And it wasn't that he had suggested sleeping together, just actual sleeping.

So that was all right then. Wasn't it?

I had a hat-box pie (chicken) and Kit had a steak. It was brilliant.

My unease gradually faded under the influence of yet more wine, and we talked and talked about so many things: films we had seen, books we had read, and our likes and dislikes. We laughed a lot too and even began to finish each other's sentences.

Then we had a nightcap. And then we went back to the motorhome; Kit jangling the van keys between his fingers and me wondering yet again if I was squiffy. Why was I doing this? I hardly ever touched a drop at home these days, but then drinking on my own had always seemed a bit... well, sad I suppose. With all this bed-sharing stuff ahead of us, it was probably not the wisest move. I tend to snore and make odd noises when I've had a few drinks. And I have been known to talk in my sleep.

God, wouldn't that be awful? If I started saying embarrassing things about him in my fuddled state. Or made a pass at him in the middle of the night by mistake. God no! Perhaps I could sleep with my arms inside my pyjama jacket.

I went off to the loo blocks to clean the salad out of my teeth and change into my pj's. When I got back, he had made up the bed with his pillows at one end and mine at the other. We shuffled around each other and he went off to the loo block. Which was a relief as my head was right up against the partition wall with the loo. We might have been 'getting on' but the thought of him in there would have been high on the excruciating stakes.

I took out my contact lenses and shortly after that Kit returned, put the light out and got into bed. Next to me.

I clenched myself up against the wall, although there was plenty of room, and lay in the gloom, listening to him shifting about, getting comfortable.

'You okay?' he said from somewhere near my feet.

'Fine,' I said, trying to sound casual.

'Comfortable?'

In one way yes, in another way no.

'Yes, absolutely,' I said.

I felt him turn over and he pummelled his pillows for a bit. Then he settled down with a sigh.

'That's better. I'm a bit fussy about pillows these days,' he said, 'they can't be too hard or too soft, don't you agree?'

'Yes, I do,' I said, 'but given the choice I like a hard one.'

I stuffed my fist into my mouth. God almighty, what had I just said?

He didn't seem to notice.

'The same goes for the mattress. This one is a bit thin, I prefer something a bit thicker. What sort of thing do you like?'

Perhaps I should pretend to be asleep? Before I said something excruciating about liking thick ones.

'Oh you know. Just something comfortable,' I said.

I scuffed my feet about. As I've said, I like sleeping with my feet outside the covers, particularly if it's warm but if I did that, I would probably stick my big toe up his nose.

'Thought we could stay on the coast road and head towards Mackay tomorrow. Unless you have any preferences?'

'No preferences at all, I'm entirely in your hands.'

He chuckled. 'Okay.'

In his hands.

Suddenly, unbelievably I imagined all sorts of filthy things.

Him with no clothes on, running his hands over me and kissing various bits of me that had remained un-kissed for years. I even thought a bit about blindfolds and ice-cream and—

Stop it. Stop it. Stop it.

I shuffled over away from him a bit more until my nose was pressed up against the wall of the van.

'Sleep well,' he said at last.

'And—,' I squeaked.

I cleared my throat and distracted myself thinking about what I would do if I won the lottery. And names of famous people with the initials J C (There are a lot.). And ice baths. 'And you.'

13

We kept to the coast road heading in the general direction of Brisbane. We also kept up our sleeping arrangements, head to toe in the double bed. I was beginning to relax, I was cool with it. Sort of.

It was very odd to wake up in the night and be aware of a man next to me for the first time in ages. He was, it had to be said, an agreeable sleeping companion. He didn't snore, hog the bedding, or man spread all over the bed. I hope I didn't either. If I did, he didn't say anything.

We got into a routine too. I would navigate using the new map when the signal to Kit's sat-nav signal failed and when I dithered or got it wrong, he didn't shout at me or huff when I was unsure where we were supposed to be going.

This made a refreshing change from my years navigating Tom anywhere. In the end, the mere prospect of doing so had made my stomach clench into knots. And my brain freeze. This meant I made mistakes all the time or missed turnings or whatever.

'For god's sake woman, are you blind or stupid?' was something Tom regularly hurled in my direction. There would then be a swerving, skidding stop and he would grab the map from me and point out where I had gone wrong.

'Well, you bloody navigate and I'll drive,' I suggested on those occasions.

This usually earned me a sneer and a comment along the lines of wanting to get there before darkness fell.

Anyway, this trip was very different. Kit didn't seem to mind if we got a bit lost, even when we somehow ended up in the interlocking roads of a vast industrial estate – Pineapple Road East, we've definitely been here before – and unexpectedly shot out of it onto our old friend the Bruce Highway, but going north instead of south. He just laughed.

We went to supermarkets and bought snacks and bottled water which I handed to him as we drove along. He liked salt and vinegar crisps and Violet Crumble which was like a Crunchie. We made salads and sandwiches at the pokey little van kitchen. I phoned Rowan every day to check on Maggie and Banjo and find out when they were due home. And every day Kit phoned work at least three times. And then got his laptop out and fired off some emails.

One evening, we sat together on the picnic chairs outside in the warm dusk, discussing our day, drinking wine, and telling each other more about ourselves. I'd been for a shower and was wearing one of my new maxi dresses. It was beautiful, in shades of pale blue and white but the beaded top was a bit lower than I was used to and every so often I had to hoik up the neckline. I could have done with a couple of safety pins to shorten the straps.

Kit told me he had been twelve when Shane was born. So, Kit was the same age as me. I'd thought he was younger. That's another thing; why does the average man usually deal better with the aging business? They don't seem to worry about wrinkles or moisturiser or grey hairs half as much as women do. They certainly don't need to obsess about the latest designer handbag because they have decent pockets in all their clothes. Perhaps men worry about other things but don't talk about it. And maybe other men don't comment if their friends put on a few pounds or aren't 'beach ready'.

The age difference meant the bond between the brothers had never been great. Added to that, Kit had been academic, Shane had been sporty. Kit had been engrossed in the family business from quite a young age. Shane had never shown any interest.

'Shane was always one step ahead of the law in his teenage years,' Kit said, 'I mean he wasn't a bad kid, just a bit rebellious. I can't count the number of times my parents had to go to the school to apologise for his behaviour or the local police station to bail him out of trouble. I'm hoping he's settled down now. Maybe your sister is a good influence?'

'It would be a first,' I said thoughtfully, 'she's usually the opposite.'

Then I told him about Tom and Dan, how I had filled my time as the years had slipped past and I could see how I had gradually changed. Doing so brought back some of the feelings I'd done my best to avoid. I suppose it was remembering the days when I'd thought I had life worked out, that I was – what had Rowan called it? – settled. And now I realised I had never been settled. I had lived on the other side of the world far from everything that I had loved and had been familiar with.

'I can't imagine you being cowed by anyone,' Kit said at last, shaking his head.

I shook off my mood and tried to sound upbeat.

'Well I wasn't exactly cowed, but it just became easier to go along with what Tom wanted otherwise he would sulk or complain or make life difficult,' I said.

Kit looked across at me in the gathering dusk.

'I think you should look up the definition of the word cowed when you get the chance.'

'Maybe, it seems a long time ago now,' I said.

My life in England and my time with Tom sat uneasily here in Australia with another, very different man at my side.

'And are you over it?'

'Over what?'

'Over Tom?'

'If I wasn't I wouldn't be here.' I said, 'When my friend left me that money, I knew immediately what I wanted to do and I just started planning it. I even had a spreadsheet. If I had discussed it with Tom, he would have probably tried to talk me out of it.'

'Well I'm glad he didn't,' Kit said, and he reached across the table and put his warm hand over mine.

I jumped.

He took his hand away. 'Sorry.'

Bloody hell! What brought that on?

'You wouldn't have had to drive all these miles or get lost in an industrial estate or eat so much junk food or snacks,' I said, trying to dilute the situation with clumsy humour.

'Yes that's true, but it turns out I don't mind,' Kit smiled at me.

I felt a bit wobbly.

This was getting ridiculous. This moment called for me to say something memorable or clever or witty.

Something that would make a difference. I should be finding a way to put a brake on things. I couldn't think of anything.

I looked down and realised my bosom was making a break for freedom again.

'Oh god, this dress,' I said, and pulled the top up.

'Relax. You look fine,' Kit said, although he wasn't actually looking at me, 'lovely.'

'Do I?' I said.

Yes, that's really memorable clever and witty. That's really putting the brake on.

I relaxed my shoulders a bit and the dress settled back down into its preferred place. Well, perhaps I could carry it off?

'You worry a lot don't you, Elin?' he said as he re-filled my wine glass.

I thought about it. 'Yes, I do. I should stop allowing my years with Tom to still make me doubt myself.'

'You should,' Kit said, 'I know, we should each make a rule for each other. Road Trip Rules.'

'Okay. What would you suggest?'

'You stop worrying,' he said.

'If you stop thinking about work,' I replied, 'I bet you can't do that.'

He considered the idea. After a few seconds, he raised his eyebrows.

'I think that would be brilliant. I like the thought of that, if I can do it.'

He linked his hands behind his head and stretched his long legs out in front of him.

'I bet you can't. I bet you don't last a day,' I said.

'You wait,' he said, closing his eyes, 'you might be surprised how easy I find it. Even at the moment when I probably shouldn't. I'm appreciating this beautiful country. This wonderful place. The sun, the sound of the birds in the trees.'

'That's poetic,' I said.

He gave a little chuckle. 'I'm glad I'm an Australian. This has to be the best country in the world. I wouldn't live anywhere else.'

We sat in companionable silence for a few minutes.

I thought about England, my little house, Dan being so far away, and I felt troubled. But then I regained my pleasure in being here, back where I had been born. Was this, after all the time away, where I belonged?

'Are you thinking about work now?' I said.

He didn't answer for a moment and then he just turned and looked at me, his eyes glowing in the dusk.

'No, Worry Police, I'm not thinking about work,' he said.

* * *

Then we reached Brisbane and, after a fairly long discussion, Kit suggested we could stay in a hotel he knew, just for a change. Separate rooms, everything above board. I'll admit I was feeling a bit excited about the thought of a proper bed, with no sand in it or having to dance around each other to make a cup of tea. I was going to have a proper shower in a proper bathroom without the risk of dropping my towel on the wet floor or having other people and their children in the next-door cubicle screaming about getting shampoo in their eyes.

We drove through the suburbs, planes taking off from the airport to our left, and then we reached the centre of town. I hadn't been to Brisbane since I was a teenager and things seemed to have changed a lot. There were high rise skyscrapers, a Brisbane Eye rotating slowly above the quay, and everywhere there were building projects underway. Brisbane felt an optimistic and vibrant place to be.

We were staying in a hotel overlooking the river and Kit drove us at a stately progress into the car park, where we parked in between a Ferrari and a Porsche. It looked a bit incongruous, as though the circus had come to town. Still, we gathered up our bags and, feeling a bit crumpled and in need of a shower, I followed Kit and went in.

It was glorious. Air conditioned, great swoops of polished

granite everywhere, and fawning staff in smart uniforms. A bit different from the places we had been staying recently, and very exciting. I expect it cost $160 to stay there for half an hour, never mind a week.

While Kit was checking us in, I caught glimpses of a dining room set with white table linen and flowers, and a bar where some stylish looking women were flashing their elegant legs and laughing at some cool-looking men in suits.

There was a man in a white tuxedo playing Barry Manilow songs on a grand piano and he nodded and grinned at us as we went past. For a mad moment I thought about going over and requesting Bermuda Triangle, which has always been a guilty pleasure of mine.

Instead, I followed Kit into the lift and up to the top floor of the hotel. After our rather constricted life in the van, the room was fabulous. I walked around with a huge grin, my arms stretched out enjoying it. I opened all the cupboards in the small, sleek kitchen, prodded the buttons on the coffee maker, explored the two massive bedrooms, each with their own bathroom and the sitting area. Each room had wonderful views over the city and there were even sliding doors leading to a balcony where there were two wicker chairs.

'Oh my goodness, this is wonderful!' I said. 'I've never been in a place like this in my life. It's gorgeous!'

Kit looked around and nodded slowly, 'Yes I guess it is.'

He let me decide on which bedroom I wanted and I unpacked. Not that I had much to unpack. There were exotic looking toiletries in the bathroom which I swept into my wash bag. I wondered if Kit was going to use his and if he didn't, could I grab them too? Honestly, you would think I'd never been in a hotel before

I had a marvellous shower, wrapped a white towel around my

wet hair, and donned the blue, waffle dressing gown I found hanging behind the bathroom door.

Back in the living room, Kit was on the phone.

'Hey! Road Trip Rules. I thought you weren't going to think about work?' I said.

He grinned. 'I'm not, I'm ordering something to drink. Room service, remember that?'

'Ah yes,' I said, 'what a great idea.'

Ten minutes later, we were sitting next to each other on the balcony drinking champagne.

Beneath us the traffic made its way slowly along the road beside the river. Boats chugged back and forth. People strolled along the Promenade. Meanwhile, I was trying to get Bermuda Triangle out of my head; it's such an earworm.

'This is the life,' I said, 'thank you for this.'

'You're welcome. You seem more of a hotel-loving girl and you're far too young to be a Silver Surfer,' he said.

'Actually, I'm neither,' I said, 'but of the two options, this is much more exciting.'

'That's good.'

'I suppose you spend a lot of time in hotels?'

'Far too much,' he said, 'and when it's business it's no fun at all. In fact it's lonely and rather boring.'

'Have you been to this one before then?'

'A few times, I really can't remember. After a while all the hotels merge into one,' he said.

I considered all my assumptions about businessmen in hotels and hoped he didn't fit the mould. I couldn't imagine him getting drunk, propositioning women in the bar, and watching dodgy films.

'Well this is a mega treat for me I don't mind admitting. It's thrilling.'

He looked thoughtful. 'It was funny when we met on the plane; you were so excited about the whole experience. I was just grumbling about the time I was wasting and being thoroughly bad tempered. I'm sorry about that. And you were having a cocktail and I just had a coffee. You must have thought I was a right bore.'

'You weren't, you were charming,' I said.

I reached out and tapped his arm in reproof. There was a tiny spark of static between us. Perhaps the plush carpets indoors were nylon?

'Not in my head I wasn't; I was bogged down with work and a business proposal I was trying to conclude. You made me realise there was a lot more to life than what I was doing, I think.'

'You should have watched *Mission Impossible 4* and had a Marmalade Martini like I did,' I said.

He laughed. 'You're absolutely right. Next time I will.'

We sat and watched the city for a few minutes, drinking our lovely crisp, dry champagne and I think both being pleased we were up here and not down there battling with the rush hour traffic.

'What do you want to do tomorrow?' he said, 'let's have a day off.'

'Something I've never done and always wanted to do,' I said.

'Sounds interesting.'

'It was something you mentioned the other day. I'd like to go to the Koala Sanctuary. I always wanted to go when I was a child, and we never did.'

'No worries! That sounds a great idea. Consider the tickets bought,' he laughed, and we clinked glasses, 'I'll ask the hotel to sort it out.'

How amazing to be with someone who didn't protest about a trip that wasn't their idea as Tom would have done.

'Brilliant, thank you,' I said.

'We can eat in the restaurant downstairs later?' Kit said, 'if that's okay with you?'

'Perfect,' I said.

I sighed and put my feet up on the foot rest. This was indeed the life. If this is where spontaneous and random choices got you, then I was all for it.

14

I changed into another of my new skirts and a plain, white top. Then I twisted my hair up with the raffia pineapple hairband. I even put some make up on for the first time in days. When I went out into the living room, I saw Kit was standing, bare-chested, ironing a shirt.

Ironing!

Bare chested!

Both things made me feel distinctly light-headed for a moment.

He was watching some financial news on the TV and he looked super cool in just chinos and bare feet. Really, completely gorgeous. Muscular and tanned and... how had this man remained resolutely off the market for such a long time? That woman he'd married and mislaid would be kicking herself now if she could see him.

When he saw me, he switched the TV off and looked me up and down.

'You look delightful,' he said.

I felt myself blush and I fidgeted around a bit with my handbag.

'Thank you. So do you,' I said.

Perhaps that doesn't work? Telling a man he looks delightful? Particularly when he wasn't wearing a shirt. But he did.

He just laughed, swung his shirt on and buttoned it up while I pretended to look at the Brisbane skyline.

We went down to the restaurant and were shown to a table by the window. There was soft music, a few glamorous couples already eating. The ceiling was covered in strings of white fairy lights. As darkness fell outside, it was magical. Far below us we could see cars edging along past the river, pleasure boats decked out with illuminations, the dozens of elegant buildings that made up Brisbane's new silhouette.

'Hungry?' Kit said as we looked through the menus.

'And greedy,' I said, and he laughed.

Then he reached forwards and moved the flower arrangement on the table (gerberas and greenery) to one side.

'That's better,' he said, 'I couldn't see you properly.'

Wow, he wanted to see me. Well, the view from where I was sitting was pretty great so I wasn't objecting. Was he flirting with me? I rather think he was. Was this wise? Was he just trying to charm me? And was this another sympathy-pity-flirt? Or the real thing? It was a while since I'd flirted but that didn't mean I couldn't.

'Here I am,' I said, and I smiled.

We ate delicious food and drank wine and chatted non-stop, and it was almost like we were old friends. Perhaps we were becoming friends now? That would be nice. I don't think I'd ever known a man who was a friend.

I'd heard people talking about their spouse in that sort of glowing terms. *He's my husband and my best friend...* I'd never for a moment considered Tom like that. Which was a bit sad really. And had I been Tom's best friend? Probably not.

'Dessert?' Kit said.

'I think I'm a bit full,' I said regretfully.

'That's a shame,' he looked at the menu, 'they have ice cream. Ten flavours.'

'You have some, I'm quite happy,' I said.

He ordered chocolate chip, and it came in a glass bowl with a raspberry coulis and mint leaves. It looked fantastic.

'Looks good,' I said.

He scooped up a spoonful and hesitated for a moment before he reached across the table and offered it to me. My lips smoothed over the spoon. The ice cream was deliciously cool, creamy and sweet. We watched each other, our eyes locked, the tension rising by the second.

'I was right, wasn't I?' he said, and he gave a small lopsided smile. 'Did I tell you that you look very beautiful this evening?'

'You said I looked delightful,' I said.

'That too,' he said.

Oh. Bloody hell, he was flirting with me! Even I could tell.

'Better than shorts and a t-shirt anyway,' I said, feeling a bit light-headed.

'It's the raffia pineapple that does it,' he said, 'you were wearing it when I saw you that morning at Rowan's house.'

'Fancy remembering that,' I said.

He offered me another spoonful of ice cream and I watched him, mesmerised.

'You shouted at me and slammed the door in my face. Of course I remember. I remember lots of things about you,' he said, 'primarily how pleased I was to see you again, the evening of your welcome home party.'

'You didn't seem very pleased at the time,' I said.

'I wasn't expecting it, but trust me I was pleased.'

How pleased?

A bit pleased? Quite pleased? Delirious?

I didn't say anything. I knew if I said something at that moment it would probably be the wrong thing. I might come out with something about other women, younger than I was, who might have caught his eye on the plane. How he might have taken their number. Phoned them. Formed some sort of relationship with them. Forgotten all about the wild-haired, travel-stained woman who drank a Marmalade Martini and spat cashew nuts out when she talked.

* * *

We got back to our room and he opened the door. There was a wonderful radiance outside the window, all the glow from the city.

He didn't put the lights on. And he turned, took me in his arms and kissed me. Just like that. Not just a friendly peck. I mean really, properly kissed me.

It was bloody wonderful too. I'm not an expert, but this was brilliant, knee-wobbling kissing. His shirt was cool and smooth under my hands, his shoulders hard and warm beneath it.

We stood there for several minutes, in front of the lights and the skyline and the city and it was like being in a romantic, glossy Hollywood film where no one ever had split ends or tripped over the rug or smudged their lipstick. I was extremely smudged, I don't mind admitting.

'Elin, I've been wanting to do that for a very long time,' he said at last, his voice rumbling in his chest against me.

'Have you? Really? You should have said something,' I said, and he laughed.

'Koalas tomorrow,' he said, and kissed my forehead.

Er, that wasn't what I was expecting. I wanted to go back to the 'you look beautiful tonight' bit of our conversation. I'd lived for far too long without compliments or flattery and I was enjoying both.

'Yes,' I said, looking up at him.

He smiled and hugged me.

'Take advantage of that big, comfortable bed,' he said, 'and I'll see you in the morning.'

And then he walked off into his room and closed the door.

Blast, damn, and bloody hell.

For a moment I thought of following him into his room, but of course I didn't. If he wanted to play it cool then so would I.

I didn't feel very cool though. I felt very hot and bothered.

Bloody koalas.

15

I certainly did take advantage of that big, comfortable bed.

I lay under the crisp, cool, smooth sheets, stretching out as far as I could but still couldn't touch the edges of the mattress. Perhaps this was bliss, in the true meaning of the word: complete happiness.

I felt supremely happy, confident, comfortable and vaguely – I searched for the word – sexy.

Hang on, I hadn't felt sexy for a long time. The sensible half of my brain tried to analyse this thought, but the other, flighty half refused to pay attention.

Things would have been even better if perhaps – shocking thought – Kit Pascoe had been in there with me. So perhaps bliss wasn't quite the right word after all?

Good God. I wasn't going to think like that. What did that make me? A loose woman? A tart? I wasn't either of those things. And yet I felt almost powerful.

At least I didn't have to sleep next to someone else's feet and my nose wasn't pressed up against the wall of a loo cubicle. I slept like a teenager. 'Sleeping like a baby' is not a phrase I agree with, not after four years of disturbed sleep with Dan.

I settled down, occasionally opening my eyes to see the glow from the city outside and stroke the lovely smooth sheets.

* * *

In the morning I sent an email and a load of photographs of Brisbane to Dan and then put in my usual phone call to Rowan. Maggie and Banjo were due home soon and they were all wondering how I was getting on.

'Brisbane? You've only got to Brisbane?' Rowan wailed, 'I don't understand what's happening. You should have been home ages ago, surely? Has there been a problem with the van?'

'No nothing, it's just taking a couple of days longer than we thought,' I said.

'So what the hell are you doing in Brisbane?'

'We are staying in an actual hotel for a change,' I said, rather proudly. 'It was Kit's idea. He stays here occasionally on business. It's gorgeous too; we are on the twenty-something floor with a fantastic view over the city.'

'And?'

'And we are taking a trip up the river to see the koala sanctuary this morning.'

'Koala sanctuary?' Rowan was incredulous, 'I thought you were bringing the van back as quickly as possible. I thought you were dreading this trip? What the blue blazes are you going there for?'

'I always wanted to see it and we never did when we were kids. I just mentioned it and Kit organised it.'

'Bloody hell, Kit this, Kit that. He seems to be featuring a great deal in this conversation. Hang on! You haven't been kidnapped, have you? He's not holding you against your will? Are you trying to give me a coded message or something? Because if you are—'

'No nothing like that.'

'—say the word – ooh, I don't know – say the word "Elvis".'

'What? Elvis? What the—'

'So he isn't letting you come home! I knew it! Bastard! I'll phone the police. Wait till I tell Shane!'

'No Rowan, please listen. I'm absolutely fine. There is no problem.'

'Okay, I get it. I'm cool with this. He's in the room with you, isn't he? He's listening to our conversation? Did he make you put it on speakerphone?'

I dragged my concentration back from a mental image of us being chased by the motorway police somewhere, until they forced us off the road and Kit was arrested.

'No, he's in his own room. We have separate bedrooms. Just listen, Rowan. Calm down. I am fine. There is no problem. We are just taking it easy.'

'You could say the word "newspaper",' Rowan suggested.

'I'm saying nothing of the sort. I am fine. We are fine.'

I eventually convinced my sister I was in no imminent danger and if I ever was, the trigger word would be "elephant", at which point Rowan would phone the traffic police, the FBI, and the CBI, plus Interpol.

I showered and rifled through my clothes, looking to find something suited to a visit to a koala sanctuary. Something comfortable and cool and yet attractive and eye-catching. Something that would make Kit look at me again the way he had looked at me last night. Hmm. I ended up with my new shorts, walking boots, and a t-shirt. And my big sunhat. I'm not sure that qualified as stunning – well, not in a good way. Then I realised I was worrying and I'd promised not to. I pulled on my clothes and thought no more about it.

We crossed the Victoria Bridge and made our way to where the tour boat was waiting to take us up river. About half of the seats were taken, and a few minutes later we set off with some exceptionally attractive and helpful crew wandering about. It was a wonderful day: blue skies, fluffy white clouds, and sunshine. Outwardly, I was bright and chatty as the guide pointed out the various bridges and fabulous houses on the riverbank that we passed. Inside, I was thinking about last night. Kit had kissed me and told me I was beautiful. No one had done either of those things for a very long time. And I'd liked it.

That day he was polite and charming. He brought me a cup of very nice tea from the boat's café and sat next to me, his arm along the seat behind my shoulders. Not touching me, just resting it there like the most natural thing in the world.

What was going on? What was he thinking? It was many years since I had dealt with this sort of situation and I wasn't sure how to handle it.

At least I had the sense not to ask.

An hour and a half later, we reached the landing stage at the sanctuary and made our way to the entrance. There was a thick cover of trees filled with birds: parakeets, kookaburras and cockatoos. The ubiquitous brush turkeys wandered around, pecking at the ground, completely unbothered about the tramping feet of tourists.

'Kangaroos, let's start with those,' Kit said, and he took my hand in his.

It was just done so easily and without any fuss or comment from either of us. The last hand I'd held had been Dan's. And yet this felt rather good, sort of comfortable and friendly. I wondered if anyone was watching, if they thought we were a quaint married couple. Not many young people hold hands these days; it's obviously not the cool thing to do.

We entered a huge field dotted with trees and at first glance empty of anything. Then an emu poked its head out from behind a tree trunk and in the distance a kangaroo bounded across in front of us.

Underneath the dappled shade of the trees, it was so absolutely, unmistakably Australian that I felt quite tearful for a moment. Then we walked over to an area at the far side of the field where about fifty incredibly tame kangaroos were lying snoozing in the sun. It was brilliant. I reached down and touched one. Its fur was warm and the body underneath it hard as iron. All that bounding and jumping, I suppose. I'd tried high impact training once, never again. And of course they did it all day.

Naturally enough, the main event was the koalas and there were dozens of them. Lounging in eucalyptus trees, chomping on leaves, and sleeping. Apparently that's what they did for most of the time. That and some energetic scratching.

It looked as though someone had taken delivery of a big box of stuffed toys and stuck them up in the trees, except some were hugging tiny koala joeys and they were beyond adorable. I'm not ashamed to admit I did a lot of delighted squeaking and cooing at this point. You'd have needed a heart of steel not to.

Then we wandered into the platypus enclosure, which was a darkened room with a huge glass sided aquarium along one side. And there they were. Surely one of the strangest looking creatures on the planet, diving and swimming through the weeds. Incredible.

We came out blinking into the heat of the sunlight again and went to the café where we had some much needed iced water.

On the table next to us a family were bickering over sandwiches and arguing about what to see next. I think by his expression, the dad had enjoyed enough wildlife for one day.

'What do you think of it so far?' Kit asked me, 'as good as you'd hoped?'

'Better,' I said, taking a long, unladylike swig of my water, 'much better.'

'I'm so pleased to be fulfilling one of your childhood ambitions.'

'Thank you. I don't altogether approve of zoos, but I do understand this place is a bit different.'

'Been here since 1927,' Kit said, reading the brochure. 'Look at this: you could have an afternoon as a snake handler if you wanted to?'

'That's not a childhood ambition. That's a nightmare,' I said.

'I'd better cancel the booking then,' he said, his eyes twinkling.

'You haven't?' I shouted before I realise he was joking.

I punched his shoulder and he laughed.

We wandered about looking at birds and something big and nasty that was lurking in a pond. Then we stopped to see the Tasmanian Devil.

We leaned our arms on the wall surrounding the enclosure, which was filled with bits of stone piping and lots of bushes that seemed to have been gnawed a great deal by something with a lot of supressed rage. Even though we stood there making encouraging noises – well, at least the sort of things we thought might be encouraging to a short-tempered scavenger – it didn't put in an appearance. From the photographs it had serious anger management issues and the face only a mother could love.

'Well that's a shame,' I said, 'I've watched Looney Toons, I was hoping to see a Tasmanian Devil. They are always so irrational and furious. Always makes me laugh. That and Wylie Coyote; optimism in the face of insurmountable odds.'

'Interesting,' Kit said, 'I know about your unusual taste in novelty pj's, so you like irrational and furious plus optimism. Does that apply to men too?'

I laughed. 'God no—' and then I stopped, realising he was asking something very different here. 'I mean, well, I don't know what I mean, actually. If I'm honest.'

'And you are always honest, aren't you, Elin. That's one of the things I like about you the most,' he said, 'it's making me think.'

You mean there are other things you like about me? What things? Give me an example?

'I try,' I said.

'No, that's the funny thing: I don't think you have to try, I think you just... well... are.' He leaned towards me, ducked under the brim of my hat and kissed me, just once, very gently.

'I are? I mean, I am,' I said. Rather breathlessly.

God, I was pathetically shallow. Just because he was being charming, was attractive, and good company. Just because he seemed to like me.

Tom had been all of those things once. I could dimly remember it: the way he swept me off my feet with compliments and devoted attention. There had been a time when Tom and I couldn't bear to be apart. He'd phoned me at all hours, sent me flowers, I'd left little notes for him in his lunch box. What had we done to ruin all that? I didn't think I had changed that much during our years together, just reacted to Tom's behaviour. It had become hard to love someone who took everything I had to offer for granted.

I lived on my own now, in my little house, with my things and my routine. Did I really need to complicate my life again after finally achieving my freedom? But surely in these days of strong, independent women, I didn't need to give that up in order to have another relationship? No, of course I didn't, and to be honest, I wasn't sure I wanted to. This wasn't what I'd expected though, that was the thing. Rowan had said something about having fun. Was this what she had meant? But with Kit Pascoe of all people?

I turned away and walked briskly along the path, swinging my arms as though I was exercising, anything to stop him from holding my hand again. Although it had felt nice.

What would my sister say? And what would Dan think? And did I really care?

I took a deep breath. Road Trip Rules.

16

We got back to the hotel just before five o'clock and had a cold drink. We sat in the bar talking about our day: the koalas, the birds we had seen. I knew we would go back up to our room soon. Whatever was going on between us, perhaps both of us were delaying the moment when other factors would come into play.

I could feel my sweaty t-shirt chill in the hotel's aggressive air-conditioning. I felt a bit odd, and at the same time excited. How long could we go on like this, just watching each other? Were we going to do anything about it? Should I? I was a single woman. I could do what I liked as long as I didn't break any laws. I liked him and he liked me, what was wrong with that?

We took the lift in silence to our room and both went into our respective bedrooms. I stood watching my closed bedroom door, wondering if the handle would turn and Kit would be standing there. I waited for a long time, and nothing happened.

I let out a long breath, sort of relieved and at the same time dissatisfied. Which was ridiculous. I'd known Tom for three weeks before he even kissed me. It was another month before we had sex. I was never sure if it was me being reluctant or him. What was I playing at?

I turned and went into my bathroom, and realised I was clenching my fists so hard my nails were digging into my palms.

Stop it, just stop it. I didn't need this sort of foolishness; I didn't do things like that.

I wasn't looking for a bit of fun or a man or a random something. Was I?

Hmm. I'd told Rowan I wasn't but maybe I was, and with him, of all people. Who'd have thought it?

No, I wasn't. I was fine as I was.

But...

I showered and pulled on my bathrobe. I could hear the television was on in the sitting room. I padded on tiptoe to the door and peeked around. Kit was standing at the window, drinking a glass of water, looking out at the city. His broad shoulders sagged as he gave a deep sigh.

'Cooled down a bit?' he said.

He hadn't turned around; how did he know I was watching him?

'Much better,' I said.

'Room service?'

'Fine by me.'

He turned around and put his empty water glass on the table.

'What would you like?' he said.

He looked at me as he held out the room service menu and there was an expression in his beautiful eyes that somehow, I knew. That moment had arrived. My mouth went dry.

It was no good having wrangling, internal monologues with myself. I wasn't kidding myself at all.

Him. I wanted him. I really did.

The starkness of the thought shocked me.

What on earth was I doing thinking that sort of thing? I hardly knew him.

I made a conscious effort to relax.

'Anything, you choose. As long as there's no goat's cheese or artichokes. Or blackcurrants,' I said. My voice was sort of squeaky all of a sudden.

'And I was about to order the blackcurrants and goat's cheese surprise,' he said, his smile very gentle.

He walked slowly towards me, dropping the menu on the table.

I thought about things. I was in a damp bathrobe, my wet hair wrapped in a towel. No makeup. No perfume. No deodorant. Just me. Was I ready in any sense for this? What did ready mean?

At last he stood in front of me and he reached out to take the towel from my hair. It fell round my face and he brushed it back. Then he stroked the back of his fingers across my cheek and cupped my chin.

'Elin,' he said, 'am I about to do something very foolish?'

My breath seemed tight, the air locked into my chest.

'I don't know. What are you planning to do?'

'This.'

He kissed me then, gently at first and then I felt his arms go around me, holding me against his body.

'And this.'

He suddenly hooked me up in his arms and looked at me for a moment. He didn't stagger under my weight either. He was waiting for something.

What should I do? What should I say? What did he expect of me? What did I expect of him? Sex: that's what I had been antici-pating. Was that the right thing to do, to think? If I did this, would I regret it?

I reached up and kissed him. Decision made.

He carried me towards his bedroom and laid me on his bed.

'And this,' he whispered.

He untied the belt of my robe and pushed it off my shoulders.

Oh, bloody hell. It wasn't too late to stop this. If that was what I wanted to do.

But I didn't.

I watched his hands as he touched me, tanned against my pale skin.

I shivered. Every nerve ending tingling as he explored me. And for the first time, I didn't feel embarrassed or reluctant. My heart was thumping so hard he must have heard it. Half of Brisbane could probably have heard it. I closed my eyes and lifted my face to his, heard him sigh before he kissed me again, his mouth warm and gentle.

Good God, I'd forgotten about this sort of thing. If I'd ever known in the first place.

Did I know what I was doing? Did I remember how this sort of thing went?

Should I tell him I was anxious? What if I did it wrong? Or in a way that he didn't like? What if we'd got this far and I didn't enjoy it either?

But I felt the sort of urgent need, desire that I hadn't felt for years. If ever.

I was doing this. I wanted to. There was no doubt in my mind.

I was going to have sex with a man who was, in the grand scheme of things, practically a stranger.

I opened my eyes and he was watching me.

I didn't do this sort of thing, did I? I wasn't like that.

Oh yes I was.

In the past I'd taken a long time to get going, to be in the mood, to really enjoy sex. This time was different. I was trembling, cold with nerves and excitement; he was warm.

This was unlike anything I had ever felt. Suddenly I was someone new, more honest, more me.

I did know how to do this, I did, I did. I didn't want to think about it any more.

And that was it. In that moment, I lost all my insecurity, all my many layers of inhibition, every reluctance or doubt. His hands in my hair, his breath on my cheek, his mouth on mine.

To find myself at last. I had been lost and perhaps he had found me.

* * *

It seemed a long time before I re-surfaced into the real world.

What had he done? What had I done? Oh yes. I remember.

Wow.

He lay beside me then, holding me in his arms.

I was aware of myself as I never had been before. I listened to the pounding of my heart, my breathing. I licked the taste of his sweat from my lips.

In the past I'd always found sex slightly odd: affection, occasional resignation mixed with embarrassment. This time had been different. Empowerment. What did I mean? His or mine? Which was right? Was there a right? Who was in charge here? Anyone? No one? Did I care?

Did it even matter?

Was that what really good sex was all about? A thing that two people did with each other, rather than something one person did while the other one thought about the ironing pile.

He pulled the bedcover over us and we snoozed for a bit as the evening outside the windows darkened into night. The cityscape in front of us blazed with lights.

I hope no one in one of the other tower blocks had a telescope.

People did that, didn't they? Scanned other people's windows to find a life more exciting than their own?

Kit turned his head towards me, his stubble scraping on the pillow, and he kissed me.

'Now, about that goat's cheese,' he said, and we both laughed.

That laugh – that shared laugh showed me a new side to lovemaking.

It could be fun. It could be hilarious. It could be a shared pleasure.

The physical sex between us had been great – more than that – but our connection, that laugh was one of the best moments of my life.

17

We ordered room service and then he had the good sense to put the do not disturb sign on the outside of the door. We drank cold wine sitting in the warm air out on the balcony as a clock somewhere in the distance struck midnight. He ordered strawberries and cream, we didn't use a spoon, and we both got very sticky. We talked and touched and laughed together and neither of us seemed inclined to go to sleep. It was as though we didn't want that night to end.

Was I allowed to feel like this at my age? Wasn't I past this sort of thing?

Apparently not.

I hadn't known about any of this. I thought I had. This was different.

* * *

It was a good job we had booked an afternoon check out, otherwise the maids would have been banging on the door wanting to service the room. Free shampoo, conditioner, body lotion, shower caps, coffee capsules, whatever they brought, none of it could have compared with that night with Kit.

At nine thirty, I woke in a tangle of white sheets, my head resting against his arm. So I hadn't dreamed it all, and he was there beside me, still asleep, his lashes dark crescents against his cheek.

For a moment, I thought back. What the hell had I been doing with this man, this stranger? And yet – I reasoned with myself – he didn't feel like a stranger; he felt like someone I'd known all my life, someone who knew me. But did he really? He couldn't know me any more than I knew him. Not really.

I didn't know the most basic facts about him. His birthday, his shoe size, his favourite colour.

Was that what most other people did in the bedroom, I wondered?

Had I been the only one missing out on all this fun?

Somehow I didn't think so.

I pulled on my robe, crept out of the room and, thirsty from all that alcohol, went to make a cup of tea in the kitchen. I pushed back the curtains. Outside the sun was high and the sky dotted with clouds.

Already the traffic in the streets far below was stopping and starting as people went to work. A van was blocking the traffic opposite our hotel and a delivery man with a red baseball cap was unloading some boxes while his companion ticked things off on a clipboard.

How much fun was this? In this lovely hotel with that amazing man asleep in the next room. I sat on the sofa and drank my tea. I wanted to sing or laugh or something. To do something outrageous, to show myself that this morning I was different. Could just a few days, one night, make that much difference to me?

I looked towards the bedroom door. Was he awake yet, stretching his long legs out in my bed? Should I fire up the coffee machine? I went to have a look at it; there were capsules and about five different sorts of coffee.

Suddenly the door opened, and he came out, his hair wet from the shower, a towel wrapped around his waist. God, he was in good shape. How did he manage that when he claimed to be at a desk or the back of a car most of the time?

Perhaps he had a basement gym at his office or a personal trainer who called round every morning. I imagined her, blonde and sleek as a whippet with a steel core and a towel around her neck.

She'd have a mean expression and be drinking one of those vile kale smoothies or 'balanced' water. I have no idea what that is. Have I been drinking un-balanced water all these years? Has that been the problem?

'Good morning,' he said.

I turned back to the coffee machine and pretended to fiddle about.

'I was just about to make you coffee,' I said, waving vaguely at the coffee machine, 'what would you like?'

I felt his arms go around me and he kissed my neck.

My knees actually did go a bit weak at this point.

'I think you can guess what I like,' he said.

He turned me round and looked down at me, his eyes sparkling.

I stifled a laugh and smoothed my hands across his warm chest. 'I'll make an educated guess.'

He bent his head and kissed my cheek, moving to whisper in my ear. 'And then come back to bed.'

* * *

We set off from Brisbane just after midday, heading for Byron Bay. This time we avoided the coast for a little while and just went south, stopping briefly somewhere to stretch our legs and have a coffee. Later in the day, we walked out onto a headland where we found a café and a beautiful view of surf crashing onto treacherous looking rocks. There was an official sign warning about there being no lifeguards and the area being prone to rip currents and unpredictable conditions.

Underneath it someone had scrawled in black marker:

If you try and surf here you're a bloody idiot

which seemed to convey the message even more clearly. It made me laugh; it was just so Australian.

As we stood leaning on the barrier, Kit put his arm around me and dropped a kiss on the top of my head.

'Okay?'

'Brilliant,' I said, and leaned against him.

We stood there, just quiet and contented.

'Hey look, look over there!'

Kit pointed out a dolphin, enjoying itself surfing down the waves, then another and another until we could see twenty or thirty of them, leaping and splashing about only a few metres from the cliffs. They were lovely; perhaps they were feeding but what it looked like was a pod of dolphins having a lot of fun in the surf. It was mesmerising.

I looked up at Kit in delight and he grinned back at me.

I felt a sudden flood of emotion: for him, for us being there together, for myself, for the whole day ahead of us. For seeing this sight, for the sea, the world, the sunshine, for the glorious beauty of Australia, for everything.

We reached Byron Bay in the late afternoon. Of course, we had left Queensland and we were back in New South Wales. If nothing else at least there we didn't risk a sixty-three thousand dollar fine if we were caught in possession of rabbits.

The road was beautiful: sunshine speckled with the occasional clump of wild woodland, the distant ocean. To me that day it was as scenic as a film set. And Byron Bay was gorgeous. Some lovely houses along tree lined streets and never far from view was the curve of the bay and the sparkling sea. The day seemed clear and clean and glorious.

The pavements were filled with loose-limbed surfers with dreadlocks, cool t-shirts, and exotic girlfriends. There were surf shops and vegan restaurants and places to get tattoos. All the girls looked as though they could be in a suntan oil commercial with their smooth, beautiful bodies and sun-kissed hair. They were so confident, so sleek and happy. So unutterably cool.

Perhaps I had been like them when I was that age and just not realised it? Had I? Was it possible to go back and try again? Perhaps I'd wasted my best years fretting about my hair and my appearance when I hadn't needed to. Kit liked me. And perhaps more importantly, I was beginning to like me too. I was kind and reasonably intelligent and thoughtful. And he'd liked my honesty. Perhaps I had more to offer than I'd realised.

Kit parked up by a rugged-looking bar and the tourist information centre, and I clasped my hands to stop myself from clapping with delight. The world was an exciting place after all; it wasn't all grey and predictable. Joyce had been right: there was a lot of world to see, and it was worth seeing.

Even so, as we explored the town it felt as though there should be an official signpost somewhere saying things like:

Welcome to Byron Bay.

If you're over 35, don't bother Mate.

If you don't surf, look cool, or backpack, don't bother Mate.

No tie-dyed t-shirt, blonde dreadlocks, or baggy shorts? Don't bother Mate.

By the time we got to the end of Shirley Street, the sky was heavy with beautiful, bellying rainclouds and the temperature had dropped. The pavement cafés were still filled with young people, digging into salads and sipping drinks. A couple were drinking bright, emerald-green smoothies. What the heck was in them?

'Looks like we might be in for a storm,' Kit said, 'we'd better find somewhere to stay.'

We found a new site for the motorhome and Kit set us up efficiently, unravelling the cables and pipes like an old hand while I looked in the fridge to see what food we had. Just after he came in, the rain started. It was as though someone had turned on a huge tap. The water drummed down on the roof with amazing energy and strength interspersed with distant rumbles of thunder.

'I was thinking we might go out for our evening meal, but perhaps that's not such a good idea, if you don't mind?' he said, peering out of the rain-streaked window.

'I'm sure I can rustle something up,' I said, 'it might not be terribly exciting or have any edible flowers on it...'

He grinned, flipped open his laptop, and logged on to the camp's Wi-Fi.

'Whatever you find will be great.'

In the event I scrambled some eggs and grilled some tomatoes and served it with some toast that was a bit burnt.

'It's almost like breakfast,' I said apologetically, 'but not a very good example. One day I'm going to cook you a proper English breakfast. Bacon, eggs, fried bread, beans – the works.'

'I shall definitely look forward to that. But for now this will do fine,' he said, 'I'm not fussy about food, you know.'

I suppose he wasn't, thinking about it. He'd accepted cheese and biscuits with as much enthusiasm as he had *steak au poivre*.

Outside the rain continued accompanied by the far-off grumble of thunder, and right out to sea we could see intermittent flashes of lightening.

Occasionally people ran past our window, their heads covered with their coats. After we had cleared away, we turned all the lights out and sat in the front seats with a glass of wine to watch the storm through the windscreen. As it came nearer, it increased in volume and fury until we could almost feel the van rocking. It was marvellous and strangely erotic.

It seemed Kit thought so too. He put his wine down and pulled me up.

'Come here,' he said, 'I need you.'

A thrill of something ran through me; he needed me. And I needed him. I wanted to be that woman, the one who looked at him from under her lashes, who curved her body towards him as though we were magnetic.

He took me to the bed at the end of the motorhome where this time we made no attempt to sleep head to toe. It was even more exciting, confined together in the humid darkness as the storm raged overhead. I looked up at him as the lightening flashed outside and it lit up his features, sharpening his cheekbones and the curve of his mouth.

It might not have been a glorious hotel room with a six-foot-wide bed, twelve hundred thread count sheets, and free toiletries in the bathroom, but it was one of the sexiest things I had ever done in my life.

How did he do this? What was he doing? More to the point, what was I doing? Was this just some sort of brief enchantment that couldn't possibly last? And what would we do when we reached home again?

18

The following day we would be driving for a longer stretch of the journey as we headed towards Port Macquarie.

Occasionally as we drove along Kit reached out, took my hand, and kissed my fingers. A simple, honest gesture but every time he did it, I felt happy. The new feeling of being in control of my future was just wonderful. I didn't have to explain myself or apologise to anyone for anything. I wanted to feel like this for the rest of my life.

I sneaked a look at him from time to time, wondering what he was thinking, what he thought of me. I mean really. Was he enjoying my company as much as I was his?

What had Tom said when I found out about Ashley?

It was just sex; it didn't mean anything.

Was I just the latest in a long line of women who had been impressed by Kit's talents in bed? He must have learned it somewhere. I wondered how.

Do men pore over magazine articles about sexual techniques and tricks in the same way women did? I had no idea.

I'd read about women being from Venus and men being from

Mars, something about them retreating into caves with elastic bands. Perhaps when they were there men discussed sex techniques or did cave drawings to pass on tips to each other. Most of them must have been using wax crayons if my past experiences were anything to go by.

We parked up and wandered around the marina, hand in hand. We were just friends. Of a sort. Friends with benefits. Nothing wrong with that, lots of people did it. Well, no-one I knew but I'd read about it.

I started to notice other women checking him out as we passed them, casting an admiring glance over him, his handsome face, his easy smile. He didn't seem to notice. I felt unreasonably pleased with myself. Our relationship was real and honest; there was no deceit lying between us.

We found a wine bar with a terrace overlooking the Hastings River and decided to have our evening meal there. At the next table was a party of eight elderly dames having a birthday party for one of their number, a silver-haired lady called Margaret. There was a great deal of hilarity, some intricately wrapped presents on the end of the table and, as we sat down, a massive cake with lots of candles was ceremoniously placed in front of her.

She looked a bit bewildered.

'Well I was planning on having some ice cream,' she said, 'but I suppose this will do.'

'It's your birthday cake, Margaret,' one of the others said loudly, 'remember? Now you need to blow the candles out and have a wish.'

'I wish I could have some ice-cream,' Margaret fired back.

One of the ladies tutted and turned around.

'We need a photograph Margaret, wait a minute.'

She flashed her dentures at us and held out her camera.

'Would you or your husband take a photo? It's Margaret's ninetieth, we don't want to miss the moment.'

Kit stood up, took the camera, and charmed the whole table in minutes.

'Oooh hello. You're not a strippergram, are you?' Margaret said, blinking up at him hopefully. 'No? That's a shame.'

'Sorry Margaret,' Kit said.

'Not as sorry as I am,' she replied with a twinkle.

I giggled into my glass of wine as Kit came to sit down again.

He threw me a rueful look. 'I'm fussy who I take my clothes off for.'

'I'm glad to hear it,' I said.

He picked my hand up and kissed my palm. What was this man doing to my head? How could this be happening? I was fifty-eight. I had a home and bills to pay. I was a mother of a son who taught maths. I shouldn't be doing this. I was used to my simple, uncomplicated life. I didn't need this, did I?

But then I had been so busy fretting about the past and worrying about the future that I had forgotten to enjoy the present. I now had my independence, my self-worth, and this. And it didn't seem at all bad to me.

* * *

We sat together the following morning looking at Google maps on his laptop and I realised we were within a day's drive of home. All those kilometres behind us and under five hundred to go. We could be home tomorrow. Back in Rowan's house, back to Kookaburra Bay, back to real life.

I couldn't quite imagine it. For days we had been in this self-contained bubble where only we existed. Apart from daily phone calls to Rowan or my aunt and the occasional email to Dan when I found reliable Wi-Fi, we hadn't had to consider anything or anyone other than ourselves. This in itself was different and exciting.

I'd reassured them all we were making good if slow progress. I don't think I'd ever really convinced Rowan that Kit hadn't kidnapped me. Every phone began with her asking, 'are you okay?' In a tone expecting the reply 'elephant'.

She reassured me that Maggie and Banjo had just returned home safely. Shane was still complaining about his leg, the surfing competition had been a success, and the café had enjoyed record takings. There were thirty-one unread messages from Tom in my WhatsApp box. I hadn't allowed myself to even think about what his grievances were. And why was he still bothering to contact me? I'd told him not to. Surely the penny must have dropped by now.

'Good grief, there are over four hundred emails in my inbox,' Kit said. 'I did tell them I was going to be off the grid for a few days. I thought they understood.'

'You really haven't been thinking about work, have you?' I laughed.

'Nope, I haven't really given it a thought. We had a deal, remember? Road Trip Rules. It's been very liberating. Have you been worrying?'

I hesitated. 'It's a lifetimes habit, hard to break in just a few days.'

He turned and grinned at me. 'Cheat. You'll have to pay a forfeit.'

'I was sure you'd crack and read them,' I said.

'I gave my word, didn't I?' He closed his laptop, leaned across, and kissed me. 'I'm finding you far more difficult to resist than my emails. And far more interesting too. Now about that forfeit... we'll never get home at this rate,' he said, kissing me again, 'I'll just keep driving around, taking smaller and smaller roads, stopping in lay-bys and dodgy campgrounds...'

'Suits me,' I said.

* * *

Later – much later that morning we set off towards Sydney.

After a while he pulled over to a petrol station to fill up and then we went into the fast food place next door.

We sat with coffee and huge slices of pie, looking out of the window at the massive trucks pulling in and reversing with pinpoint accuracy. At the solid looking men getting down from the cabs and lighting cigarettes, talking in a huddle, pointing up towards the road. I felt quite friendly towards them, sweaty vests, greasy baseball caps and all. They were Australians, my people. A gritty, hardworking race forged by individuals from all the races and countries of the world. People who were perhaps descendants of the thousands who had settled here over the generations. I realised with a rush of emotion that I was falling in love with my own country again. This wide brown land.

I had a home and a son in England, but suddenly the thought struck me: did I belong here after all? I felt rather wobbly for a moment.

'I shall miss all this,' I said, stirring sugar into my coffee with a wooden stick.

'What, this truck stop? Or Australia? Or our road trip?'

'All of it,' I said, 'just all of it. Actually...'

I stopped. What was I about to say? That I didn't want to go home to England? But I had to.

I had a home and a son and a life. I needed to pull myself back into the real world and stop being so naïve. We would be home soon, and he would put his suit and tie back on and become Kit Pascoe again, dealing with bespoke financial whatever.

And me? What would I do? Go back to England and Tom's looming presence? Dan bringing his washing for me to do? Was I going to shrink back from everything I had learned?

'Actually what?' Kit said.

'I like this,' I blurted out.

He kissed my cheek and squeezed my hand. 'I do too. Forget about Sydney for the moment. Let's run away one more time. Come on, don't be sad, let's go and see the Blue Mountains.'

* * *

After another overnight stop, we pressed on into the Blue Mountains. I know it was something to do with the eucalyptus gum evaporating in the heat but that morning they really did look blue. Added to that as we drove steadily up into the wooded hills were illuminated roadside signs warning about something called 'controlled burning'. I assume that the forest authorities were doing it for some good reason, but the smell of smoke hung heavy in the air. It was almost ominous. On both sides of the road the forests stretched for miles, as far as I could see, it wouldn't be surprising to know no person, settler or indigenous tribe, had ever set foot under those trees.

It was all the courageous and determined parts of civilisation right next door to absolute wilderness. The conflict and choices of two different sorts of life. Just like mine.

Occasionally there was a beautiful house set high on a bluff. I pointed them out to Kit when I could.

'Their views must be incredible,' I said.

'Glorious,' he agreed.

'I'd love to live somewhere with a wonderful view. It would be amazing to wake up somewhere like that every morning.'

'My house has a perfect view over the ocean,' he said.

'Where is it?'

'Just south of Sydney. I bought a plot of land ages ago and left it for a long time. Then five years ago I had a house built, one that I helped design. A friend of mine is an architect, and he knew what I was hoping for.'

'Sounds brilliant,' I said.

'Would you like to see it?'

I held my breath for a moment. 'I'd love to.'

'Really?'

'Yes, I would.'

Kit had a life too. Of course he did; I had to remember that. One that involved his successful business, probably a group of chic, sophisticated friends, and his house overlooking the ocean.

He would have cool parties with everyone talking about the environment and being intellectual and woke. He wouldn't just sit in the garden with an array of liqueurs creating cocktails with rude names as Rowan and I had done the other week. He had a life that I had been and would be no part of. And that was fine. I didn't need to grab on to him like a drowning swimmer grabbing for a lifebelt.

We came to an incredibly twisty part of the road, and he had to concentrate for a few minutes, then we were off again, the road gradually climbing all the way up above the valleys below.

At last we reached Katoomba and drove down the straight, busy road lined with cafés and interesting little shops until we parked and went to the viewing platform to look at the mountain range for which the town was famous. The Three Sisters. I know I had been brought here before as a young child, but I didn't remember it being so full, with coach loads of tourists swarming all over the place, taking selfies and admiring the view.

Kit went into the gift shop and returned a few minutes later, stuffing a paper bag into his pocket.

'This is fantastic,' I said, enjoying the feel of the cool wind blowing into my face, bringing with it the faint scent of eucalyptus and smoke. The sensation of foreboding, being about to lose something, was growing stronger. Perhaps I could cling onto it for just a day longer.

We walked away from the crowds and went down one of the little tracks into the cool shade of the trees. Paths had been cut into the bush to see the waterfalls, I marvelled that anyone had ever managed to build the road up here. It was truly breath-taking. Kit was right: this country was beautiful. Irresistible. Unforgettable. And yet I'd forgotten.

Kit stood next to me, a solid, comforting presence.

'You and I, Elin…'

I turned. 'Yes?'

He took a deep breath.

'You and I have surprised each other, I think.'

'Yes I think so too,' I said.

'And I think I was more surprised than you were.'

'Don't count on that,' I said.

'I'm not saying this very well. What I meant to say was I… the way I reacted. To you, I mean. The way I reacted to you. It wasn't what I'd planned.'

I frowned, a little tick of anxiety registering in my brain. What did he mean, it wasn't what he'd planned? How had any of this been a plan?

'You asked me once if I was married and I didn't tell you the full story,' Kit said.

'You don't have to,' I said.

'No but I want to. Now.'

Kit leaned his arms on the railing in front of us and watched the waterfall as he spoke.

'I haven't talked about this to anyone before. It was a long time ago. She was beautiful and flirtatious and had a wild streak that at the time I found irresistible. We had some great times together, and then she would disappear for weeks. On business, she said. Which seemed to make sense at the time. Then she said her mother was ill and she had to look after her. Of course, she asked for money. Of course, I gave it to her. Finally, after three months, she came back. Filled with excitement and crazier than ever. I should have seen the warning signs, but I was blind to it all. I was in my early twenties at the time and naïve. Well, that's one word for it.'

'So what happened?' I said.

Kit turned and flicked me an ironic smile.

'We were married in Las Vegas. Then two weeks later some bloke turns up at the door, punches me on the face and asks to see her. I have scar as a memento.' He pointed at a small, crescent-shaped mark on his cheekbone.

'Good God!' I was giddy with shock for a moment.

'Turns out he thought we were having an affair.'

'I don't understand. How—'

'She was already married. Married to him. And I think her husband had finally lost patience with all her excuses as to why she was away all the time, why he found it hard to contact her. She'd told him she was looking after her mother too, who was apparently dying. In fact her mother was alive and well and living in Singapore. Her husband had hired a private detective who had tracked her down to my apartment. I was incredibly embarrassed. As far as my family were concerned, I'd just gone on holiday to Las Vegas with a girlfriend. I never told them about the Elvis impersonator or the Little Chapel of Happy Days in the Valley or whatever it was called. It makes me cringe just thinking about it.'

'That's terrible. What an absolute bitch.'

He gave a short, ironic laugh. 'Well, yes.'

'So what happened?'

Kit shrugged and looked down at his hands. 'She went back to her husband as far as I know and they moved to New Zealand, so I never saw her again. He must be the forgiving type. Our marriage was annulled; I signed the papers put in front of me. I didn't press charges against her – I don't know if the authorities did – and that was that.'

'I don't know what to say, that's shocking.'

'Well, yes,' he said, 'I questioned myself, other people. I didn't want to trust anyone like that again. To allow myself to be vulnerable. But I hated being so lonely. Not having anyone to talk to. I just wanted to find someone who would be honest with me, someone I could trust. Someone kind. Someone I could laugh with.'

I realised he could have been describing me. I'd been lonely and vulnerable too. We had laughed together, we had been straightforward with each other

I was thoughtful as we walked back up the trail, going back on my memories of our time together over the last few days. The intimacy, the warmth, the honesty. But then there had been so much more: his gentleness towards me, his thoughtfulness. The way he had taken his jacket off and put it around my shoulders when I was cold one evening. How we had laughed together over silly things. How he had cared for me, looked after me. Asked for my opinion of the route we took or the places we stopped to eat. I wasn't used to that. And every morning he had asked if I wanted to drive and every morning I had replied truthfully that I didn't. Still it had felt nice that he had been kind, and surely there was nothing about that I could object to.

I didn't want or need a man sorting out my life; I'd proved I could do that for myself. But he said he'd had a plan. I'd glossed over that throwaway comment. What plan?

If I had been twenty years younger, I would have imagined myself falling in love with Kit. Thinking about us having a future together. But at my age, the fact that we lived on different sides of the world, it didn't work like that.

'You're very quiet,' he said, 'have I shocked you?'

I looked up at him, a shaft of sunlight pierced the tree canopy and shone on his hair, making it gleam.

'Well yes, of course I'm shocked. Why do people like us, perfectly reasonable people, allow ourselves to be bullied and lied to? It's like we have no self-respect. I'm never going to be like that again. I deserve better.'

'You won't share this with anyone?'

'Of course not,' I said firmly, 'I've told you things in confidence too, things I haven't even told my sister.'

'That's quite something,' he said.

Hand in hand we walked towards to the car park and at one point the path was crowded with yet another coach party heading for the viewing platform, so Kit walked ahead of me. I looked at his broad shoulders, his beautiful profile when he turned to make sure I was okay, and I shivered because I knew without a shadow of doubt that after just a few days, this adventure had made me feel differently about myself; despite my protestations, I knew it was possible to love him.

What made one person love another anyway? What were the odds of that person feeling the same way? And how did you know they were sincere? The whole thing was improbable and terrifying.

But I knew when we parted I would miss his company. The way we saw life, the way we talked and listened to each other. That didn't need to involve love or need or dependence, did it? I never wanted to feel dependent on anyone again. This could just be friendship. We shouldn't gravitate towards each other just because we made each other laugh. Just because we were surprised or grateful. Should we?

19

_____

The next morning was going to be our last travelling together. We were less than three hours from home, from Rowan's house anyway. What did I mean by 'home' these days?

We packed up the van and stowed away our things in the many cupboards, both of us making sure everything was properly locked following one episode when we had gone around a sharp bend and all the saucepans had shot out across the floor.

At last all the pipes and cables were safely stored and we were ready.

Sitting up in our seats where we had shared so many kilometres and snacks and bottles of water, Kit put the keys in the ignition and we looked at each other.

'All set?' he said.

'Pretty much,' I said.

'Then let's ride.'

We set off down the road that took us away from the Blue Mountains and undulated through the National Park until we turned off, avoiding the outskirts of Sydney and taking us past small townships and glimpses through the trees of huge lakes and hidden houses.

Occasionally Kit would catch my eye and one of us would say something cheerful. How much we would enjoy being able to sleep in a proper bed again, or we were looking forward to getting some fresh clothes. That sort of thing. I don't think I believed any of it. I don't think he did either.

We hardly talked for several miles and then Kit put the radio on. I fiddled with the dial, trying to find a station that was playing something other than political news or weather reports. In the end we listened to a radio station where the presenter insisted on playing one miserable love song after another and talking about someone called Cindy and how depressed he was. He must have had a bust up with his girlfriend last night or something.

In the end I turned it off.

'Any more of his music choices and I'm going to lose the plot,' I said. 'Why doesn't he just apologise for whatever it was he did, bring Cindy a mahoosive bunch of roses this evening, and ask her to wipe her feet on his neck?'

Kit laughed. 'Yes that might do it.'

'Here's the turning for the B88,' I said, looking down at the road map on my knee, 'that means we'll be home in under an hour.'

'So you really would like to come to see my house one day?' Kit said.

'I'd love to,' I said.

'Really?'

'You sound surprised. Why? I'd love to see what sort of house you created.'

He grinned. 'I just wasn't sure, you know, what was going to happen when we finish this trip. Okay then, it's a date.'

A date? What an old-fashioned word. I hadn't had a date for

decades. And he had been thinking about what would happen after our road trip. That was interesting. Maybe he had been having the same sort of thoughts I had.

'Deffo, mate!'

He laughed. 'You've been wandering around truck stops and little towns for too long.'

'Doesn't feel too long to me,' I said.

'Nor me,' he said very quietly.

Just before midday, we pulled up outside Rowan's house and she shot out of her front door before the engine had even stopped. Maggie and Banjo hot on her heels.

'At last! Are you okay?'

I got down from the cab and went to hug her.

'I'm fine Rowan, I told you not to worry'

'How was the trip?' Maggie said, waiting for her turn for a hug.

'Great,' I said, 'absolutely great. We had a fab time.'

'Any problems with the grey water hose?' Banjo asked.

Kit reassured him everything had worked like clockwork. No damage done, everything safely stowed away. Kit and my uncle went to look over the motorhome, chatting quite easily.

Rowan threw Kit a highly suspicious look and hissed at me.

'Well as long as you're sure you're all right.'

'I told you, everything is great.'

'I don't think you've told me anything actually,' Rowan said, 'and you certainly haven't told me where you've been all this time.'

Kit and Banjo got out of the van still talking like old friends.

'We've had a great trip, haven't we Kit?' I said.

Kit came to stand next to me, his hand just touching the small of my back for a second. It was only a small gesture, but it felt like something that was just ours, a little connection that no one else saw.

'Excellent. I'm sorry we took longer than you were expecting. How are you both? And Shane?'

'Oh Banjo and I are fine, absolutely back on top form,' Maggie said.

She looked better, the colour back in her cheeks, the familiar sparkle in her eyes.

'Shane is too. Although his leg means he can't empty the dishwasher, tidy up after himself, or cook anything. I'm hoping this phase will pass, even if it means boot-up-the-arse therapy. Which I am more than happy to administer one day very soon,' Rowan said.

At that point Shane appeared at the front door and came to greet us, limping rather dramatically. He shot Kit a wary look and turned to me.

'Hey, you're back!' he said. 'Had a good trip?'

'Great thanks,' I said.

The brothers stared at each other for a moment. It didn't look particularly friendly and the little frown line between Kit's eyebrows was back.

'Well, I'd better be getting along. I'll drive the van over to your house Banjo, if you like?' Kit said.

'I suppose I need to follow you and take you home afterwards?' Shane said.

Kit nodded. 'If you're safe to drive?'

'I'm fine. And we can – you know – '

What did that mean?

I went into the van to start collecting my stuff. The next few minutes were spent getting my clothes and toiletries out and into Rowan's house.

'Right then' Kit said at last, 'I'll be off. He looked at me, unsmiling, no hint of the relationship and the feelings we had shared. 'I've got your number; I'll be in touch. And thanks for your company.'

'No, thank you,' I said politely, 'it all worked out well.'

We were standing in the hallway, our last few seconds alone before our road trip ended.

We felt stiff and formal with each other, as though we had concluded a business transaction, but when he took my hand I leaned forward and kissed his cheek. His skin was warm and slightly stubbly and smelled of soap and sunshine.

Then Rowan hurried out of the kitchen towards me.

'Come in and I'll make you some tea,' she flicked Kit a look. 'Thanks for everything Kit, we really appreciate what you've done.'

'My pleasure,' he said.

And he left, closing the door behind him. Everything suddenly felt a little less vivid and exciting.

We went into the kitchen as Kit and Shane drove off with my uncle and aunt to deliver the motorhome back to their house.

'Right, now you can tell me: what have you really been up to?' Rowan said her eyes narrowed suspiciously.

I widened my eyes in an attempt to look innocent.

'Me? Nothing. I haven't been up to anything.'

She shook her head and then turned to fill the kettle.

'You're such a bad liar, Elin. You always were. Your mouth goes a bit funny when you lie. What happened?'

'Oh Rowan, leave it.'

Her mouth tightened. 'Has he upset you? Did he make a pass at you? I wouldn't put it past him after what Shane told me!'

'We had a pleasant trip. We took in a few sights and we both enjoyed it. What did Shane tell you?'

She didn't enlighten me. 'So explain why did it take you twice as long as it should to get back here?'

'We stopped at places and went to see things. That's all. He thought it might be a good opportunity for me to see a bit more of Australia after so long away. And he wanted to as well. What did Shane tell you about him?'

Rowan opened the cupboard to find clean mugs, went into the drawer for the teabags.

'Oh, this and that. Kit sounds like a bit of a player, that's all,' she said at last.

'Based on what evidence?' I said, suddenly defensive.

'Oh I don't know, just a series of women over the years.'

This didn't sound right to me at all. It wasn't the impression I had.

'Really?'

'Apparently. Shane wasn't very clear on that point. So you're okay? You're sure?' she said at last.

'Of course I'm okay,' I said.

Rowan turned and looked at me, thinking. I could feel my face getting hot. And then her eyes widened.

'Oh, Jeez Louise! Elin! You slept with him, didn't you?'

'Rowan—'

'I knew it! The way you were looking at each other! You did, didn't you? You slept with Kit Pascoe!' Her voice was somewhere between a scream and a yelp.

I turned to go into my bedroom, wanting to get away from her questions. Rowan was close on my heels.

'So?'

'What?'

'Don't what me,' she said furiously, 'what happened?'

I sat down on the bed.

'All right, I enjoyed his company, he made me laugh, we got

on, despite all the things you may think of him, he's a nice bloke. We were honest with each other.'

'Oh really?'

Perhaps I shouldn't have said any more. Stopped digging. But then I suddenly wanted to. I didn't want his departure to be the end of it. I wanted to talk about him, just a little bit.

I looked up at Rowan, standing waiting, her hands on her hips.

'Yes Rowan, and I slept with him, several times if you really need to know, and I bloody enjoyed it.'

Rowan huffed, disapproving. 'Aren't we getting a bit too old for random sleeping around?'

I stood up, defensive and angry. 'It's funny Ro, but so many people – you included – have been telling me I'm not too old to do stuff. Make a new relationship, have adventures, seize opportunities. And yet now I am too old, apparently. I don't think that's completely fair.'

Rowan twitched in annoyance. 'Oh, right, well forget I said anything. As long as you're okay with that.'

'I am very okay with that.'

'Then there's no more to be said, is there?'

'Is that a promise?'

Rowan made a dismissive noise. 'I care about you and your happiness Elin, so sue me. I care if you get tangled up with someone who – who might not be – who might make you unhappy. Now of all times when you've got away from being bullied and cowed.'

There was that word again. Had everyone seen me as a browbeaten wife? Perhaps I had been; the doors closing in on me so slowly and subtly that I hadn't even noticed. But I wasn't that woman now.

I took a deep breath.

'I know you care Ro, and I love you for it. But I'm not that person any more. I'm not. And it might surprise you to know that in the last few days I've learned about myself and what I want and, more importantly, what I don't want. I'm never going to go back to the way I was. Trying to win approval by being a doormat. Now what was that you said about tea? I've been gasping.'

'Yes, I bet you bloody have,' Rowan said rather tartly.

20

The following day, I started doing my laundry and sorting out my clothes. Each new garment seemed to hold a memory. The skirt I had worn when we had dinner in the hotel, the dress with the neckline I had thought was too revealing, the shorts I'd worn to the koala sanctuary. I even clasped my sunhat to my chest rather dramatically, remembering how Kit had ducked underneath the brim to kiss me. I felt warm and sentimental, ridiculous really.

Maggie and Banjo came over later that morning to see how I was getting on and have a good chat. My uncle looked fine apart from a super strength support thing on his wrist, and Maggie was back on top form, excited to see me safely back, and trying to hide her curiosity about how I had got on with Kit.

'And what about my favourite boy, Shane?' Maggie said. 'Where is he, anyway?'

'He went down to the Wipe-Out and he's not back yet.'

'Where does Kit Pascoe live, by the way?' she asked, never one to be diverted from a topic she found interesting.

'Somewhere near Wollongong, he said. On the coast road.'

'Nice spot, if you can afford it,' Maggie sniffed.

'He said the traffic was bad?' Banjo said. 'They've been doing roadworks north of here for weeks.'

'That's Australia for you: one big road building project at the moment.' Maggie looked at her watch, 'Now tell me how you got on with Kit.'

Here we go, the fourth degree.

'Fine,' I said airily, 'he's a nice chap. I know he got off on the wrong foot with us, but he was very nice to me.'

'Very nice,' Rowan said, 'very, very nice. Terrifically nice.'

I gave her a shove with my elbow.

Luckily at that point Shane came back, his VW van chugging up into the drive.

'Well, here we are,' he said, 'back safe and sound and twice as handsome.' He went to give my aunt a kiss on her cheek. 'Good to see my best girl Maggie back safe again. And Elin, are you sure you're okay?'

He didn't meet my eye but came to give me a hug. One which was slightly stiff and awkward.

'I'm fine, thanks Shane.'

'I'm glad you're back. I hope my brother wasn't too much of a miserable bastard like he can be.'

'He was fine,' I said, sick of saying the same thing over and over again.

And whatever Kit was like with Shane, he had been something very different with me. I wondered if perhaps Kit wasn't the whole problem here; perhaps Shane had some explaining to do.

'Yeah, well,' Shane almost said something else but then he stopped himself.

* * *

Kit sent me a text message the following morning, asking if I was free that afternoon. He wanted to pick me up and take me to see his house. My heart did a jump of excitement. I was going to see him again.

I replied telling him I wasn't doing anything particular, and I'd look forward to seeing him. And then after a bit if dithering I added a kiss to the end. Then I deleted it. And then I added it again.

I showered and picked out one of my dresses, the blue one I had been wearing when he told me I looked lovely. Then I twisted my hair up into a knot and secured it with my trusty pineapple hair tie. It had almost become a lucky talisman. Then I left a note on the kitchen table telling Rowan where I was going and reassuring her I would see her later.

Kit arrived at three o'clock and I hurried out to the car before Rowan could come back from the Wipe-Out unexpectedly and start asking embarrassing questions.

In the time since I had seen him, I wondered if I had imagined how lovely he was but one look at him confirmed I hadn't been wrong. He was in a blue shirt and black jeans and he looked marvellous. I slipped into the seat beside him and we sped off up the coast road.

'How are you?' he said. He reached over and squeezed my hand.

'Brilliant,' I replied.

He grinned. 'This is like old times isn't it? It seems ages.'

After a while, we left the highway and turned onto a private road which led directly towards the ocean. A thick screen of palm trees hid the house at first, but then we passed through electric gates which closed silently behind us as we got out of the car.

The house, set on a rocky bluff overlooking the sea, reared up in front of us like a white cliff face. The weather that day was clear and glorious and the ocean was a dazzling aquamarine colour that set off the gleaming walls of the house to perfection. We walked through the huge front door into a white hallway with some sort of figurine in the middle. It might have been a tree, or it could have been a thin elephant, I wasn't sure.

I felt some sort of comment was expected but I couldn't think of anything to say. Apart from, what the heck is that?

The living room was furnished with black sofas, white cushions, and a long glass coffee table. The room seemed devoid of any signs that anyone even lived there. It was rather disappointing. No photos or ornaments. No clues as to how he lived his life here. No signs of a welcome home party, no glasses left on the floor. No piles of post or newspapers. No clock or mirrors.

There seemed no imprint of the man in this house. I thought back to the wall of family photographs on the wall in my sitting room, the little collection of ornaments Dan had bought me over the years, the shelves filled with books and photograph albums. The silly cushion with 'World's Best Mum' that Dan had bought me for Mother's Day when he was fifteen.

Here there was only one huge picture on the wall: a gigantic wave crashing onto rocks. But there were the most incredible views over the Pacific, which sort of made up for everything.

Far below us were boats of all shapes and sizes moored in the bay. Two jet skis were whizzing across the water and a few white gulls were wheeling photogenically across the sky.

'Oh my god, that is stunning,' I said.

'You like it? Really?'

To be brutally honest, I meant the view, not the décor. In fact, I wasn't sure if I did. It didn't feel like a home; it felt like an architect's impression of one. Perhaps this was all too much for me? Was this really the sort of man he was? Someone who apparently lived in the middle of a style magazine, buttoned up and obsessively tidy. I hadn't seen that coming at all. Not after the time we had spent together in the motorhome, the barbies, the informal meals and outings.

I took another look around. It was spectacular, no one could deny that. And he had appreciated my honesty, so perhaps it was more polite to skirt around what I really thought. And it was a house he had designed and planned. You can't tell someone you don't like their home the minute you walk in, can you?

'It's amazing,' I said.

Which of course it was; I probably didn't have the sophistication to fully appreciate it. Like those houses on the television program which look like concrete bunkers or prisons and are described as 'ground-breaking' or 'architecturally on point.' I never get them either.

'Do you want to have a look around?'

I turned to him, feeling suddenly more confident. He was still Kit even if he didn't have a hook for keys by the front door or any photos on the walls.

'I want two things.'

He raised an eyebrow.

'Firstly, I'd like to see around,' I said.

He took me through the house. There was a dining room with a white marble table and twelve black chairs, then a kitchen which was bigger than the footprint of my house. The staircase was blond wood, wide and curving with those little lights set into the edges like you get in cinemas.

Upstairs there were several massive bedrooms and bathrooms and a door on the landing leading to a roof terrace open to the sky which was furnished with white wicker chairs with fat, grey and white cushions. The sun was hot here, the light from the ocean below us dazzling.

We went back into the cool of the house and into his bedroom

which unsurprisingly was painted white with a huge grey and
white bed and a daring scarlet armchair in one corner. Did he
have a monochrome fixation?

'It's amazing,' I said, 'it really is.'

'There's something about it that isn't quite right yet,' he said,
'but I don't know what it is. I've been talking to someone... now,
what was the other thing you wanted?'

I slipped off my jacket and recklessly threw it onto the red
chair where it lay, making the room look slightly untidy.

'I want you to kiss me,' I said.

God, this was bold for me. But I did. I wanted him to kiss me
so much that I couldn't really concentrate on anything else. Not
the house or the view or the day or the time.

He stood looking at me for a moment, and for a nanosecond I
wondered if I had misread the situation. But then he smiled, and I
saw that look in his eyes again.

He stepped towards me and pulled the raffia pineapple from
my hair so it fell loose around my shoulders and then he kissed
me. Oh boy did he kiss me. It was as though he hadn't thought of
anything else since we had parted.

'I remember this dress,' he murmured as he pulled it off over
my head.

'I remember this shirt,' I said as I pulled it off over his.

Through the open windows I could hear the sea ebbing and
flowing against the shore, imagine the waves foaming against the
rocks. Just like the picture downstairs. It was like something from
a particularly suggestive and Freudian Open University tutorial. It
was blooming marvellous.

* * *

We lay in bed together, his arm around my shoulders, watching the sea and drinking champagne. I mean how much better could this get? Then as the heat of the day cooled, we put on dressing gowns and drifted outside onto the roof terrace. We sat in the darkness on the white chairs and watched the lights from the marina, listened to the surf, counted the flashes from the lighthouse out on the bluff. It was wonderful.

'I bought you a present when we were in Brisbane,' he said, 'I forgot to give it to you before I left. Your sister was there and I don't think she approves of me.'

'Ooh, I love presents,' I said.

'Well don't get too over-excited. It's just something I saw that I liked. And I thought it might help you remember me. Stay there, I'll go and get it.'

I didn't think for one moment that I would ever forget him, but a present is a present and always welcome. Unless it has a plug attached or is that weasel thing: a joint-present. I'm not much fussed by either of those.

He came back with a small paper bag in his hand and gave it to me.

Inside was a small, very sweet toy koala holding a eucalyptus leaf between its paws.

He sat on the edge of the bed and grinned at me.

'Silly, isn't it? But you did seem to like them.'

We seemed so happy, we seemed to get on so wonderfully. I was actually beginning to believe in myself more than I had thought possible. I hadn't ever thought I would get to the point when I could trust or relax with another man. And yet here I was doing both those things.

And just for a fleeting moment as I looked out of the window into the dark night, I thought I could smell the eucalyptus and smoke of that day in the Blue Mountains, and I shivered.

21

'This house,' I said to him the following morning as he scrambled eggs in his pristine black kitchen and I perched on a rather uncomfortable bar stool, 'it's very stylish and glossy. But just about everything is black or white. Don't you like colour?'

'I got an interior designer to do it. He came highly recommended, and I didn't really have the time or inclination to do it myself. Perhaps that's what's wrong with it.'

'It's not wrong, it's just very masculine and minimalist.'

He leaned over and kissed me. 'I'm a masculine sort of guy.'

'Well I know that,' I said.

'I've been talking with someone who might have some ideas though,' he said, 'friend of a friend.'

If it had been my house, I would have had a load of ideas. Some flashes of colour or texture. Some of those gorgeous little wooden sea birds on spindly legs. Perhaps a table with shells, some of the beautiful dot art that the Indigenous people did. But it wasn't my house, and maybe he wouldn't have liked my taste in things.

That morning he had to go to his office, so he drove me home first. Watching the early morning rush hour, all the other commuters in their cars and trucks, I felt rather pleased with myself.

Hey, look at me, I'm here, in this car with this man. We really seem to like each other. And we made each other laugh. No off-putting habits as far as I could tell and he was kind and generous. Added to that, he recently helped out a relative stranger in an emergency just for philanthropic reasons.

He pulled up outside Rowan's house and leaned over and kissed my cheek.

'Have a good day,' he said.

'And you.'

'I'll try,' he said.

When I went inside the house, I found Shane asleep on the sofa, snoring like a buffalo, his games controller still in his hand. The room stank of alcohol and the ashtrays were full of cigarette ends. It looked like he and his mates had enjoyed another all-night session. Surely they were all too old for this?

As I closed the door behind me, he woke up and looked at me rather blearily.

'Oh you're back then?' he said.

'I thought you'd be at work by now,' I said.

He didn't answer but stood up rather unsteadily, rubbed his eyes, and went into the kitchen to get a glass of water. He sounded as though he was still drunk or monstrously hungover or both.

'How is good old Kit?' he asked.

I dumped my handbag on a chair and took off my jacket.

'Fine,' I said.

'Fine,' Shane echoed, and he muttered, 'I've been talking to Ro, he's a piece of work.'

'You're still drunk Shane, just leave it,' I said.

'Oh good old Kit eh?' Shane mumbled.

'What's the matter with you? He's been a lifesaver as far as I'm concerned. Agreeing to come with me to Cairns, driving the van back here. He didn't have to.'

'He was just being kind, was he?'

'Yes of course he was. He was terrific. I couldn't have done it without him.'

'Just out of the goodness of his heart?'

'Well, yes.'

I was rather annoyed and not liking the way the conversation was going. Shane might have his opinions, but so did I.

Shane re-filled his water glass and took a long drink.

'Nothing to do with business then?' he said, wiping his mouth with the back of his hand.

'I don't know what you're talking about,' I said, 'and perhaps you should stop now.'

He ignored me. 'I like you, Elin. You're almost like family. Well I suppose you are family. D'you know when I first asked him, he refused. He said you were nothing to do with him, that he couldn't be responsible for all the waifs and strays I stumbled across.'

I didn't want to believe this.

'Kit wouldn't-'

'As far as he was concerned, you could sort it out yourself.'

'But—'

'Until he came up with a plan.'

I felt suddenly cold, despite the heat of the morning.

That day in the Blue Mountains. What had Kit said?

It wasn't what I'd planned.

'Plan? What do you mean, Shane? What plan?'

'Surely you know there's always a plan where Kit is concerned?'

Something bad was coming. I wanted to know what he meant

but at the same time I wanted to stick my fingers in my ears and not hear anything.

Shane looked at me with bleary eyes.

'Remember that paperwork he wanted me to sign? I kept refusing because it was the only hold I had over him. I enjoyed seeing him squirm, just for once. I said if he helped you out, I would sign it. I knew I would sign eventually, I'm stubborn not stupid. He tried to argue with me at first, said why should he have to drag some – and I quote – "snappy, old woman" halfway across the country. But then he saw sense, said he would arrange the flights to Cairns, that he would sort everything out on the condition that when he got back, I would sign the paperwork immediately. And I said yes.'

I felt my heart chill and the memory of the smoke grew stronger. This moment. I knew there would be something like this. There had to be. There always was.

'And I said he either did it or I'd keep him hanging on for months. He's trying to sell the company, do you see? He didn't mention it? No, I bet he didn't. My father's company. There's a London firm wants to acquire it, Kit stands to make a lot of money and make no mistake, that's what makes Kit tick. Money. I bet he was charming, wasn't he? I bet he was all over you like a rash vest. You do realise he was probably just enjoying himself? Taking full advantage of the situation.'

'He wasn't! Don't be ridiculous!'

Shane wagged a warning finger at me.

'Aha! He's really got round you, hasn't he? I wondered if he would just be his usual rude, grunting self, but Kit's cleverer than that, isn't he? Oh yes. There's always a deal where Kit is concerned, remember? I know what he's like. I've seen him in action. He's always been the same.'

I couldn't help it; I turned away and put my hands over my ears.

'You're wrong, Shane! Stop it! It wasn't like that!'

Shane walked around the kitchen table and looked at me again.

'Wise up Elin, you've been had. In every sense of the word from what I hear. Now I've signed the paperwork, you won't see him for dust.'

'No, you're wrong Shane. You're wrong! Why did he invite me over there yesterday? Tell me that?'

I was almost crying now. Angry and embarrassed. It hadn't been like that at all. It had meant something to me, to both of us. Hadn't it?

Shane flapped one hand at me.

'He wanted to show off that house of his, that's my guess. You've been plutoed. He made you think you were special but the novelty's worn off now and the paperwork is signed. Just think of it as a farewell shag and have done with it.'

Rowan came into the living room just as I slapped Shane's face.

'What the hell is going on?' she shouted, 'I could hear you pair from the end of the house!'

'I'm just putting Elin straight,' Shane muttered, rubbing at the red mark on his cheek, 'I've told her about the contract.'

'You promised you wouldn't!' Rowan cried, her face twisted with distress, 'you said it would stay between the two of you.'

'Yeah well, I like Elin. I don't want to see her getting hurt,' Shane mumbled. He dropped his head into his hands. 'Christ my brain hurts.'

'I'm not sure you even have a brain half the time,' Rowan snapped.

I looked at my sister. 'You knew about this as well?'

Rowan was having trouble meeting my eye. 'Shane told me after you'd left for Cairns. That's why I was so worried about you.'

I sat down and tried to think straight.

'You didn't think to tell me?'

'I wasn't supposed to know, Shane told me by mistake.'

'By mistake? God, Shane you must have been a great loss to the Secret Service. So you practically blackmailed Kit into it?'

'You don't think he would have done it otherwise, do you?' Shane mumbled.

I felt quite sick. My disappointment rising into my throat, choking me.

Suddenly everything I had believed was in doubt. But surely I hadn't imagined it all? The growing friendship between us, the emotional connection, the laughter, the fun, the flirting. Could men do that: have thrilling, passionate sex with women just to get a deal done with their annoying, younger brother? The whole idea was ridiculous. And yet...

I took a deep breath. 'I don't believe you. I don't believe Kit would do that.'

'Believe what you like. Kit wants to sell the company. I stopped him. I'm an equal partner, he couldn't do anything without my agreement. It's been dragging on for months, maybe two years. Before I even met Ro. So it might be longer. Solicitors coming and going and arguing and changing things. Every time they think they get somewhere I stick a spanner in the works. It's been rather fun if I'm honest.'

'Shane... you wouldn't do something like this... you can't think this is just fun?' I said, my voice fading.

At the back of my mind, a little nagging doubt was developing. I thought back, remembering the places we had seen, the conversations we had enjoyed. From my perspective they had been honest and straightforward. Two lonely people unexpectedly finding each other. Perhaps Kit had seen it very differently: a bit of a laugh, an advantage taken.

Shane wouldn't look at me. All the old bravado and cheekiness gone; he just looked guilty. He sank his face into his hands. 'Leave me alone. I don't want to talk about it; you haven't had to put up with him lording over you all his life. Being Dad's favourite, getting all the attention. And now, just when I thought it was all over, I have to go with him to bloody London. I didn't realise that was on the cards. How long is that going to take, eh? Imagine how much fun that trip is going to be.'

'Christ Shane, how old are you anyway?' Rowan said.

'I'm okay with the way things are,' he said. He sounded a bit unsure of himself now. 'This company sale is going to change everything. Look, I'm sorry. I shouldn't have said anything to Elin. I dunno. I'm really upset.'

Rowan threw up her hands in despair.

'So what have you got to be upset about? Because you told her or because you're an idiot?'

'I'm not upset about the deal. I'm just an idiot,' Shane shouted back.

'Well I'm glad we got that sorted,' I said.

'Elin—'

'I'm too old for this,' I said, 'and so are you, Shane.'

Shane rubbed his hand over his stubble and then ruffled his hair.

'You can see what he's like though, can't you? I bet you were even fooled for a bit. All that charm in one big dollop,' he muttered

I didn't say anything, because yes, I had been fooled. Done up like a kipper.

My phone pinged with an incoming text message.

It was from Kit.

I couldn't stop myself. I read it.

Good to see you yesterday.

And that was all. Not even a kiss at the end. Should have I expected one? How had I got this so wrong? Yet again. It was embarrassing.

22

I went and showered and then I did some more half-hearted sorting out of my clothes. Perhaps I should keep some of them after all. Perhaps I wasn't entirely that exuberant, optimistic woman who wore colours and gold sandals and tied her hair back with a raffia pineapple.

I wanted to spend proper time with my family before I had to think about going back to England. That's what I should have been doing. I had left them, gadding about on a road trip with someone I hardly knew. Behaving like that. Kit was a stranger. I must have been mad. I should have been braver and just gone on my own, not allowed Kit to be dragged into this at all. And yet...

Just when I was starting to believe in myself, getting my life back on track it felt like it had all gone wrong, that I had made a mistake. It was as though all the doors I'd been slowly opening could shut in my face.

I picked up a cardigan, a tailored shirt, my sensible wedge heeled sandals, and stared at them. They seemed to belong to someone else, not me. They looked like a stranger's clothes.

I took a deep breath. I didn't want to be that woman again. I liked the change I was feeling, I wanted to keep going with my new belief in myself. It had felt exciting. Could I manage that?

Right. I stuffed most of my dull clothes into a black bin liner, ready to take them to a charity shop the next time I went out. No matter what happened next, I was going to be rid of that person, the one who allowed herself to be uninteresting and unremarkable. I refused to be – what had Kit said? Cowed.

I wanted to be more than that now. I was going to be more than that.

Whatever the truth of the matter, my encounter with Kit Pascoe had made me realise I wasn't finished yet. The Australian sun had risen for me. There was life and courage in me. I wasn't going to lose those just because I felt a fool. There are worse things in life than making a mistake.

Then I moved a jacket and underneath was the koala toy Kit had given me.

I almost cried.

Oh yes. I remembered the sweet, easy feeling of that day, the wonderful view over the Blue Mountains. The soaring beauty of the Three Sisters. The little pathways and the waterfalls cut into the unfathomable forest. The way he had confided in me. Had that all been a load of lies, a way to seem vulnerable? A way to trick me into trusting him the way that other woman had tricked him all those years ago? Perhaps he was more damaged than either of us had realised. How could I believe anything he'd said to me?

For a moment I held the little bear over the bin, ready to drop it in, but I couldn't do it.

It was early evening, which would make it morning in England. I picked up my phone and dialled Dan's number.

'Hi Mum, I'm a bit busy. Anything wrong?'

'No just wanted to hear your voice, catch up with you,' I said, trying to sound cheerful. 'I'm back with Auntie Rowan. Safe and sound. Banjo is back home, he's on the mend.'

'That's good.'

'He and Maggie send their love. They say you should come and visit.'

'Gosh, if only. I'm loving the pictures you've sent me. Look, I've got a lesson in five minutes. Let's talk about it when you get home. I'm walking and talking. I can't wait till the end of term, not long now.'

'Everything okay? How is Skye?'

'Fine, everything is fine. I'm just tired. Skye is working in a vintage shop in Clifton now, she loves it. Have you heard from Dad?'

'No he sends me texts but I don't read them. Why, what's happened?'

Dan sighed. 'Then I might as well tell you. He and Ashley have split up,'

I gasped. Thunderstruck. 'You're kidding?'

'I'm not; he's staying with a mate of his. He says Ashley was driving him to drink. He keeps asking me when you're coming home, and I keep saying I don't know. He said you weren't replying to his texts, I think he wants to talk. I wouldn't blame you if you didn't.'

I bet he does, I thought.

'I'll let you know—'

'Look I have to go, I've got 3C next and from the noise they are making, they are probably smashing up the desks.'

'Lots of love!'

'Yes, see you soon.'

Tom and Ashley had split up. He'd be angling to come to me for sympathy. I could almost hear him. In an irritating, little-boy voice that he assumed was likely to win me over. What a ghastly prospect that was: listening to my ex-husband droning on about how his wife didn't understand him.

I might have a nagging doubt about Kit, the horrible feeling that I had been so wrong about him, but life with Tom had been far worse. I was never going to be taken for a fool again.

I borrowed Rowan's car, packed all my charity shop recycling into the boot, and drove over to see Maggie and Banjo. They were happily watching cricket on TV with the sound turned down and munching through a bowl of popcorn. In front of them on the coffee table was a book of maps and a notepad.

'We're planning our next trip,' Maggie said, passing me the bowl, 'we thought we might nip across to Tasmania. Patty and Malc have suggested a meet up, and after all we did miss them when we had the accident.'

'When are you planning on going?'

'Well, after you go back to England. But never mind about that, tell us more about your trip; we haven't had a chance to catch up properly, have we? I must say it took you long enough to get home. Did you get lost?'

We spent the evening chatting and exchanging news. They told me all about their stay in hospital and I gave them highly censored highlights of my road-trip. My attempts to gloss over everything didn't work.

'We got the impression you and that Kit Pascoe man were pretty friendly, the way he was talking about you when he called in,' Maggie said at last. She used the same airy tone of feigned disinterest that she always had in the past when asking about my boyfriends. She somehow imagined it would get me to spill the beans.

'He was okay,' I said, 'you know. Okay.'

'Well that's not the impression we got did we Banjo?'

My uncle looked around guiltily; obviously he had been trying

to follow the silent television and not listening to her at all.
'What?'

'I said we thought Kit Pascoe and Elin were friendly.
Didn't we?'

'Did we?' He looked puzzled.

Maggie clicked her tongue at him. 'You're useless, Banjo. You
remember what you said?'

He pulled a face. 'No, what did I say?'

'You said... oh for heaven's sake Banjo. You're bloody hopeless.'

'Is it okay if I stay here tonight?' I said, hoping to change the
subject.

Maggie's face lit up. 'Of course, you can love, you can have
your old room. That would be lovely. Any reason?'

'I just wanted to spend some more time with you both before I
go back to England,' I said, trying to look innocent.

She wasn't fooled. 'I know that look, Elin. I know you're hiding
something.'

'Nothing at all,' I said, 'absolutely nothing.'

My childhood bedroom had once been decorated with my choices
of lime green paint on the walls and citrus yellow woodwork.
More proof that I had liked colourful things when I was younger.
Plus I'd collected a terrible montage of pop stars and girlhood
crushes on a corkboard. Now all that had gone and been replaced
by pale-blue walls and a cross-stitch picture of kangaroos in the
bush. The dressing table at which I had spent so many hours
trying to cover up my teenage spots was still there. Where had the
time gone?

I unpacked the few things I'd brought with me for the visit
and there at the bottom of my bag was the toy koala, the silk euca-

lyptus leaf between its paws a bit crumpled now. I straightened it out and put it on my dressing table. We stared at each other for a few minutes. I didn't know what to think. I wished the sick, sad feeling in my heart would go away.

* * *

No sooner had I sat down at the kitchen table the following morning than my aunt started the inquisition.

'So, Kit Pascoe?' she said.

'Oh Maggie! What about him?'

'Did you and he... you know, have some sort of thing going on? I said to Banjo the moment I saw you that there was something. I could always tell with you girls.'

I took a deep breath to try and formulate some sort of answer and realised I couldn't be bothered.

'I don't really want to talk about him,' I said.

Her eyes lit up. 'I knew it, I knew I was right! You don't fool me Elin, never could. I remember that lad from Gerringong. All that sulking and shouting and pretending.'

'Jeff Baker,' I said, remembering being dumped on Christmas Eve for someone else who I assumed was my friend.

She got the silver bangle that was supposed to be mine. And every time we'd met up in the weeks afterwards, she'd flashed it at me with a smug smile of triumph. 'I wonder what happened to him?'

'He works in the bank. I saw him only the other day. Married to some Chinese girl who does nails.'

'She could do mine,' I said, looking at my bitten nails and ragged cuticles.

'She works in the precinct, near Coles. You could ask.'

'I could,' I said, 'I wonder if she's any good?'

I don't know what I was thinking. I'd rather have my hands daubed with mud and set on fire than find out if Jeff Baker's wife was a good manicurist.

My aunt was not easily diverted. 'Kit Pascoe. So you and he…?'

'Look, I'm nearly sixty, I'm not going to discuss my relationships, real or imagined. I can take care of myself.'

'I'm not going to interfere,' she said with a wide-eyed look, 'perish the thought!'

'Not much!' I said.

'Don't be so tetchy. If you want to know what I think—'

'I don't.'

'—Well I'm going to tell you anyway; I liked him. Banjo said he was a good sort. And he's certainly very handsome. Kit I mean, not your uncle. Although to be fair, Banjo was quite the looker back in the day. He had more hair then, and of course he was a cheeky sod.'

'Whether or not someone is handsome shouldn't make a difference.'

'Well, maybe not but I could see why you'd feel the pull,' Maggie said, looking a bit wistful. 'I wish you'd just tell me what the matter is. We both thought he was okay, and he looked at you in that way.'

'What way?' I asked, despite myself.

'That way, you know. He liked you. And he was certainly kind helping us out. Malc and Patty said he was lovely. Couldn't have been more helpful.'

'Yes, well there are always two sides to every story,' I muttered.

'Go on then, tell me,' she said. She stood up. 'I'll make some tea.'

'It's difficult to explain,' I said.

'Algebra, why people watch TV reality shows, banker's bonuses, they're difficult to explain,' Maggie said, waving one hand in the air, 'so is politics, why tourists go into the outback without any water, why people are so rude. Telling me what's the matter should be fairly easy.'

'I really don't want to talk about it.'

My phoned pinged with the arrival of a text message. From Tom. I bit down a strangled cry of rage and looked at it.

Please phone me. I'm in a bit of a fix.

'That's Tom, yet again. He and Ashley have split up. Daniel told me.'

Maggie laughed. 'Really? Karma come back to bite him on his arse, has it? I can't say I'm surprised.'

She reached over as if to take my phone, but I pulled it away.

'I'm guessing he's looking for sympathy.'

She bristled. 'Pah! Not from you I hope?'

We had a fairly brisk chat which diverted her attention nicely, about Tom and his many faults and character flaws.

* * *

That afternoon, wanting to get away from the questions, I went food shopping.

In the middle of all this, I received another text from Kit. My heart did a bit of a tremor when I saw Kit's name.

What are you doing this evening?

Nothing particular. Fending off questions from my aunt. Some laundry.

I decided not to reply. Then half an hour later, I had another from Kit.

I wondered if you would like to meet up for dinner this evening?

No kiss at the end. Nothing special. No mention of if he'd missed me. Was I okay? Did men get that personal when they were messaging? Or was I reading too much into it?

I found a parking space, went into the supermarket, and picked up a few things I needed. As I got back to the car my phone rang. It was Kit.

I let it ring out and didn't answer. A few seconds later, he rang again.

I looked at the screen for a few moments, wondering if I should ignore him. In the end, curiosity got the better of me.

'There you are at last, I was wondering,' he said.

'Wondering what?' I said, my tone decidedly frosty.

'If you were okay? If you received my texts?'

'Yes I am and yes I did.'

'Well?'

'I didn't reply,' I said at last.

'Well I know that. Can I take you out? Tonight?'

'I'm busy,' I said, 'I have to go.'

I ended the call and drove home, my thoughts in turmoil.

He wasn't going to drag some snappy, old woman halfway across the country.

Let's just call it a farewell shag and have done with it.

I wouldn't let it upset me, I wouldn't.

As I unloaded the shopping outside my aunt's house, a car pulled up behind me, its engine purring in the way expensive car engines do. I knew it would be him. I could sense him getting out of the car, hear the solid clunk of the driver's door closing behind him.

'How did you find me?' I said.

'I needed to talk to Shane and Rowan told me where you

were,' he said, 'very unwillingly I might add.'

I turned and looked at him over the top of a brown paper bag filled with vegetables. A tuft of carrot tops was sticking out and tickling my nose so I made a great fuss about swatting it to one side so I didn't have to look at him any longer. Kit stood in the sunshine, a check shirt, jeans.

'Are you okay?' he said.

He tried to take the bag from me in an attempt to be helpful. I clutched harder at it and for a moment we wrestled with my aunt's groceries.

'Look, I don't need your help,' I said.

He backed off, holding up his hands in surrender. 'Right, I see.'

'What do you want?' I said at last.

He looked mystified. 'I wanted to see you of course.'

'Of course you did,' I said rather sarcastically.

'Look Elin, what's the matter?' he said.

I looked away. 'Nothing—'

'Obviously there is something,' he said. 'Something's changed. The other day—'

'The other day was the other day,' I said furiously, 'this is another day, this day.'

I realised I sounded a bit ridiculous even to myself.

He frowned, trying to understand me. 'I just wanted to ask you out for dinner. I didn't realise it would upset you this much. What's wrong?'

'I'm just a snappy old woman. We get like that you know—'

He looked even more puzzled.

'—and I have things to do. I'm staying here for a few days.'

'How is Banjo? Is he fully recovered from his accident? I bet he was glad to get safely home?'

I fidgeted a bit and looked towards the front door wishing I could make a run for it.

'He is fine, thank you. Yes, he's very glad to be home. What a stroke of luck you were around to help out. I hope it wasn't too much like hard work,' I said in a tone that could only be described as pointed.

'It was a pleasure—'

'Yes, I bet it was. Not so bloody miserable and snappy after all was I?'

'Elin, I have no idea—'

'Well I know now what you were up to and why you did it, so just go away and leave me alone.'

I walked away from him towards the front door. He dodged around me and blocked my path.

'Elin. What's all this about? I don't understand.'

'Really?'

His face tightened. His eyes were cold. 'So, I'm guessing you don't want to come out to dinner with me?'

'No, I bloody don't. Not tonight or any night. I'd rather—' I tried to think of something rude and pithy but at the same time clever, but I couldn't. Doubtless I would come up with the perfect put down at three o'clock tomorrow morning.

Instead I went into the house and kicked the door closed behind me in a marked manner.

'Elin? What's all that shouting?' Banjo called from his chair in front of the television.

'Nothing and no one,' I said.

'Didn't sound like no one,' he said mildly, 'and it didn't sound like nothing either. Sounds as though you were having a bit of a row.'

I didn't answer. I went to put the groceries away in the kitchen, slamming the cupboard doors closed, pushing things into the fridge, hardly able to see through unshed tears.

23

I had forgotten how persistent Maggie could be when she had her teeth into a subject, and it was getting more and more difficult to avoid her constant questions. Where was Kit? Why was I in such a mood? What had happened? Had anything happened? And most embarrassingly: should Banjo have a word with him?

I was catapulted back to being sixteen again when my uncle had harangued Ben Lincoln outside school after he had dumped me. I don't think I had ever got over the shame.

When I got back to Rowan's house, I could hear quite a commotion coming from her bedroom where I found Shane crashing around trying to pack a suitcase. Rowan was sitting on the bed looking miserable.

Shane needed to go to London with Kit to finalise and sign the contracts. The deal was being concluded; at long last their father's company was being sold. Solicitors and businessmen would probably assemble in some glass office block near the Thames with their pencils sharpened, coffee brewing, and avaricious glints in their corporate eyes.

'Don't talk to him,' Rowan hissed as I came in. She pulled me into the kitchen and closed the door behind her. 'He's in a bloody foul mood. He's flying to London with Kit on Friday; he won't be back for ages. He's going to be impossible. Never mind the jet lag, he's probably going to be arrested on the plane for having a fist fight if someone looks at him the wrong way. I just hope to God they aren't sitting anywhere close to each other. Well, not within punching distance. Kit sent some bundles of documents over with a driver yesterday. For Shane to read through. Like that's going to happen. He's tried to convince Kit he doesn't need to go but Kit's not having any of it. A car is coming back to pick him up at four thirty and until then I'm going to hide all the glasses and keep out of the way. My bet is Shane's packing all the wrong stuff and he will end up in some boardroom in his board shorts. The green ones with the lobsters, just to make a point. I'm not even sure if he has a suit. Or a tie other than his old school tie which he chewed the end off.'

'Oh, good grief,' I said.

'Well he'll just have to put up with it. Apparently he will come out of the deal with a shed load of money but even that hasn't cheered him up.'

'Some people are never happy.'

'Talking about people not being happy, how are you? Maggie said you were very down in the dumps. And you had a flaming row with Kit on the doorstep.'

'I might have,' I said.

'And she told me that Tom and Ashley have split up? Is that true?'

'Apparently.'

'God you are going to have to be careful, otherwise your bid for independence will be very short lived indeed.'

'No it won't, I've learned my lesson,' I said, 'neither of them are anything to do with me any more and I intend to keep it that way.'

'So what about Kit?'

I shrugged. I wanted to pretend I was indifferent. Offhand. Inside I was anything but.

'What about Kit?'

Even saying his name gave me a little twinge of pain inside. This was ridiculous. Immature. If this was where unexpected crushes got me, then I wouldn't bother in future.

'Nice try, Elin,' Rowan said, 'I think we both know there's more to it than that.'

The car turned up at the house bang on schedule and Shane stamped out towards the car with very ill grace. Personally, I would have thought a business class flight was something anyone would enjoy but apparently not. He had even moaned about that to Rowan, wondering if he could swap his seat for one in Economy so he didn't have to sit near his brother. I told him I didn't think he would have any difficulty doing so if he really meant it.

I left Rowan and Shane to a long hug and rather tearful farewell on the pavement outside the house while the driver loaded Shane's case into the boot and then went to sit in the front, staring tactfully ahead from behind mirrored shades. Shane opened the window and waved madly as he was driven off and then Rowan came back inside and opened a bottle of wine.

'Oh well, he'll soon be back,' she said rather miserably, 'I thought he was just going to be away for a few days but apparently not. He has to talk to their lawyers and heaven knows how many meetings to go to. And apparently the paperwork is going to be like *War and Peace*. He'll absolutely hate it. I will miss him so much; we've never been apart for so long.'

She gave a little gulp.

I gave her a hug. 'He will miss you too. But at least it will be worth going? And he won't have to do it again. Look how many times Kit had to do that trip.'

And Shane didn't, because he had refused to co-operate.

Rowan gave a nod of agreement as she slugged back some of the Hunter Valley's finest and choked as it went down the wrong way. I looked at the wine bottle label; a crest, lots of writing, a stylised view of a verdant landscape. I remembered Kit saying he wanted to go to the Hunter Valley, but we hadn't fitted that detour in. It made me feel sad all over again.

'Shane's already planning what to do when he gets back. So really all this protesting about not wanting the money is a bit hypocritical. He wants to refit the Wipe-Out, install a bigger kitchen and build an extension so he can start a surf school.'

I put the bottle down on the table. 'That will cost a lot won't it?'

Rowan gave me an old-fashioned look. 'He's getting a lot. Didn't you and Kit actually talk to each other or were you too busy clawing at each other's clothes and having hot sex?'

'I never said we were having—'

'Oh please, spare me. I think I can recognise a couple who have been doing some enthusiastic horizontal dancing when I see one. And I don't think you went over to his house to play backgammon, did you?'

'Well, no.'

'Look Elin, I'll be honest, I've been thinking about it a lot and I can see things more clearly now. Shane was being needlessly diffi-cult, putting Kit off for all that time. He was deliberately making a bad situation worse. Rather childish if anything. It was going on before we even met so the only perspective I had on Kit was what Shane told me. There was nothing stopping him from signing those papers years ago except sheer bloody mindedness. And if he had you wouldn't have got caught up in this mess. I've had time to think about it and I blame Shane as much as anyone.'

'Thanks,' I said. 'It doesn't make me feel any better, but thanks.'

We sat at the kitchen table knocking back wine and chatting for a while until we finished the bottle and Rowan opened another.

'Don't argue with me,' she said, 'I feel like getting pissed.'

'I wasn't arguing,' I said, 'I do too.'

'So tell me about Kit?' she said temptingly.

'I was a mug,' I said, the flood of my feelings breaking out at last, 'believed all that charm nonsense, the careful campaign to make me think he was okay. I can see now it was a game. Maybe one he plays for his own amusement. What a fool I was.'

'Bastard,' Rowan said, topping up my half glass of white wine with the newly opened red.

'Bastard,' I agreed.

There was a knock on the front door and Rowan tottered off to answer it.

She came back a few moments later with an enormous bouquet.

'These are for you,' she said, 'this must have cost a pretty penny. Who is it from?'

I searched without success for the card. 'No name but I think I can guess. They'll be from Kit, won't they?'

Rowan looked a bit wistful. 'Shane has never sent me a bouquet like that in all the time we have been together. He bought some garage flowers once; we'd had a row about the recycling. They were reduced and he didn't even bother taking the price tag off. This is about a hundred dollars' worth by the look of them.'

I sat looking at them for a moment and then, consumed with

fury and fired up with alcohol I took them outside and whacked them against the wall before dumping them in the compost bin. There were leaves and blossoms all over the ground which I kicked at and missed.

'Well that's a shame,' Rowan said mildly. She opened a packet of crisps and started munching, 'but I'd have done the same. Probably. So go on, tell me about you and Kit?'

'Oh for heaven's sake – we had sex and it was brilliant, so what?' I said. 'Anything else you need to know?'

'Dunno. Was he nice?'

'He bought me a koala,' I said.

'A real one? What the hell are you going to—'

'A toy one Rowan, don't be daft.'

I went to fetch it and I placed it on the table between us. It sat, still clutching its eucalyptus leaf between its paws.

'That's sweet,' Rowan said, 'oh don't!'

She reached out as I flicked the little bear on its nose and she caught it before it could fall onto the floor.

'S'nice,' she said, a bit slurred, 'it's cute.'

'A stuffed bear. Bloody man.'

'So what made you do it?'

I sat pulling the koala's ears and thinking.

'I'm beginning to understand how lonely middle-aged women get conned by people on the internet. It's been such a long time since I felt... oh I don't know... felt anything. I thought we had something different. I thought he was being honest with me, but it turns out he wasn't. I was just part of a plan.'

'Oh. Well... I don't know what to say. Want some crisps? Soak up all this alcohol?'

'I need the loo,' I said and went out into the hallway where the first thing I saw was a small white envelope on the floor. With my name on the front. Presumably where it had fallen out of the bouquet.

I opened it.

Sorry Elin. I was a fool. I can't wait to see you again. Can we talk?

Just as my foolish heart began to race, I realised who it was from.

Lots of love, Tom xx

24

Three days later, two things happened.

Firstly, Rowan received a phone call one evening from Shane. After a great deal of yelping with excitement and telling him how much she was missing him, she put him on speakerphone.

'Well I'm here,' he said as we crouched over the phone, 'did you get my texts?' There was a lot of static noises on the line which was a bit off-putting.

'Yes, I did. Are you okay? What's London like? Have you had anything really English to eat? Like roast beef and Yorkshire pudding?' Rowan asked.

'Hardly Ro,' – *crackle* – 'bloody boiling here. Everyone told me it would be cold and it always rains but it's really,' – *crackle* – 'sunshine and everything. We're staying at a hotel overlooking the river and there are people everywhere. And,' – *crackle* – 'all over the streets and policemen on horses. Tourists in big groups taking selfies all over the place. I don't know if I'm coming or going half the time.'

'It's a terrible line, Shane. But you're okay?'

'Yeah I'm fine,' – *crackle* – 'bit buggered with the jet-lag.'

'What time is it with you then?

'Nine forty,' – *crackle* – 'morning. I'm shattered. But Kit's gone into the London office to get some work done. Sod that for a game of cricket, I'm still in bed. Pity you're not here too, Ro.'

Rowan exchanged an anxious look with me. 'And is Kit okay too?'

'Yeah seems to be,' – *crackle crackle* – 'an evil bastard.'

The line was even worse at this point and all we could hear was Shane complaining about the coffee and then there was silence.

'I think he's lost the connection. At least they got there safely.'

'How long are they going to be away?'

'They're back a week today. Shane said he didn't want to bother trying to get over the jet lag. He was just going to work on Australian time.'

'He won't get to see much then, will he?'

'Does he ever? I do miss him though; I've got used to the noise and the mess. Wet suits everywhere, those terrible t-shirts he wears. And the bed seems too big without him. I wake up some-times, and I'm patting the pillows, wondering where he is, and then I feel sad.'

'You old softie.'

I felt a little envious, hearing her talk about Shane like that. When Tom and I had split up, one of the things I had enjoyed most was having a bed to myself. In contrast, sharing a bed with Kit had been lovely. And then I thought about Kit a bit more, thousands of miles away, and felt a bit sad too.

* * *

The second thing to happen was an email from my neighbour Lizzie.

Hi Elin, hoping you are having fun. I'm not sure when you are coming home, but I thought I should tell you that Tom seems to be living in your house. Is this okay? I don't remember you saying anything about it—

'Oh for heaven's sake! No! No! No!' I shouted.

Rowan turned to look at me. 'What's the matter?'

I was so furious I could hardly spit the words out.

'Bloody Tom! I've had an email from Lizzie, my friend back home. She says Tom is living in my house!'

She came towards me, still holding one of Shane's old t-shirts that she had been carrying around like a comfort blanket.

'How the hell did he get in? I thought you'd changed the locks?'

'I did! Listen to this,' I read out the rest of the email. '"Tom said he's staying to keep an eye on the place until you get back and you told him where the spare key is. I don't want to interfere, but I remember the incident with him and the recycling bins and thought I'd just check. If it is fine with you then I apologise for disturbing your holiday. The weather here has been sunny and warm but probably not as hot as Australia. Anyway, just let me know? Love Lizzie."'

'Bloody hell! He must have got into the key safe, he must have guessed the code. I always use my date of birth because otherwise I'll forget it. I must be mad! And now he's moved in!'

'That's a bloody cheek. He could have asked you first,' Rowan said.

'He didn't ask because he knew I'd say no!' I said, furiously, 'I might have guessed he was up to something. I'm not putting up with this and he's a fool if he thinks I will. He really is a—'

'Yes, but what are you going to do?' Rowan asked.

I sat with my face in my hands for a few seconds and tried to think clearly.

'I could ring Dan, I suppose. No, he's busy with all the end of term stuff. I can't involve him. Can I?'

I clenched my fists in front of my mouth and gave a frustrated scream. I tried to imagine Tom in my little cottage, his feet up on the coffee table I'd sanded and painted. His dirty clothes in a pile next to the washing machine. It was so vivid I could almost hear his voice asking for something to eat.

'Look Elin, calm down, let's think this through sensibly. Perhaps you need to talk to him.'

I was feeling quite ill by this point, my stomach clenched into a tight little knot of fury.

'I'm going to email Tom. No, I'm going to ring him. What time is it in England?'

We did the calculations. It was the very early hours of the morning in England. Possibly not the best time to ring someone.

I rang him anyway.

While I waited for my call to be connected, I imagined Tom asleep in my bed. His snores rumbling through my room, the smell of his balled-up socks on my floor. I'd have to throw everything out when I got home and fumigate everything.

After several rings, Tom answered.

'Mnah?' he said.

As I expected, he'd been asleep.

'What the hell are you doing in my house?'

Next to me, Rowan gave a fist pump.

There was a lot of coughing and rustling his end. He was sleeping under my new feather and goose down duvet that made that satisfying crackly noise. Which was a joke when he'd always insisted he was allergic to them and needed a nasty, sweaty, hypoallergenic one. He'd better not have been wiping his nose on my new, John Lewis, William Morris patterned pillow cases. The thought of him in my room, rummaging through my things, fumbling about in my drawers was too horrible.

'Are you still there?' I shouted.

'M'yeah, god Elin what time is it?' he said.

'Time you got out of my house,' I yelled, 'there must be a room at a hotel? Why didn't you just go into one of them? Or go and sleep in the staffroom. Lizzie next door has told me you're living in my home. That's trespass.'

Tom snorted. 'Interfering old busybody. I needed some space and some peace and quiet. And I asked if you had any objections,' he said. This was followed by a lot of sinus clearing noises and harrumphing. Rowan and I both flinched back from the phone in disgust. 'And you didn't say anything. I texted you. Christ what time is it? I've got to get over to school in a few hours.'

'I told you I was ignoring your stupid texts. I wasn't agreeing!'

'Well I don't remember that,' he said, sounding hurt, 'that's your fault. You should have told me you were ignoring me.'

Rowan made a confused 'huh?' face at me.

I was furious.

'If I'd told you I was ignoring you again, then I wouldn't have been bloody ignoring you, would I? Only you could try to make this my fault, Tom. Well you know now, so sod off back to Ashley and don't come back!'

'What's that? Sorry can't hear you Elin,' there was a lot of rustling noises and broken words that I wouldn't put it past him to be faking and then the line went dead.

I tried ringing him again but he didn't answer. I wandered around the kitchen cursing and swearing for quite a long time and then Rowan grabbed me, pressed a cup of tea into my hand, and made me sit down.

'You could ring the police?' Rowan said. 'Say there's been a break in and your neighbour thinks there's a squatter.'

'Ha! You're joking. He'd have to be growing cannabis in the attic or running a prostitution ring in the garden shed before the police did anything. Maybe not even then.'

'Oh. Well you could make something up to tell them? Drug dealing to kids next to the ice-cream van after school? Or the smell of burning? Or your neighbours heard gunshots and someone screaming last night?' Rowan suggested helpfully. 'Oh I wish Shane was here, he'd know what to do. Perhaps I should ring him and send him round to sort Tom out.'

'I don't think that would be a very good idea. Knowing Shane, he'd just get himself arrested and deported.'

I did a bit more cursing and then settled for grumbling and muttering under my breath.

I sent him a text.

You have no right to be in MY HOUSE. You have entered illegally, and I did NOT agree to you being there. Leave now and I will not involve the police.

I received a mis-spelled reply almost immediately.

It's a blody emergancy

So I sent another one.

I have not given you permission to use my house as a hotel and I want you to leave NOW. Do not leave any tissues, dirty underwear or half eaten food anywhere. Or mouldy coffee mugs.

Unsurprisingly there was no reply. Ironic: now it was his turn to ignore me.

I sent a text to Dan next simply because I couldn't think of anything else to do.

Your father

(I've noticed this. Divorced parents always refer to the ex-partner as your father or your mother)

has let himself into MY house. He does not have my permission to be there. No one does. If he contacts you, tell him to bugger off out of there. I'll ring you later.

Then I emailed Lizzie to tell her no, Tom was not supposed to be in my house but not to worry, that I would sort something out.

I pondered on this problem for hours. I would need to either go back early, which I really didn't want to do, or involve Dan. And of course, there was Skye. I brightened up a bit at the thought of her. She wasn't the sort to take any nonsense from anyone.

Was this going to ruin the end of my holiday? Was I just going to fall back into being cowed and compliant? No, I damn well wasn't. Not now, not ever.

I sent Dan a message.

Can we have a Zoom call on Saturday? Can you and Skye go to my house? I need your help. I know your father is there too, don't let him slope off.

Dan replied, agreeing and suggesting Saturday. Mid-morning for me and evening for them.

This is about Dad, isn't it? I phoned him the other day and he said you wouldn't mind him being there. I said you would. Skye says we should go over there and boot him out.

Well good for you, Skye; I couldn't agree more.

* * *

The following day, Rowan organised a meet up with some old school friends who still lived in the area. I hardly recognised most of them; they seemed so different from the young, fresh-faced teens I'd known. I probably did too. We all looked a bit old and battered. Although it didn't stop one who had been a bit of a heart throb back in the day – but wasn't any longer – from making a clumsy pass at me when he heard I was divorced.

Why do men do that? I wondered. Did the unfortunately named Lorne Rainger really still see himself as the clean-jawed, bright-eyed, muscular rugby player he had been rather than the paunchy, bearded, bespectacled dick he had become?

Maybe somewhere there was a woman who would respond enthusiastically to Lorne and his clumsy jokes about riding the range together, but it wasn't me. Bloody men: they all seemed to think they were irresistible, and they weren't. But perhaps some of them were more resistible than others?

There was a tiny part of me that still believed there were nice men out there; I just hadn't met many. Certainly not Simon Bateman, who used to be lithe and blessed with an impressive head of hair and was now, as Rowan had said, bald and the size of a small house. I talked to a woman who had been in my actual class at school but really was unrecognisable as she seemed to have spent most of the last few years having cosmetic surgery: June Webster, who used to be little and mousey and was now blonde, impressively busty and looked permanently surprised. But then as I wandered around with a glass of rather good red wine, I wondered what I looked like to them.

I had been slim, tanned, athletic, and extrovert. I'd seen the photos. Now I must have looked very different. And yet inside I didn't really feel any different. Not now I had shed – as Rowan put it – sixteen stone of dead weight when I got rid of Tom.

Perhaps we all felt the same way? Changed outside by the passing of the years, but pretty much the same inside. Battered by our life experiences but still standing.

25

Eleven o'clock on Saturday, and I had settled myself in Rowan's kitchen while she hovered around out of view of the webcam on my laptop. We both had large mugs of strong coffee and Rowan was crunching nervously on a biscuit.

'Do you know what you're going to say?' she said. She had already asked me this several times that morning, 'I mean, have you got your notes?'

I shuffled several pieces of paper on the table in front of me. I had expected to be apprehensive, but I wasn't, in fact I was surprisingly calm.

Bang on eleven, the call connected.

'Hi Mum, how are you? You look great!'

Dan sat there, thousands of miles away and yet as clear as though he had been in the next room. The wonders of modern technology. My heart swelled with love for him, and I realised how much I had missed him.

I was very conflicted. I wanted him here with me, but I didn't want to be there with him.

He was dressed as he usually did, in a dark sweater over a polo shirt, and he looked rather stressed. Somewhere in the room, which I recognised as my sitting room, there was a crash.

'It's okay, that was just Skye knocking over a chair.'

Skye dipped down behind Dan and waved at me.

'Sorry, just me being clumsy. Great to see you,' she said, 'just getting a chair for Tom.'

She had her black hair in several plaits and a lot of silver chains around her neck. A certain look passed fleetingly over her face and then she disappeared from the screen and Tom lumbered into view and sat down next to my son with an enormous and rather self-satisfied sigh.

It was the first time I had seen Tom for a long time and at the sight of him, some of my negative feelings came flooding back. Like seeing a teacher in the supermarket during the school holidays, one I hadn't liked. I took a deep breath.

Tom smoothed his hand over his hair, which was greyer than I remembered.

'Ah, there you are! Well this is all very clever, isn't it?' he said. He peered at the screen. 'You look very tired, Elin. Positively washed out. Have you been ill?'

Gaslighting comment number one. Well, he hadn't wasted much time.

'Not at all,' I said firmly, 'I'm feeling great.'

Tom shook his head. 'Well okay, if you're sure. Now this is fun; it's been ages since we saw each other. Lots of water, lots of bridges, eh? It's almost like one of our famous family pow wows, isn't it? You must miss all that. Now you have been living alone. By yourself with no one to talk to. Week in, week out.'

Oh for heaven's sake... what family pow wows?

'Wrong again, Tom. And I'm with Rowan and I've met so many interesting people. I'm having a fantastic time over here.'

'Oh, bless you. Always put a brave face on things, don't you?

Still, it's probably good that you were able to visit before you get too old. You wouldn't believe how hard I have been working. It's been one damn thing after the other. I don't know how they would get anything done at that school if I wasn't there to chivvy them along. How's the weather? You never were any good in the heat, I expect that's why you look so drained.'

I shuffled my papers and picked up a pencil.

'I'm perfectly fine,' I said, 'I just wanted to know why you are in my house, and more importantly, when you are leaving?'

Tom picked up a glass and took a sip. Ice clinked against the side. I peered at the screen.

'I see you've helped yourself to my gin,' I said.

He looked bewildered, almost hurt. 'I didn't think you'd mind. While you've been off enjoying yourself, I've had an awful few months. No decent meals, not enough sleep, no alcohol except at the weekends. Ashley treats me like a child half the time. When are you coming home?'

'I want you to pack up your stuff and go.'

Tom's mouth dropped open in shock, and his eyes bulged.

'What? But I asked you! You didn't say I couldn't!'

'I told you only the other night that I wanted you to leave.'

'I thought you were drunk; I didn't think you meant it.'

Next to him I could see Dan, leaning away from his father as though he didn't much want to be there.

Tom put on a mollifying tone. 'Oh come on Elin, sweetie. I've told you I'm in a fix. Ash has chucked me out and for no good reason. I've nowhere to go. I stayed with Charlie for a couple of nights, but his cow of a wife doesn't like me.'

I took a deep breath. 'Nor do I, that's why we got divorced.'

'You must see reason. I'm on my uppers here; I just need a couple of days before I can go back and sort out this thing with Ashley,' Tom said, 'she needs time to calm down.'

'What have you done this time?'

He didn't reply; he just looked shifty.

I looked at my ex-husband and sighed. He looked older, greyer, and rather rumpled.

Tom mistook my sigh for sympathy and his face relaxed.

'Just a couple of days,' he repeated, 'we were married for such a long time. Such good friends. Don't forget.'

'I certainly haven't forgotten. You were the one with the dodgy memory,' I said.

Dan stood up at that point.

'I'll leave you two to talk for a bit,' he said, 'and then I'll come back.'

This was typical of Dan; hopeless at any sort of confrontation. But then Skye appeared behind him and pushed him back down into his chair.

'I think your mum needs you here, Dan,' she said, 'remember what we said?'

Tom fidgeted. 'I've been doing a lot of thinking and I appreciate...'

'What? That the grass wasn't actually greener?'

'You don't understand. Josie is such a difficult baby,' Tom said mournfully. He clapped Dan on the shoulder. 'Not like Danny boy here.'

Dan flinched.

It was on the tip of my tongue to remind Tom what a terrible baby Dan had been and then I realised he was, as always, steering me off the point.

'I don't care, Tom. I'm telling you now to give your door key back to Dan, pack up all your stuff, and get out of my house. Now,' I said, 'or I'm phoning the police.'

On the other side of the table, Rowan gave a silent fist pump.

'I'll give you a hand, Tom,' Skye said silkily.

Tom looked annoyed and glared at her.

'I don't know why she... this... creature is even in here. It's family stuff, nothing to do with her. Sticking her pierced nose and her tattoos in where they're not wanted.'

Dan rose to the insult. 'Don't speak to my girlfriend like that!'

Skye went to stand behind Dan and gave me a cat-like smile. She was still a bit heavy handed with the eyeliner I noticed, but remarkably pretty under all the make-up. Then she moved like lightning and picked up a bunch of keys on the table.

'This one I think, isn't it?'

She unhooked my house key from the key ring and put it in her pocket, while beside her Tom twittered his outrage and made a grab for Skye's arm.

She dodged neatly out of the way and laughed.

'Come on Dan, let's help your dad get all his stuff together.'

'Give me that back! Don't you dare touch my things you – you stupid, interfering, boss-eyed... witch!'

Dan stood up at this point so all I could see was the bottom of his sweater.

'Don't speak to Skye like that. Mum's right: you shouldn't be here. Get your stuff together. Or I'll be the one phoning the police. And Skye's uncle is a police sergeant; he could be here in half an hour.'

Tom turned back to the screen, his mouth in a tightened line, his nostrils flaring as they always used to do when he was crossed.

'See what you've done, Elin? You've split this family into bits, all because of your stupid, provincial, unchristian attitude.'

Opposite me, Rowan stood up and adopted a boxing stance and threw a few jabs and punches into the air.

I bit back a laugh, adopted a disappointed expression, and looked at my watch.

'You've got twenty-five minutes then, Tom. Better get a shift on.

It wouldn't look good for the headmaster to have a police record, would it?'

Tom threw me another furious look and stood up with such force that his chair fell over. I saw Skye hurry round to pick it up; it looked as though she was wearing trousers patterned with pirate flags.

'My God, you've changed, and not for the better I'm sorry to say. I just came on this call to catch up and ask if you were having a nice holiday,' he snarled, 'I didn't realise that going back to Australia would destroy your better nature.'

I looked at my watch again.

'Twenty-two minutes. And don't try messaging me because I'm blocking your number.'

Tom gave a strangled growl of rage and disappeared from view.

Skye came to sit in his empty chair, her face one big grin.

'I think he's going,' she said, her voice a bit squeaky, she held up the key, 'and he won't be coming back!'

I laughed and Rowan came around the table to give me a hug. I felt triumphant, thrilled that at last, at long last Tom was out of my life. I should have done this a long time ago.

'I'd better go and keep an eye on him,' Dan said.

Skye and I grinned at each other across the miles. I felt a burst of affection for her and I wished I had taken the chance to get to know her better before all this. That was something else I needed to do. She seemed fun and assertive. Perhaps she was giving Dan the jolt of self-confidence he needed.

'Well that was exciting,' she said.

'You were brilliant! I can't thank you enough,' I said, 'you deserve a medal!'

'So apart from that, are you having a nice time? Is that Rowan, your sister?'

Rowan waved at the screen, and they called hello to each other.

'We are having a great time; I want to tell you all about it.' A thought suddenly came to me. 'Have the school holidays started?'

Skye nodded. 'Another two weeks to go. Poor old Dan the Man has been getting greyer by the day. I wish we could afford a holiday; he really needs a break. I mean, we could go to my auntie in Sussex, but that's not exactly excitement city, is it?'

'No. So what's happening now?'

Skye cocked her head to one side.

'There's a lot of thumping noises going on upstairs. I think Tom is stamping about. Oooh, I can hear shouting. Should I go and look?'

She disappeared off for a few minutes and then came back chuckling.

'You should see him. Tom tried to take the pillows and the duvet off your bed, and Dan stopped him. And then they had a row. And Tom was shouting "you should have some respect for your father" and Dan said, "if there was anything to respect, I would".'

'He'd better not steal my bedding! Those are new!' I said furiously.

'Oops,' Rowan said, 'perhaps he's planning to sleep in his car.'

The three of us waited for a moment in silence, all of us trying to hear what was going on.

Then Skye shouted over her shoulder, 'Dan, shall I phone Uncle Patrick? At the police station? Ooh, I think they are coming back downstairs. Ew, Tom's left two pairs of pants drying on the radiator. I hope he doesn't forget them.'

We waited for a few minutes and then Tom appeared, breathing heavily, and clutching a handful of underpants. I recognised them; I'd bought them for him in M&S.

'Right. I'm not staying here to be insulted and I'm not putting up with this any longer. I'm leaving.'

'Not putting up with what?' I said. 'Trespassing? Trying to steal my pillows?'

Tom made an unintelligible, harrumphing noise and left. A few seconds later, he came back.

'We could have sorted this out, you know. You are the one who chose to be unreasonable. You'll regret it when you find yourself alone, living on ready meals, surrounded by cats. And when you do, don't come crying to me.'

I held my hand up in a Brownie salute. 'I promise not to.'

I was actually enjoying this. I had put up with such a lot over the years. If only I had realised the best way to deal with Tom was to either ignore him or laugh.

Tom pointed an accusing finger at Skye, 'and you are the cause of all this. It's a mortal sin you know, coming between a son and his father.'

Skye scribbled something on the back of an envelope and handed it to Tom.

'Malignant narcissism. Look it up when you get a chance.'

Behind me, Rowan roared with laughter.

'Trollop!' Tom shouted.

At this point, Dan came into view, shoving his father aside with some force so that the handful of underpants flew up into the air and landed on the table in front of Skye. Her face was a picture.

With a great deal of muttering, Tom collected them up and stamped off.

And then I heard the front door slam shut.

Rowan, Skye, and I all cheered. I felt terrific. At last, after all this time, I had stood up to Tom and got the better of him.

Dan went to the window.

'He's gone.' He went and put an arm around Skye. 'I'm sorry about that. You okay?'

'Oh I'm fine,' she said, 'I've worked in pubs when the World Cup was on. This was nothing. Oh gawd, there's a pair of his pants under the table. Get the barbecue tongs, will you, Dan?'

'Blimey, what time is it? I think I need a drink,' Rowan said.

26

For the rest of the week, Rowan and I spent a lot of time down at the Wipe-Out. With Shane away, there was always a possibility that no work at all would get done at all. We rather enjoyed ourselves, sorting out an old stock room, cleaning the shelves where the pots and pans were stored in the kitchen, and clearing out the fridge.

'Can salt go off?' Rowan asked. 'This pack has passed its expiration date.'

'By much?'

'Four years.'

'I wouldn't have thought so, but better safe than sorry.'

The beach was quieter during the week, the weather still beautiful, the waves whipped up by the wind, so only the keen surfers were out there. Standing at the sink while I was washing up some dusty glasses I had found in a cupboard, I looked out of the window. Perhaps I would like to try surfing again. What was the worst that could happen: a mouthful of salt water?

I could see someone who looked like Trev the Tank out there, skimming down the side of a wave, looping skilfully over the top and sitting down on his board to wait for the next one.

'I think I will give it another go, you know?' I said. 'Surfing. It might be the last time I get to try it, if...'

I stopped. If I went back to England, that's what I had been about to say.

'If what?' Rowan said.

'Oh nothing. Well, I was just thinking. I don't think I would try surfing in England.'

'Well, Shane would teach you if he was here. You could always ask Trev, or Elliot.'

'I just might,' I said.

'Shame to waste that new cossie. Did you wear it on your trip at all?'

Ah yes, I remembered that day: Norm's birthday, when we hadn't gone swimming.

'No, I never had the chance.'

'I'd better go, there's a queue building up at the counter.'

I carried on washing up. Kit and Shane were due back the following day. I had to stop thinking about Kit, stop going over our conversations, stop remembering him.

Perhaps now their company was sold, Kit wouldn't have to go to England ever again? I wondered what he would do instead. He didn't seem the sort of man who would just sit in his monochrome house admiring the view.

Then of course I allowed myself to think about him some more. And even worse, I decided to dry my hands and torture myself one more time and look at the photos I'd taken on my phone.

My photos catapulted me back to the time before I got involved with Kit Pascoe. There was Shane, pulling a pop-eyed expression as he held out the washing up bowl full of prawns,

Rowan leaning against him and laughing. Photos of my aunt and uncle at that first barbeque; Banjo looking slightly mad with his cork-brimmed hat, Maggie tickling his nose with the blue feather decoration. There I was shopping with Rowan, posing with a silly expression when I tried on all those clothes at Jilly's shop.

And then there was the first picture of Kit. Or more accurately his head as he turned to speak to the attentive stewardess on the flight to Cairns, his lovely profile, his polite expression. Dusty Jack, campsites, wonderful, deserted beaches, the hat-box pie. Yes, I know it's naff in the extreme to take pictures of your meal but... well...

Then pictures of the view from the hotel in Brisbane with all the lights sparkling. An extravagant floral display in the reception area, the river cruise to the koala sanctuary. I seemed to have taken a lot of pictures of Kit. I looked at those pictures and my gaze went over his face countless times trying to work out how I had got things so wrong.

Had he taken other women to that hotel, maybe even to that same room? I bet he had. That's how he knew it was the perfect scene for seduction?

He's a bit of a player.

Perhaps I shouldn't even think about that part of it.

I thought about deleting the pictures, but I couldn't do it. Perhaps later. I rummaged about in my bag and my fingers touched soft fur. I pulled out the little koala toy, remembering how happy I had felt when Kit gave it to me.

Then I went back and looked at the pictures again, plunging myself into misery. All that waited for me back home was the possibility of an unwanted ex-husband lurking about, a pile of post, an overgrown lawn, and a load of laundry to get through.

* * *

Shane came back the following morning, crashing through the front door with his luggage just after eleven o'clock.

'I'm back!' he yelled, 'and I'm never going away again.'

Rowan ran into his arms, almost crying, she was so pleased to see him again, and they stood hugging and laughing for a few seconds before Shane turned to me and hugged me.

'Great to see you!'

'Did you have a good trip?'

'It was okay, I suppose. Nice to see a few things in London, but good to be back home again. I have to say all this flying business isn't all it's cracked up to be. It takes forever. I think I realise why Kit was so fed up with it if I'm honest. The jet lag is killing me.'

Well thank heavens he had at last realised that.

'But it's all sorted now?' Rowan said.

'Yes, everything signed, sealed, delivered. I've never seen Kit so relieved.'

'And he's back too?' I said casually.

'Yes, the driver took him back home before she dropped me off. I must say that house of his is very impressive. I'd not seen it before.'

'Did you go in?'

Shane looked a bit vague. 'Only into the hallway, he said he had people working there, doing some alterations. Now then, I need to have a shower and get sorted. I can't remember if I'm supposed to go to sleep now or stay awake.'

Rowan gave him a friendly punch on his arm. 'Stay awake as long as you can. Anyway, I want to talk to you.'

'And I want to talk to you,' Shane said and grinned.

* * *

I did a bit of tidying up and then went out to the shops to pick up a few things, more to give them some privacy than anything.

When I got back, they were in the kitchen and Shane was making some tea and whistling very cheerfully.

Rowan was sitting at the kitchen table, her hands in her lap, looking rather stunned.

'Everything okay?' I said, dumping my shopping on the worktop.

'Shane bought me a present back from London,' she said.

'I should hope so too.'

Rowan slowly lifted up her hand. For a moment, I didn't know what I was looking at and then I realised. It was a ring, set with a whopping great sapphire.

I let out a scream of delight, which Rowan echoed.

'You're engaged!'

'I am! Shane went down on one knee and everything! Then he had to grab me because he'd knelt on a coat hanger and nearly fell over, but he actually proposed.'

'Bloody hell!'

'I know!'

'I'm so happy for you!' I said, almost tearful.

Rowan beamed at me. 'So am I! Isn't it great? I never expected to get married. I never wanted to – until now.'

'So when is the big day?' I asked.

'Soon as we can arrange it really. No reason to wait. You can't go back to England now. You've got to be there!'

'I wouldn't miss it for worlds!'

'You have to be my bridesmaid!' Rowan said, 'I've waited years for this. I shall put you in a vile, salmon-pink dress.'

'You dare!'

'Well you made me wear that awful flowery thing.'

'I didn't think it was awful; I thought you looked lovely! And who is the best man? Baz? Trev?'

Shane grinned. 'Kit of course!'

'What? Kit? I thought you couldn't stand each other?'

'I know! I thought that too, but things have changed. We sorted out a few things when we were in London. I mean, first of all we had a fight in the middle of Heathrow airport.' Shane put Rowan in a friendly headlock. 'Joining the family, aren't I? Are you pleased?'

'Couldn't be more pleased,' I said truthfully.

And I was. Shane and Rowan made a great couple; they complemented each other perfectly. At the same time, I felt a little pang on envy.

'And Banjo and Maggie will be pleased too. Now she really can be my mum,' Shane said, proudly.

I laughed. 'Lucky her!'

Shane beamed. 'We need to go over to their house and tell them, and I'm going to ask Kit to pop round for a drink soon. We need to celebrate!'

I caught my breath. I hadn't seen Kit for a while now and hadn't heard anything from him either while he was away. How would it feel to see him again? Could we both draw a line under what had happened and be civil to each other?

* * *

The next day it was raining so Shane closed the Wipe-Out and he and Rowan went off for the day to sort out a few details. Where would they get married, who would do the ceremony.

I decided to do something useful instead of just wandering around eating toast and watching the rain. Fired up by my work in the café, I'd been cleaning out Rowan's kitchen cupboards and marvelling that she had so many things that were out of date. I mean seriously; I found a jar of ground cinnamon which was best before 2001, and it wasn't the only one. There were three others, all needing a decent burial.

Consequently, I was hot, the front of my shirt was splattered with chilli sauce because a jar from 2002 had exploded over me when I opened it, and I was surrounded by black bin liners full of rejected foodstuffs. Then of course there was the recycling to be done. The jars and tins had to be emptied and washed out and put into the right containers, cardboard needed to be squashed, plastic sorted. So I was in a state of mind that was partly feeling smug and ecologically aware and partly knackered and wondering why the blue blazes I was bothering and if I would ever complete my task.

There was a knock on the front door.

Oh great, I looked a complete mess, my hair held back with an elastic band, my fingers stained with a spilt jar of turmeric, so it looked as though I smoked ninety a day. Not to mention the Jackson Pollack disaster across my chest.

With a groan of possibly early onset arthritis, I got up from the floor and went to answer it.

'Hello, I'm glad you're in,' he said. He glanced at my shirt, 'good grief, have you hurt yourself?'

I staggered back, clutching on to the door frame for support.

It was Kit Pascoe.

Standing on my doorstep. In a dark raincoat with rain dripping off his hair. Looking just wonderful. I shouldn't have thought that. I shouldn't have cared.

I stood there for a moment, my mouth open. I must have looked a complete idiot.

'Hello,' I said at last, 'it's chilli sauce.'

'I didn't know you were such a messy eater.'

We stood and looked at each other and neither of us moved until he wiped his wet hair out of his eyes.

Then he pulled a huge bouquet of pale pink roses from behind his back.

'I'm so sorry, Elin. Here are the roses, would you like to wipe your feet on my neck? That's what you said would be the right way to apologise.'

'Oh Kit!' Suddenly I felt like crying.

'And can I come in? It's a bit damp out here.'

I made some sort of reply that sounded a bit like 'Blemeyeah' and then I stepped back and let him in.

I took the roses and buried my face in them while he stood in the hallway, unbuttoning his coat and shaking the rain off himself.

'Sorry about this,' he said, 'perhaps I should have phoned.'

My mind went completely blank.

'What are you doing here?' I said.

'I wanted to see if you'd forgiven me. Great news about Shane and Rowan, isn't it? He told me he was going to propose when he got back. I went with him when he bought the ring.'

We were still standing in the hallway, and he was still holding his wet coat.

I couldn't think of anything sensible to say. It seemed I was just going to stand there and look at him, not quite able to believe that he was here.

'I'm sorry, please come in,' I said at last, 'I must find a vase for these lovely flowers.'

He followed me into the kitchen which looked like the aftermath of a supermarket car-boot sale.

'You're looking well,' he said.

I looked down at my turmeric-stained hands and ruined t-shirt.

'That can't possibly be true. And you're going to be Shane's best man?'

'Yes, I bet that surprised you?'

'A bit. The last time I saw you with him, you two were far from friendly.'

'We have sorted out some issues now, I'm glad to say.'

'Good.'

Gosh, this conversation really was stilted. I wanted to say so much, but at that moment I couldn't find the right words.

I was remembering some of the feelings I'd had. Anger and disappointment and humiliation. I wasn't ready to forget or forgive now that the shock of his arrival was fading. Could I do this? I wasn't sure that I could.

We sat in silence and I flicked him a nervous glance. And then of course we both spoke at the same time.

'Look Elin—'

'Kit I don't—'

'Sorry,' he said, 'you go ahead.'

'No, you,' I said, I think I was breaking out in a nervous sweat. I rubbed my palms against my trousers, dislodging some random fragments of stale pasta onto the floor.

'Elin, are we ever going to speak properly to each other? I thought we had a lot to say.'

'Oh God.'

'Why are you so tense? I'm the one who should be worried,' Kit said.

'You should?'

'God, yes. Of course! After everything, the terrible things I said.'

Oh yes, the things he had said.

'I realise now what happened when we got back after our road trip. After you had been to my house. Shane told you, didn't he? It's okay, I know he did. It was one of the things he chucked at me; how appallingly rude I had been. How it looked as though the only reason I helped you was because Shane blackmailed me into it and then – well remembering how things turned out between us – you must have thought I was a right mongrel.'

'I didn't know what to think,' I said, 'I felt so stupid.'

He shook his head. 'I'm so sorry. It was the last thing I wanted to do, the very last thing.'

'So?' I said. I folded my arms, suddenly defensive.

'I told you before, Shane and I were never close. I spent all my time flogging around the world, doing deals, drumming up business. Shane spent his days at the beach surfing or in the café. The workload never seemed fair to me. But what could I do?'

'I don't think anyone would disagree with you,' I said, 'even Shane realises now what a strain of all that travelling must have put on you.'

'Well, that's something. Then when my father died and the business passed to us, the problem got worse. Shane didn't want to be involved but was happy to take the dividends that came his way. Dad always tried to involve him over the years, see if he wanted to take over some of the workload, but Shane never did. He always said he was happy the way it was. And I suppose it did go well for a few years. The company grew. We did well out of it; in a way it was better that Shane didn't interfere. Dad and I used to make a good team.' He stopped, looking thoughtful. 'We were wrong; looking back, I can understand why Shane felt left out. I can see we didn't try hard enough.

Then three years ago we attracted the attention of bigger companies who could take things on to the next level and were prepared to pay a handsome price. At that point I was ill with overwork. I was depressed, I was lonely and tired, I was burnt out.

I can say it now, although at the time I would never have admitted it.'

'It did sound dreadful,' I said.

'And just as I could see the possibility of escape, Shane stalled everything. He put up pathetic obstacles, he "lost" paperwork, he didn't reply to letters, and as you know he didn't sign anything. We were at a stand-off. I know it all sounds incredibly immature now, on both our parts. I handled it badly, but I couldn't see any way through. And it went on for years. I heard through the grapevine the UK company were looking at another business in Melbourne. After so long, both of us were stubborn; we weren't communicating. And then you came on the scene. Shane used you as his lever. If I would help you bring the motorhome back, he agreed to sign. As I'm saying this, I'm ashamed, ashamed of behaving the way that I did and appalled at the things I said.'

I could hardly breathe. Watching him, so happy to see him again, to hear his voice. But I wasn't going to let him get away quite so easily. He needed to know how I'd felt. I deserved an explanation.

'I was humiliated. And very hurt.'

'I'm so sorry. Shane and I weren't sitting together on the plane but when we reached London, I tried to talk to him about you. How I felt. And he admitted he had told you everything. We'd just got to Heathrow; we were waiting for our luggage and we were late. We were both tired, but it was the last straw. We had a real humdinger of a row. We said a lot of things we should have said a long time ago. But in stages perhaps, not all at once. And certainly not in the baggage reclaim area.'

Where was this confession going? Was he genuine? Did he mean all this?

'I'm sorry, Elin. I said those things out of anger at my brother because I was overworked and tired. Because I didn't think. Because I was at the end of my tether. Because I was an idiot.'

'So you didn't mean it?'

His face relaxed. 'Oh God no, Elin. I didn't mean it. I didn't mean any of it. When I saw you at your sister's party that first evening, I couldn't believe it. I wanted to take your number on the plane, but I was afraid you'd think I was trying it on. You were the first person in a long time I felt I could talk to. The first person who made me laugh, who seemed to understand. I wanted to see you again and I had no idea how I could find you. And what did I do? I went and had another blistering row with Shane. That's a way to make a good second impression, isn't it?'

I wasn't going to be fooled again. And yet...

'The opportunity to help you and your family was too good to be true. Of course I agreed. I would have agreed without Shane and his nonsense. He didn't blackmail me into anything. I wanted to do it.'

'Oh,' I said.

I sat very still for a moment collecting my thoughts. I felt quite sick with nerves.

I had been fooled by a man before – Tom with his compliments and flattery. Talking himself out of difficult situations. Perhaps like many women my age who were lonely, I was vulnerable to this sort of thing. I didn't want to be one of those women who just pathetically accept attention, whoever is giving it. Who put up with being treated badly, being taken for granted.

'I was very hurt, I don't mind admitting. And then when I thought you... when we... when we got together...'

'You thought I was just taking advantage of the situation?'

'Something like that,' I said.

He reached across and put his hand over mine. His fingers were cold.

'I'm not like that, Elin.'

I pulled my hand away, and looked at him properly then, remembering what we had meant to each other, the way we had been with each other, the way he had made me feel.

'So what do you want?' I said.

'Do you forgive me?'

'Well, I'm not going to wipe my feet on your neck,' I said.

He gave a funny little grin that turned my heart. 'That's a relief.'

We sat in silence for a while. I sneaked little looks at him. It was surreal. Could I really trust him? Could I ever trust any man?

He looked up. 'Will you forgive me, Elin? I mean really?'

I hesitated. 'I want to but...'

I'd had feelings for him I'd never expected. I'd thought I was past all that: the fear of putting my trust in someone. The sadness and the disappointment.

I could say no. I imagined him going back out into the rain. Perhaps he would turn and wave as he went out through the gate, and struggle with the catch which was a bit tricky. And then he would get into his car and I would stand and listen as the motor started and I would watch until he turned the corner and was out of sight.

How would that make me feel? Could I bear the thought of it?

Life had more to offer me than now than I had thought. It was time to believe in myself and try it again my way. But did my way involve him?

And he stood up and so did I and he looked at me with those beautiful eyes that were sometimes hazel and sometimes greenish and his face relaxed. And suddenly I knew exactly what I wanted him to do.

'Elin,' he said, and he took the final step towards me.

'Thank you for the flowers. You've given me a lot to think about,' I said, 'now I'd better get on with clearing up all this mess.'

And I stepped back.

I closed the door behind him and didn't watch him leaving. I didn't watch his car disappearing into the rain. I just went back into the kitchen and looked at the empty chair where he had sat, the drops of water on the floor where his raincoat had dripped.

Should I have followed my impulse to throw my arms around him and rest my head on his chest?

No, I was different now. I was wiser. I knew what I needed out of my life; I wanted to make my own decisions and choices. In my own time.

27

I spent the rest of the day clearing up, drinking tea, and occasionally crying.

It wasn't as though I was actually sad either; I was annoyed with myself for being such a fool for so long. I'd begun to suspect where things had gone wrong in the past and now it was obvious. If this wasn't a lesson learned, I don't know what was.

My life seemed to be filled with clearing out cupboards, trips to the tip, throwing things away, and not feeling any better for doing it.

This was not improved by Rowan and Shane when they got back

'God, what's happened?' Rowan said.

I was sitting at the kitchen table still in my food splattered t-shirt, drinking a gin and tonic.

'Kit's been here,' I said.

'Really? Your Kit? Really! That's good. Isn't it?'

'He's not my Kit, I wasn't in the mood. He apologised, accepted he'd behaved badly, and everything seemed to be okay again.'

'Did you sleep with him?'

'No I bloody didn't.'

'Why not?'

'Because I didn't want to.'

'Really? Well you could always ring him?'

I took a deep breath. 'No, Rowan. I need time to myself. It's over. He's apologised, I said okay, and he left.'

'Well, in other news, we've set the wedding date,' Rowan said, 'August fourth, before it gets too hot. Nothing worse than a sweating bride. And the registrar has a space then. After the wedding, we're thinking we could have a party at Maggie's house. But we might change our minds. She's already started making bunting and she's terribly excited. She called me three times today with suggestions. If we have giant prawns on the barbie, do I want to borrow her washing up bowl, that sort of thing. And Banjo's getting a new suit. Well more accurately, getting a suit. I don't think he has one. And then we need to go shopping to find the lime-green jumpsuit I'm going to buy for you.'

'Yes that sounds lovely,' I said, not really listening. I was wondering where Kit was, what he was doing.

'And a bouquet of plastic wattle flowers with some glitter glued on to the petals.'

'Yes, brilliant,' I said, gnawing at a thumbnail.

'You're not really listening, are you? And Kit will be around a lot more now he is going to be best man, so you can sort everything out properly.'

'Yes, I suppose so,' I said.

Kit would be there. How did that make me feel?

'Hang on Rowan! A lime-green jumpsuit? Are you completely mad?'

* * *

I had another Zoom call with Dan later that evening. I'd been thinking about things more clearly and I'd had an idea.

'I want you and Skye to come to Australia. It will be the school holidays; you both need a break and some fun. And I know Rowan and Shane would love you to be here for their wedding. And I would pay your airfares. What do you think?'

Dan's mouth dropped open and Skye screamed and almost fell off her chair with excitement.

'Say Yes, Dan! For heaven's sake!'

Dan frowned. 'I thought you wanted to go to Sussex to see…'

'No, I really wouldn't! How can you even think that!' She turned to the screen to look at me. 'Go to Sussex to see Auntie Fay, who is as batty as a bat, and locks up the house at eight thirty? She doesn't have internet and there is nearly always a cat sleeping in the bed.'

Dan grinned. 'Just checking!'

'We'd love to come, absolutely brillo. Yes please and thank you a million times! Shall I find out about flights? I think I've got some Avios miles we could use, although probably only enough to get to Birmingham one way. What shall I wear? Is it going to be hot? Will it be posh?'

'Please do find out about flights and I'll transfer the money into Dan's bank account. Wear something you feel good in and no, I don't think for a moment it will be posh. It should be warm; remember it's autumn here, not summer.'

I felt a real burst of excitement. Not only would it be Rowan's wedding, but Dan would be there too. I couldn't have been happier.

* * *

Two days later, we went shopping for Rowan's wedding dress. Like a lot of brides, she didn't really know what she wanted, except she would know it when she saw it.

In the end, after a lot of wandering about in bridal shops and department stores where we didn't find anything, Rowan eventually bought the only dress she tried on.

We had gone back to her friend Jilly's shop in Kookaburra, not expecting to find anything remotely suitable but the minute we appeared, Jilly pounced on her.

'I have such a beautiful dress for you. When you told me you were getting married, I put this away in the storeroom. It's supposed to be an evening dress, sort of captain's dinner cruise wear. But I think you would look smashing in it.'

Shyly, Jilly unzipped the bag and swathes of shaded blue chiffon fell out.

I gasped. 'Oh God, Ro! Put it on!'

With a great deal of giggling, she did, and it wasn't what I'd been expecting but she looked wonderful.

It had a simple white lace bodice, elbow length sleeves because Rowan (like most women) wasn't happy about her upper arms, and a full, floor-length, layered skirt that was every shade of blue. It trailed onto the ground so it wasn't what could be described as practical. Jilly found a plastic crate for her to stand on.

'You look like a mermaid,' I said, rather tearful.

Jilly dabbed at her eyes and passed me a tissue. 'Doesn't she look gorgeous? And look, it's even got pockets! How great is that? Why don't more dresses have pockets?'

Rowan stuck her hands in the pockets and swished the skirts of the dress around.

'I love it. It's exactly what I wanted, although I didn't know it. And Maggie's making my bouquet. And it's blue and white.'

'She doesn't know one end of a flower from another!'

'Ah but she's making them out of fabric and paper. She got so into making bunting that she couldn't stop. Honestly, it will be brill.'

Jilly blew her nose, still rather overcome with emotion.

'And Shane? What's he wearing?'

'A linen suit and a new shirt,' Rowan said proudly, 'and not one with ketchup stains down the front. I'm hiding the new one so he can't wear it before the wedding day.'

I raised my eyebrows. 'Shane in a suit? You're joking!'

'I'm not. He wanted to wear board shorts and a Hawaiian shirt covered in hula dancers, but I think he saw sense. Oh God, this dress is so gorgeous! It's given me an idea for the wedding theme.'

'I knew the moment I saw it... and what about you, Elin? I think we might have something which might suit you too,' Jilly said, 'I had a delivery of things yesterday, I haven't had time to unpack everything yet...'

She went into the back of the shop and we heard her crashing about, the noise of cardboard boxes being ripped open, and some muffled cursing.

'I ordered you a lime-green jumpsuit,' Rowan said, 'I did tell you.'

'Very funny,' I said.

At last Jilly returned and presented a dress still swathed in plastic which she pulled off with a great flourish.

'Whadda you think?' she said, her eyes hungry for my approval.

I pulled it out and gasped.

'It's lovely,' I whispered.

The dress was absolutely gorgeous. Knee length ivory silk with a border of hand painted coral, fish, and shells around the hem.

'It's a sign!' Rowan said. 'Are you sure you like it? I mean that ghastly Liberty print thing you put me in when I was your brides-maid... well, I didn't want you to wear something like that.'

'I loved it,' I said, 'and Liberty print was all the rage back then.'

I shrugged off my skirt and top and tried my bridesmaid's dress on; it was perfect.

'Oh my, you little beauties!' Jilly said, 'and I'll give you discount even though they are fresh in.'

'Then it's a done deal! Come on, let's get out of our finery, go home, and have a glass of wine to celebrate. Or champagne! We've been given two bottles and Shane doesn't like it. Gives him heart-burn. I want to tell you all about the Hen Night my friend's organ-ising and the wedding decorations we've planned. Shane's having the Wipe-Out re-painted and bought about five miles of fairy lights to put up. I think he wants us to have the wedding on the beach.'

So that's what we did. We sat in the back yard with the flocks of parakeets twittering in the trees and talked weddings and hair and make-up in a way we hadn't for years.

They were an unusual couple; they would do it their way. People would turn up and they would be married and undoubt-edly it would be marvellous.

'So what news of Dan and Skye?' Rowan said. 'When do they arrive?'

'They fly out from London on Thursday. They will be stopping off in Singapore for two days; I hope they don't get up to anything. Or bring anything suspicious with them.'

Visions of the Singapore police with batons and handcuffs loading my only son and his girlfriend into the back of a van swam before my eyes. I almost practised my 'sad face' for the photographs as I was interviewed by the *Daily Mail*, pleading for his release.

Rowan laughed. 'They will be fine, don't be daft. Lots of young people go travelling these days; they have a fabulous time and hardly ever come to grief. Maggie and Banjo are so thrilled they are coming over to stay. And they can go walkabout for a bit. I'm sure Banjo would lend them the motorhome.'

'They would love that. Any news of Kit?' I said, trying to sound unconcerned.

Rowan looked uncomfortable.

'Oh yes, well I shouldn't say anything. I'm probably wrong. Well, Shane is probably wrong.'

'And?'

'Oh Elin. You mustn't think about it. I think he's been seeing someone. You know, *seeing* someone.'

My heart did a sudden diving swoop. Could this be right? Surely not?

'But it's only five minutes since – never mind. So what else?'

'Shane said he and Kit went out to have dinner together at the weekend just to go over a few last details of the sale, and there was a woman. A redhead. Stacked apparently. You know – very obvious. She came over when they were still on their starters – Shane had prawns and Kit had—'

I was spluttering with impatience. 'Rowan! I don't care what they had to eat. Perhaps this was just a work colleague? Or a friend?'

Rowan looked uncomfortable.

'Apparently, she was all over him, very touchy-feely. Talking about how much fun she'd had and how she was looking forward to getting down to it, that sort of thing. Shane said they seemed to know a lot about each other. Her name was Pookie or something, Shane's hopeless with details. And Shane saw her before that when he went to Kit's house to drop him off when you got back from the road trip. And she was upstairs when he got there, because she came down and kissed him goodbye.'

'What do you mean? Kissed or snogged?' I said trying hard not to wail. I shouldn't care. I had sent him away last time. He had the perfect right to move on, just as I did.

'I don't know. I told you, Shane's a typical man, doesn't tell you any of the important bits.'

I thought back. 'He had a phone call with someone called Sukie when we drove to the airport together.'

'It could have been Sukie. So Kit must have been carrying on with her even then? God what's the matter with men?' Rowan said crossly. If Shane ever did that to me I'd... well, I'd...'

Rowan stuttered a bit as she tried to think of something bad enough.

'...I'd scratch my initials into his surfboard. There, that would show him, and then I'd cut out the crotch out of his new wetsuit.'

'Rowan, stop working yourself into a state!' I said, 'look, I don't mind,'

That was a lie; I realised that even as I said it. The news had squished all my excitement at the prospect of seeing Kit again. Had I thought we would see each other across a crowded room (or beach more likely) and run into each other's arms? Not that I was very good at running any more, especially not on sand. And not with a stacked redhead called Sukie in my way.

Unless I could just run over her, kick sand in her face or something. No that was not the way to go. Dignity, always dignity.

Perhaps she was just a friend. A friend with benefits. Just like I had been. Someone who kissed him in public and didn't mind who saw them. Perhaps he had been phoning her while we had been on our road trip, wishing he was with her and her stacked, redheadedness.

Rowan patted my hand. 'When Kit sees you in that gorgeous dress he will dump Ginger Pookie and sweep you off, I bet you.'

'I don't think I want him to actually.'

'No, right, you need to know where you stand. A dog with two masters. Riding two horses at the same time. Never a good idea,' Rowan said.

'Er, do you think you could pick your metaphors a bit more carefully,' I said, 'I don't really want to be thought of a horse. Or a dog.'

Rowan topped up my glass with more champagne and I tried to process how I was feeling. So many emotions were swirling around in my brain. The excitement of Rowan's wedding and seeing Dan and Skye again soon were positives. But on the other hand, the negatives of knowing I would not be here in Australia for much longer, that any thoughts I might have had about Kit had been foolish.

Well, I would focus on the good things: helping to arrange the wedding, looking after my sister, enjoying my remaining time here. And then, only then, perhaps I would worry about what I would do next.

Rowan's house grew more and more chaotic in the following days.

There were piles of clothes everywhere, wet suits hanging from the curtain rails and most of the sitting room was taken up with cardboard boxes. Some of them were presents from friends and family, but most were full of crockery and cutlery and glasses they had borrowed for the wedding party.

After a lot of late-night discussions, they had decided to hold the ceremony on the beach with outside catering plus Bazza in charge of a huge barbeque Shane had found on eBay. I didn't say anything but I thought they might need to rethink this part.

Rowan had posted a notice of intended marriage the day after

Shane's proposal, a friendly marriage celebrant who was Trev's cousin had been booked, and people had been invited. Rowan had wanted to email people, and Shane just asked anyone he knew. So by their reckoning they had between thirty and one hundred people due to turn up.

28

The Hen Party. Oh boy.

Not that I have been to more than a handful of these occasions and the last one was seven years ago and not really much fun at all. Six of us had gone with the bride for two days to a damp cottage in the New Forest where we had painted names onto pebbles for the table settings. And there were only three bottles of wine between us. And I took those.

This time I didn't quite know what to expect, but Rowan's friends had got it all worked out. That Saturday, my sister and I spent the morning getting togged up in our finest party gear because Rowan had insisted we would all meet up in the afternoon because she didn't want a late night. Which seemed surprisingly sensible knowing the sort of hours my sister had kept during her teenage years. It was the last sensible part of the event.

'So are we taking a bus? Or a train into Sydney?' I asked, 'and where are we going?'

Rowan laughed. 'Noleen has it all arranged, don't worry about a thing, and Shane has organised the transport.'

'We're not surfing into Sydney harbour, are we?'

'Just wait and see.'

Rowan looked wonderfully exotic in a scarlet, knee-length dress and she had brought me an identical style in sea-green. Just after midday a long, black limo pulled up outside her house with eight of her friends leaning out of the windows and screaming with excitement. Three were waving champagne bottles so it was obvious the party had already started.

'Right, I'm only going to do the introductions once, so listen,' Rowan said as we piled into the back of the limo. 'Jilly in blue you know already. Lulu in yellow runs a café on the esplanade, the one where we had ice cream. Noleen is in the purple and she's arranged all this; Fee in orange, they're both teachers. I used to work with them before I escaped.'

'Lucky cow,' Noleen shouted from the far end of the limo.

'Zoe in pink works in Jilly's shop and Jackie in the lavender manages a hotel in Sydney. Okay? Got it? Everyone – this is my sister, Elin.'

Someone pressed a champagne flute into my hand and everyone cheered and we clinked glasses.

'Selfie!' Jackie shouted and we all clustered together, champagne glasses and smiles gleaming in the disco lights in the limo roof.

'Now Elin, tell us all about the horrible husband,' Jilly said over the hubbub.

'Ex-husband,' Rowan said, clinking my glass again.

Everyone cheered again and someone refilled my glass.

We drove for about an hour into Sydney, past the road works and rebuilding which seemed to be everywhere in Australia. There were legions of hard-hatted workmen in their high-viz jackets, all of whom got a cheer from our car. We stopped right next to one group because of the traffic lights and took another selfie with the windows open and some cheerful workmen grinning in to the windows behind us. By the time we piled out at the Rocks, we were all in the mood for fun.

'Here you are, bride-to-be,' Noleen said, pulling a pink sash over Rowan's head and hanging some L plates from her neck, 'it's party time!'

We walked along Circular Quay, watching all the ferries buzzing to and fro, from Manley, the zoo, and Darling harbour. There was a massive cruise ship docked there too, with people standing looking out at the view from their balconies. I wondered what it was like to come into one of the most famous waterfronts in the world on board a ship. With the Harbour Bridge and the Opera House, it must have been spectacular.

Then we stopped at one of the waterfront bars to order cocktails and nibbles.

'So tell us what first attracted you to Shane?' said a young woman in orange, which meant she was Fee, 'was it his lovely nature? Or his abs? Tell us all about it.'

Rowan re-told the story of Shane juggling apples in the supermarket to entertain a toddler and then carried on.

'It was his abs the second time I met him,' Rowan said, 'I was down on the beach at the Wipe-Out and he came in from the surf. And he peeled off the top half of his wet suit, you know how they do, and kerpow, I was hooked before he'd said a word.'

'So shallow,' Jilly said, 'and predictable.'

'And then he just stood there and gave me that grin, so I knew he was doing it to show off, and he asked me if I wanted a drink. And I said do koalas like eucalyptus and he laughed and that was that. He moved in two weeks later.'

'You were still teaching with us then,' Noleen said, 'and you gave your notice in a month after. We all thought you were mad.'

Rowan held out her arms to the afternoon sun. 'And here I am, not sorting out Class Five, not sorting out paperwork for the government, not breaking up fights in the yard. Instead I'm marrying the nicest bloke I ever met. Living the dream, ladies.'

'Like I said before: lucky cow,' Noleen said.

At that point, the tray of cocktails arrived and everyone cheered the young waiter who blushed and stammered at having so many women staring at him.

'Selfie!' someone shouted, and the poor chap was dragged into the middle of our group where he gave a nervous grin and then scarpered off as fast as he could.

'I wish I could meet a nice bloke,' Lulu said, her face rather glum, 'all I seem to find are losers and creeps.'

Jackie huffed. 'You don't go out anywhere to find anyone. Look at the number of times we've asked you out and you always make some excuse not to come.'

'I'm usually too busy making ice cream. All the blokes I meet online are fakes too,' Lulu said taking a slug of her drink, 'they say they are tall and fit and handsome and when they turn up, they aren't any of those things. The last one I agreed to meet looked like a retired sumo wrestler who'd been smacked in the face with a frying pan. I'm beginning to think all men are liars. What do you think, Elin?'

Rowan finished her cocktail and waved at the hapless waiter to order some more.

Over at the bar I could see him arguing with one of his colleagues, trying to get out of serving us. I didn't blame him.

'Elin is unlucky in the love department. She married a loser and then she had a thing with Shane's brother...'

'What sort of thing?' Jilly asked, 'and isn't Shane's brother a big dick?'

'Well, only Elin is qualified to answer that. Do tell us all about him,' Rowan said with a wicked gleam. 'She went off with him for days in my uncle's motorhome and they got on very well indeed.'

'That's not quite how it happened,' I said.

At that point some baskets of fries arrived and luckily everyone was distracted for a moment.

'So go on then,' Fee said, 'was he any good in bed? Tell us all about it?'

'All what?' I said.

'What's he like?' Noleen asked, taking a handful of fries, 'is he like Shane? Has he got abs too?'

I felt distinctly uncomfortable. I could answer all these questions, but under no circumstances was I going to.

Thankfully, a seagull swept down at that moment and perched hopefully on the railing near our table. Rowan gave a scream.

'Shoo it away, someone.'

Jackie flapped a menu at it without success.

The seagull was joined by another beady eyed companion. Rowan threw her arms over her head.

Suddenly behind us there was a lot of fierce wuffing and growling and the gulls flew off screeching.

'Sorry about that ladies.' There was a young man hanging on to the dog's lead; he stood patting his dog's head and grinning. 'Hen party is it?'

'Oh my word. Brilliant as well as beautiful,' Zoe said looking at him dreamily, rocking slightly.

The newcomer had a wide and very attractive smile and long dark curls which waved in the sea-breeze as he scanned us all. Next to him, his dog found a bowl of water and did some noisy lapping.

'I'm Stevo the seagull patrol and this is my brave dog Chip. You must be the bride,' he said to Rowan.

'You chase seagulls?' I said.

Stevo pointed to his dog's high-viz jacket which was emblazoned with 'Seagull Patrol' on the side.

'Brilliant,' Lulu said, 'I love dogs. Isn't he the cutest thing?'

'Who, me or me dog?' Stevo said with a cheeky wink.

Stevo brought Chip round to the other side of the table for Lulu to stroke.

'You going to be a bridesmaid?' Stevo said, fixing her with a penetrating look.

'Oh no, I'm just a guest,' Lulu said, with a shy glance up at him.

'Well, hope you and your boyfriend have a good day at the wedding,' Stevo said.

'I'll be on my own,' Lulu said blushing.

His face brightened. 'You don't say? Well, I got to get back to work; me and Chip have a job to do, can't hang around here chatting up pretty ladies,' he said. He looked back at Lulu, 'perhaps you'll be back here later, maybe?'

'I could be. I probably will,' Lulu said blushing furiously.

Stevo gave her a wink and wandered off to chase more gulls away, Chip pulling energetically at his lead.

'Get your overnight case; you've pulled!' Rowan said.

'Bloody hell!' Lulu said, marvelling, 'I think I have. I wonder if he likes ice cream. We should have got a selfie with him.'

'He's a real looker too. Now we've got you set up with someone, let's go back to the far more interesting subject of Shane's brother,' Jilly said, and once again all eyes turned to look at me.

'There's nothing to tell,' I said.

This was greeted with jeering.

'Is Shane's brother good in bed?' Noleen asked.

Mercifully she then distracted everyone by telling us in some detail how unsatisfactory her latest partner was in that department and then we took another selfie with everyone pulling miserable faces in sympathy.

We finished our latest round of cocktails and went off to look at the Opera House which was standing gleaming golden in the evening sunlight. With that and the view across to the Harbour Bridge, it was an outstanding setting. Naturally enough, we clustered together again for another selfie, all of us shouting 'opera' at the same time. The gang then decided on another waterfront wine bar, pulled two tables together, and ordered wine.

Rowan came to sit next to me and put her arm around me.

'Okay love?'

'Yes, your friends are fun,' I said.

She rocked with laughter. 'They are a nosey bunch I'll give them that.'

'Happy?'

She nodded emphatically and then stopped and grabbed hold of the edge of the table. 'Oooh I shouldn't do that, everything has gone a bit wobbly. So, have you heard from Kit again?'

'No,' I said, 'I didn't expect to.'

'Muppet. Messing my sister about like that,' she said fiercely, 'I'll get Shane to punch him. I'll give him a piece of my mind when I see him. I'll tell him what I think of him.'

'No need for that, Rowan,' I said, 'everything is fine. No need to tell him anything.'

'Ah, well I did tell him something,' Rowan said, suddenly looking a bit guilty.

Further down the table, the rest of the gang had already finished the wine and were waving the empty bottles and taking selfies before ordering some more. They could certainly speed-drink, I had to admit it.

'What did you tell him?' I said, feeling a bit uneasy, 'and when did all this happen?'

Rowan, who by now was obviously more than a bit squiffy, stabbed at the table with one finger. 'I saw him at the house; you were out. I told him you deserved an apology—'

'He did apologise,' I said.

She wasn't listening. '—and I told him if he let you go, he was an idiot. A bloody idiot.'

'Oh for heaven's sake, Rowan!'

'No, no I told him. I told him you were the best sister anywhere,' at this point she flung her arms around me and started getting a bit emotional, 'I did, I told him he wouldn't find anyone better than you.'

'Oh God, what did he say?'

Rowan straightened up and thought for a moment.

'He said he knew that. He didn't need me to tell him. And I said well then? And he said well then? And then I said he had no business hanging around with whatever her name was. God, I didn't mean to tell you this. I must be pissed. And then I told him to think.'

'Think what?' I said.

'Exactly!' Rowan said, which under the circumstances was a bit unsatisfactory. 'And while we are confessing things, I did take that lipstick when you were twelve and I was ten.'

'I know you did Rowan; it was all over your face and your sheets.'

'Was it? I thought I'd got away with it,' she said.

A tray of mini burgers arrived at that point and the gang all cheered. And three seagulls swooped down to take a look.

Immediately, there was another bout of enthusiastic wuffing and Stevo appeared at our table with the ever-eager Chip.

'Here we are again, ladies,' he said with a grin at Lulu, 'me and Chip the Wonder Dog are on the case!'

Lulu grinned back. 'Do you like ice cream?'

* * *

It was a great night. What I remember of it.

Having declared she didn't want to be out too late, we ended up going with Rowan from one wine bar to another chattering and laughing. We met up with another hen party of beauty therapists and apparently swore lifelong friendships with total strangers and took several group selfies and asked passing tourists to take pictures of us too. We ate hot doughnuts and drank more cocktails. We danced in front of one of the street entertainers – whether we helped or hindered his takings that evening, I couldn't say. But the main thing was we had fun, and even in my fuddled state I exulted in being free to enjoy myself, make new friends, and not feel my age or any responsibility.

We ended the evening shortly before midnight, staggering back to the limo, after first prising Lulu and Stevo apart from a passionate, snogging embrace down by one of the ferry terminals while next to them Chip – tired out from his official duties – lay flat out, patiently waiting on the ground. It was a brilliant night.

29

Two days later, after double checking that Rowan's driving license was valid, we went to pick up Dan and Skye from the airport.

It was so wonderful to see them both, coming through the gate at arrivals, towing their cases behind them. They both looked tired from the long journey, but they were full of excitement with tales to tell about their trip.

'Singapore airport is absolutely fantastic,' Skye said, hugging me, 'there's a massive waterfall, gardens, shops, ponds with the biggest fish, everything. Why aren't all airports like that? I would have stayed there.'

I think her many plaits were standing out at all angles with her enthusiasm. Her eyes were sparkling with delight. Beside her, Dan seemed just as animated which did my heart good to see.

'Well you two are stoked to the max,' Rowan said, hugging them both.

'Hiya Mum,' Dan said with a huge grin.

We hugged and rocked for a bit, and I shed a few tears, I was so pleased to see him. He seemed pale and rather skinny to me. He needed a few of Shane's barbecues and some sunshine.

'Congratulations on the engagement, Auntie Rowan,' he said over my head.

'Skip the auntie business,' Rowan said, 'and whatever you do, don't try calling my beloved Uncle Shane! He'd be horrified.'

'Can't wait to meet him,' Dan said, 'so after all these years you actually got someone to propose.'

'Cheeky sod,' Rowan said, 'I'll have you know I'm in my prime! Come on, let's get you two back home. Maggie and Banjo are dying to see you. Now, where did I leave the car?'

They spent the whole journey telling us more about the wonders of Changi airport, until we both wanted to go there. There were theatres, light shows, wonderful places to eat, even a butterfly garden.

'You're going to find Kookaburra a bit tame after all that,' Rowan said, 'but we do have the beach and you can't beat it. And you'll get free stuff in the Wipe-Out.'

'Beer too?' Dan said, beaming.

'Does Trev put up tents? I should say so!' Rowan said. 'Now look: don't miss this view of the ocean. It made your mother cry when she saw it again.'

'Wow, it's fabulous,' Skye said, her face pressed up against the car window, 'but why did it make you cry?'

'Because I hadn't seen it for so long, except on Google Earth. It made me a bit emotional to be back,' I said.

I was feeling much the same at that moment and did a bit of sniffing and clearing my throat. Leaving this place was going to be doubly hard now. The thought of that made me want to cry even more.

'Why did you leave it so long to visit?' Skye said.

'I've thought about that a lot over the last few weeks, and I'm blowed if I know,' I said.

'So when do you have to go back?' Dan asked after a few minutes.

'I was tempted to return when I heard about your father being in my house. And then we sorted it out between us, and Rowan and Shane got engaged.'

Dan tapped me on the shoulder. 'Which reminds me, Skye's dad went over to your house and changed the locks. And he fitted some window locks too. Just in case. Here's the new keys.'

'Oh Skye that's so brilliant, thank you!' I said, the relief washing over me, 'let me have the bill, won't you?'

Skye laughed. 'He did it for nothing; he said Tom was way out of order, doing what he did. He was pleased to help.'

'I'm so grateful.'

I looked down at the keys in my hand. They were new and shiny and there were a lot of them. For a moment, I could hardly remember what my house looked like. I jingled the bunch of keys and then put them into my bag and clipped it shut. I imagined walking up to my front door and unlocking it. And it wasn't something I was looking forward to at all.

* * *

Shane was there early the following morning, already in his wetsuit, munching on a piece of toast and slurping at his tin mug of coffee.

'Trev's got a few days off,' he said as I came into the kitchen, yawning.

And this affected me how?

'That's nice for him,' I said, pouring myself some tea.

'Yeah, he's finished putting up tents for the moment and he's going to catch a few. Before they change their minds at Tents Tents Tents and make him start taking all the tents down again.'

'A few what? Tents?'

'Waves, silly. Rowan said you wanted him to teach you to surf. He's proper good too, got more patience than me. I'd just shout at you. He said he'd meet us at the beach,' Shane looked at his watch, 'ten minutes ago. So, get your skates on. You can use Rowan's stuff. She's working in the shop today; you won't see her for a couple of hours. And Dan won't be up yet.'

'I'm not sure actually—'

'Come on, it's bitchin' out there.'

Was this good or bad?

'I haven't tried this for years. And I never could.'

'It's like riding a bike, you'll be fine. Go and put this on.'

Shane threw a wetsuit across the table at me, knocking the milk carton over. We spent the next ten minutes clearing up the mess and before I could think of any excuses we were in the van, roaring off down the road to the beach.

It was a beautiful day, the sun rising above a picture-perfect sea. The waves about two feet high. Some little kids were out there already, one of them couldn't have been more than five or six, and he was managing. It was very impressive. I didn't know they made wetsuits that small.

'Right, now where is he? He should be here,' Shane said, shading his eyes, 'I'd better go and see what's going on in the café.'

We found Trev, sitting with a bacon sandwich in the Wipe-Out. He was leafing through a copy of Australian *Woman's Weekly* with a picture of Elle MacPherson laughing in a bikini on the front. She looked about thirty-five. Genes are very unkind sometimes; she was the same age as I was. Still, if I looked like her, I'd probably be laughing all the time too.

'Ah, there you are,' Trev said, 'Shane-o says you want to learn to surf. Well look no further; I'm always up for a challenge.'

'Don't you think I might be too old?'

Trev looked at me and grinned. 'Nah, you'll be right. And you're short so your centre of gravity is lower. Like a bulldozer. You're a proper Betty.'

'A Betty?'

'An older girl. It's a compliment.'

'Okay, I think. It doesn't sound like a compliment. And I'm not very fit.'

Trev chuckled. 'You will be by the time I've done with you. You know the basics? Like how to pop-up on your board?'

'Yes. In theory, although I never managed to do it. Shane says it's like riding a bike.'

I looked over to him for confirmation, but Shane had picked up the discarded magazine and was squinting at the pictures inside.

Trev scratched his head. 'Well, I've never known anyone drown on a bike, but you never know. Let's just give it a go.'

We waded out, the sea a bit cold for my liking, and in no time Trev was sitting astride his board beyond the breaking waves, waiting for me.

I paddled as hard as I could, my arms aching after only a few minutes effort. This didn't bode well for the next hour.

'I thought you'd changed your mind and buggered off home,' Trev said cheerfully as I reached his side, already gasping and spitting out salt water.

'So, go on then,' he said, 'show us what you got and we'll take it from there.'

I turned back towards the shore and promptly fell off my board.

I spent the next part of the lesson falling off, swallowing sea water, and trying to hear Trev's bellowed instructions

'You need to practice your pop-up, noodle arms,' he shouted at last.

'I have no upper body strength,' I gasped, 'I never did.'

'Forget the pop-up then. Just try catching one and slide down. I'll show you.'

Trev caught a wave and glided down towards the beach.

'See?' he said as he paddled back to my side.

I fell off again and I hadn't even done anything. I was just lying on my board in calm water. I was beginning to wonder if this was even possible.

'It's good fun though, isn't it?' he said, as I heaved myself back onto my board.

'Terrific,' I agreed, wondering whether the café was still serving bacon sandwiches.

I was starting to remember why I hadn't managed to do this all those years ago.

Rowan had been quite good when she was younger, certainly much better than me. The little kids in the shallows were good. A few yards away, a man was even surfing with his dog on the board, and the dog had a better idea of what to do than I did. It even had the time and energy to bark at the same time.

'You're Australian; it's in your blood,' Trev said encouragingly.

I think by then my blood was 25 per cent sea water.

'I'm hopeless,' I said.

'No you're not, them nippers over there have been surfing all their lives. And so has that dog, probably. You're not going to catch on in twenty minutes.'

We'd only been out there for twenty minutes?

'Look, you're shivering. let's call it a day for now, and try again tomorrow,' Trev said kindly, 'Just give it one last go on the way back in.'

So I did. I positioned myself properly and tried to look over my shoulder at the waves forming behind me. Which in itself was difficult. As my neck was a bit stiff.

And then magically, I found myself in the right place at the right time; I could feel the head of the board sliding down in front of me and I was getting up speed. I imagined for a glorious moment the might of the Pacific urging me on towards the shore. It was very exciting. Perhaps I could do this after all. I briefly imagined myself bulldozing down the wave but in an elegant way. Managing the pop-up. One hand out in front of me, knees bent.

There were more people on the beach now, I hoped no one was watching me too closely. Perhaps I could do this after all. Should I actually try a pop-up?

'Keep your head down,' Trev shouted.

This went against all my survival instincts.

The wave broke over my head, the nose of my surfboard dipped under the water, and I was unceremoniously hurled off.

I felt the sand under my hands, the water roaring in my ears, and to add insult to injury, as I surfaced, my board – attached to my ankle with a strap – ricocheted and slapped me on the back of my head, so I fell over again.

I dragged myself to my hands and knees, coughing and spluttering, my mouth full of sand, and found myself looking at a pair of feet in the shallows in front of me.

'Having fun?' said someone.

I looked up, squinting against the sun and my hair which was all over my face. And I'd taken my contact lenses out too.

I realised it was Kit. Of course it was.

'Shane said you'd be here, that you wanted to learn. I've been up the other end of the beach,' he said, 'I thought I'd come along and see how you're getting on.'

'Cheers Shane,' I gulped.

Next time I saw Shane, I would probably kill him.

Kit laughed and I squinted a look up at him.

It was almost worth the aching arms, the salt water in my stomach, and the complete lack of dignity to see him.

He was wearing some board shorts and a rash vest which was – as it should be – tight around his chest. So I could see just how muscular he was. Wow. I bet he could do pop-ups and if he had a dog, I bet the dog would too.

I reached out a hand and he pulled me to my feet.

'I was rubbish,' I panted.

'I'm sure you weren't,' he said kindly.

Trev had just surfed up to us and picked up his board.

'She was too,' he agreed happily, 'really bad, but it's only the first go, she'll be right. If you've had enough, I'm going to catch a few.'

'Thanks for trying, Trev,' I called out as he paddled away.

'So a qualified success?' Kit said.

'I wouldn't go that far,' I said, pushing my hair out of my eyes. It felt like my face was covered in sand; in fact, most of me was. Some of it in very uncomfortable places. I bet Elle MacPherson didn't end up like this when she went surfing.

'Coffee to warm you up?' Kit said.

'That's the best idea I've heard today,' I said. 'Where have you been? I haven't seen you for a while.'

'Adelaide,' he said, 'sorting out the wedding present.'

'What is it?'

'It's a surprise.'

'Hmm, Maggie said she and Banjo had organised a big surprise for the wedding day too. Everyone is being very mysterious.'

'You'll see, all in good time,' Kit smiled.

As we sat down at the café, Lyn and Cheryl suddenly appeared as though by magic. Or perhaps their ESP had alerted them to the presence of an attractive, single man? There was a great deal of hair flicking and giggling on their part. I watched him, his bare feet in the sand, his strong, tanned forearms, his broad shoulders, the way his tight vest clung...

'Mmm, muscles,' I murmured, rather distracted. 'I mean, I haven't got many muscles.'

'Give yourself a chance. Not long until the big day,' Kit said, 'two days. I thought your son was going to be here?'

'He and Skye are staying with Maggie. They've borrowed Banjo's van. They wanted to see a bit of the area. They should be back sometime today.'

'It must be great to see him again. I hope he doesn't have any problems with the grey wastewater hose.'

He looked at me and his eyes twinkled. I don't know what he was remembering but I was having some alarming flashbacks.

'I'm sure they will be fine,' I said. 'Now, wasn't coffee mentioned? I could do with something to take away the taste of the Pacific?'

30

The wedding day dawned bright and sunny with a sky that matched Rowan's dress, shading from palest cornflower where the sky met the sea, to a vibrant sapphire overhead. It was as though nature was doing its best to make her day as beautiful as possible.

I went down to the beach to take the last boxes of glassware to the café and saw the overnight tide had swept the sand to a smooth, glossy backdrop. Overhead, a few birds wheeled in the warm air.

And the car park was full of motorhomes. I mean absolutely rammed with them. There wasn't room for a bicycle, let alone any cars. People were starting to emerge, doors were open, and the early morning air was scented with bacon frying and coffee.

'Hey there! Elin! It's me! Patty!'

I turned to see a familiar figure trotting towards me, her face one big smile.

'Patty! How great to see you again! What's all this?' I said.

'Well Banjo and Maggie invited us, didn't they? It's a surprise! The Silver Surfers wouldn't miss this for the world! We're all here. Alice, Stew and Deb. Frank and Hilary. Teddy, Hannah and Sally.

All the gang from Cairns and then some. Two have come over from Perth, but then Geoff and Claire have got a whopping van. They brought Jim and Dinkie with them because their van is off the road. Well that wasn't going to stop them! Dinkie's a demon behind the wheel, you know that! Over there is Vic and Edie, Henry and Evelyn, and next to them is Arthur and Mabel. Oh we don't miss a good party when we're invited!' She beamed proudly and did a little skip in her excitement. 'Banjo and Maggie co-ordinated it all so we arrived last night when the car park was empty. We had such a great meet-up last night; there will be some sore heads this morning, I can tell you. We've had the police round telling us to move on. For a bit I thought they meant it but then Malc gave them all a bacon roll and a cup of tea and they soon cheered up.'

'How wonderful to see you all here!' I said. 'Rowan will be thrilled.'

'Don't tell her just yet; it's supposed to be a surprise!'

As she spoke, another massive van pulled into the entrance of the car park and Patty gave a cheer.

'It's Norman and Frank! He said Norm's got some new teeth specially! He wouldn't want to miss all this! I'll see you later and I'll introduce you to everyone. I've got to go and move those traffic cones. I've been saving a place for him.'

Patty hurried off and I stood with a daft grin on my face watching as people got out of their vans to greet the newcomers. There were a great many bush hats and scruffy shorts and smiles. They might be older and some of them might not be in the best of health, but they certainly knew how to have fun. The Silver Surfers were an inspiration.

Down on the hard-packed sand, they were starting to put out chairs: plastic chairs from the café, deckchairs, camp chairs, and canvas stools. There were wooden crates and cool boxes and even a couple of up turned boats. I spotted Shane helping to pull them all into neat rows and hurried over to say hello.

He turned, a huge daft smile on his face, and gave me a hug.

'G'day sister-in-law-to-be,' he said, 'how is the bride?'

'She was in the bath when I left, getting the jitters I think wondering if everything is going to go okay.'

'Course it is; tell her not to be daft. We're just putting the finishing touches to everything,' Shane said, 'and Kit's just arriving with the balloons. Good job it isn't windy, eh?'

And there he was, walking along the water's edge towards me like something out of a film. He was barefoot, wearing chinos rolled up to the knee and a dazzling white t-shirt, holding on to a massive bunch of blue and white helium balloons.

God, at the moment I really could have run towards him and hurled myself into his arms, but of course if I had, he would have lost all the balloons and I didn't want to be responsible for that. And I wanted to be rather more careful before I hurled myself at anyone in future.

'Hello again,' he said, smiling down at me, 'I thought I'd find you here. This all looks fun, doesn't it?'

'Marvellous,' I said, my heart thumping in my chest.

'Better than surfing?'

'Absolutely, I've only just got the sand off from last time.'

Oh God, I was going to make a fool of myself. I was going to start saying random, stupid things.

No I wasn't, I was going to be sensible and level-headed.

'How is the bride this morning?'

'Excited,' I said, 'and nervous.'

'Everything is going to be fine,' he said.

'I'd better go,' I said, 'lots to do.'

* * *

Rowan, still in her dressing gown, was sitting with Maggie at the kitchen table, trying to eat some toast.

'You have to eat something, Ro,' I said, 'or you'll be fainting instead of getting married.'

'I can't,' Rowan wailed.

'One bite for you and one for me,' Maggie said pushing the plate a bit closer to her.

'I'm not a toddler,' Rowan said crossly and took a bite.

'How are things at the beach?' Maggie said.

'Excellent, looking great,' I said.

Rowan wheeled around in her chair. 'Is Shane there?'

'He was,' I said.

'He should be getting ready; he's not supposed to be at the beach,' she moaned, 'I bet he's going to be late!'

'He won't,' I said, 'he has Kit with him.'

'So he's turned up at last! Where's he been?'

I decided not to tell her.

'No idea,' I said.

'Have any other guests arrived?' she said.

I exchanged a look with my aunt. 'A couple,' I said, 'there's no need to worry. Everything is going to be great. Time to start on your hair and make-up.'

Rowan put her forehead into her hands and then drooped onto the table.

'Oh God, what if Shane changes his mind? Or backs out at the last minute? Or just doesn't say "I do", or is it "I will"?'

'Rowan, he won't change his mind. He's looking forward to it just as much as you are. You two are perfect together.'

'But I'm so old!' Rowan wailed.

'You're not old, but you'll have a wedding day slap if you carry on,' I said firmly, 'that's part of my bridesmaid's duties.'

'You're so reassuring,' Rowan said, looking up at me. 'Come on then, let's get on with it.'

Two hours later and we were both ready. It was nothing short of a miracle. Banjo, unbelievably smart in a blue and white striped blazer, some light slacks pressed into knife-edge creases and jaunty straw boater, came to collect Maggie, who by then was decked out in a rather successful turquoise dress and jacket, a pink feather fascinator in her hair.

That left just the two of us in the suddenly quiet house. Perhaps I should have left Rowan with Banjo but that wasn't what Rowan wanted.

I sent up a silent prayer that Shane would be there, sober and ready.

'Is the taxi outside?' Rowan shouted from the bathroom.

I looked. There was a car, but not a taxi. I looked more closely. It was a sleek, black limo; it was Kit's car. And yes, standing by the driver's door, attired in a tight, dark suit complete with mirrored shades was the blonde driver, Sam, looking more like a secret agent than ever.

'Yes,' I shouted back, 'the car is here, it's time to go.'

Rowan came out of the bedroom, holding her bouquet in front of her like a shield. Her dark hair was curled, plaited, and decorated as it had been when I saw her on that first visit, with feathers and tiny shells.

Looking at my sister in her beautiful mermaid dress, I felt the tears welling up. She looked twenty years younger; Shane was a lucky man to have her in his life.

'You look wonderful,' I said, rather choked up, 'absolutely glorious.'

'So do you,' Rowan said, her voice a bit wobbly. She held out her flowers and swept a hand though her skirts, which rippled like sea water. 'Well this is something I never thought I'd be doing, I don't mind admitting.'

'You just needed to wait for the right man to come along,' I said.

'Shane's the right man,' she said more confidently.

'He is; just make each other happy.'

Rowan whirled around.

'Do you know what I realised in the middle of the night?'

'What?'

'Kit is the right man for you. He is, don't look like that. He's the right man for you and you are the right one for him. I just know it.'

'No, I'm not. We had a bit of a fling, that's all. He's got the redhead now,' I said, 'it's all in the past.'

Rowan flapped a hand. 'I'll sort her out. I'll wrestle her to the ground, take her out to sea in Baz's boat, and chuck her over. Or perhaps I'll go for her with a harpoon gun? Or dig a hole in the sand and push her in.'

I laughed. 'Now come on Bride, we need to get you to your wedding.'

'Okay. I'm okay. I can do this,' Rowan said. She took a deep breath and pushed her feet into her wedding shoes, which were blue flip flops which she had decorated with a great deal of glitter and some more tiny shells. 'And don't say anything that might make me cry.'

Outside, she took one look at the limo and turned to me, her eyes wide, mouth open.

'I don't think that's Tommo's Taxi, do you?'

'Nope,' I said grinning, 'I don't think it is.'

'It's no good, I'm going to cry, I know I am.'

* * *

When we got to the slipway leading to the beach, Rowan gasped.

'Who are all those people? Why are they here? Shane didn't tell me anything about a festival going on at the same time!'

I squeezed her hand. 'It's not a festival Ro, it's your wedding.'

'What? All of it? There are balloons! There are people all over the place! There are beach tents and gazebos! And there's Maggie's bunting! And all those motor homes in the car park! Oh, just look at that beautiful blue VW Splitty van over there!'

'Focus, Rowan, focus.'

'But who are these people? What the hell is going on?'

We got out of the limo and an absolutely massive cheer went up, startling all the sea birds who were dodging in and out of the retreating surf. There must have been three hundred people there, all of them smiling and taking pictures on their phones.

Suddenly Dan and Skye appeared from out of the crowd and came to give Rowan a hug. Dan in jeans and a surfing t-shirt and Skye in a beautiful orange sari.

'You both look fantastic!' Dan said with a massive grin. 'Isn't this brilliant?'

'You both look incredible,' Skye said breathlessly, 'in a good way.'

'Where have you been?' I said, hugging them both.

Skye looked blank. 'Not sure really, around and about.'

'We'll catch up later,' Dan said, giving me another hug, 'off you go!'

'Jesus!' Rowan said, as we walked along the path which had been swept of sand, the edges decorated with shells and strands of seaweed. 'Who did all this?'

'Shane's mates and their girlfriends,' I said, 'everyone wanted to help.'

'Oh God, I'm going to cry again,' she whimpered.

At last we could see Shane was there as he'd promised he would be. Smart in a pale linen suit and pristine white shirt. Next to him was Kit. I heard Rowan give a strangled gulp and she grabbed my hand. Then Banjo was there at her side, offering her his arm and I walked away from them towards the front of the rows of chairs where Maggie was already dabbing at her eyes with a tissue.

Kit and I looked at each other for a moment and then he smiled and winked at me.

The celebrant was there with one of the tables from the Wipe-Out covered with a white cloth. She was a small, neat woman with a shock of white hair, dressed in a yellow and white polka dot dress and red jelly sandals.

As Rowan reached Shane, they exchanged a look that said just about everything. Until Shane pulled a funny face to make Rowan laugh and they hugged each other. Then she pulled back to look at him.

'Jeez Shane, you're not crying, are you?' Rowan said.

Shane rubbed briskly at his eyes. 'Nah, I'm still sad about One Direction splitting up.'

'You idiot!' Rowan said, bashing him with her bouquet.

The celebrant cleared her throat.

'G'day everyone. Thank you all for coming. My name is Susie Hatch and I am a civil celebrant here today to conduct the marriage of Shane and Rowan.'

The ceremony had begun and, apart from the sound of the retreating surf, you could have heard a pin drop.

There were the formalities to go through and the exchanging of rings that Kit fished out from his pocket after, of course, first pretending he had forgotten them.

'I now pronounce you husband and wife.'

And just like that, they were married.

Shane swooped in to kiss his new wife with a very impressive dip over one arm and everyone, even the tourists and bystanders standing up on the edge of the car park railings, roared their approval. And two of the policeman shook hands and clapped each other on the back.

* * *

The party started almost immediately: music blared out from the loudspeakers, the barbeque flamed into life nearly taking off Baz's eyebrows, and in a few minutes, there were queues for the Wipe-Out and the beer tent, and it seemed that everyone was laughing. There were even four policemen and a traffic warden standing enjoying burgers on the edge of the car park. What was going to happen when all the motorhomes started moving or other people wanted to park was anyone's guess.

I met up with Rowan's hen party friends who were all in good form and teasing Lulu about her new boyfriend, Stevo. Chip the wonder dog was there too, looking very smart in a white collar decorated with a big blue bow.

And then I saw her. A redhead, dressed in an exquisite, emerald-green dress which shimmered in the sunshine, hanging on Kit's arm and laughing in a controlled and sexy way. She had an impressive set of white teeth emphasised with very red lipstick. There was a touch of the Jessica Rabbit about her. Damn. That could only be Sukie.

I wandered around trying to avoid her, which wasn't difficult as I didn't seem to have a moment to myself. Chatting to people, hearing about Dan and Skye's trip in the motorhome, having my dress admired, and answering questions about Rowan and Shane that made me wonder if some of the guests even knew the happy couple. Oh well, it looked as though there was plenty of food. A constant stream of hot dogs and burgers, bowls of salad, chilli, platters of cheese, and huge bowls of fresh fruit. Shane had even organised an ice cream van which was handing out cones and ice lollies.

Meanwhile, the Silver Surfers had set up their own encampment of picnic tables, gazebos, and chairs on the sand and were deciding where they were going next.

Everywhere I went, I seemed to see the redhead out of the corner of my eye, and she was never far from Kit. It was very disappointing.

* * *

Gradually, the afternoon cooled and with much ceremony and a lot of slightly drunken shouting from Shane's friends, Shane stood up, still clutching a pint of beer.

'I'm not going to make a speech because I don't want to make a complete tit of myself—'

'Why break the habit of a lifetime Shane?' someone shouted.

'—but if you look up, you'll see how I feel,' Shane said.

Obediently we all looked up at the clear sky and a small plane buzzed overhead and started skywriting. Somehow, and heaven know how they do it, it spelled out 'Rowan I love you' and another huge cheer went up.

Rowan was crying like a baby as Shane hugged her. It was beyond romantic.

Then as the plane flew away, leaving the message to gently fade into the blue sky, Kit stood up to give a speech.

'Thank you everyone for coming along today to help us celebrate Shane and Rowan's wedding. For those of you who don't know, I'm Kit, Shane's older and slightly taller brother.'

There was a cheer of approval at this, led by Shane's surfing buddies.

'I'm not going to talk for long—'

Another cheer.

'—but I want to congratulate them and wish them every happiness for the future. Rowan is a great, feisty, and lovely woman and I can't imagine why she would want to marry my brother, but love's a funny thing and here we are. Shane, you're a lucky guy.'

There was another roar of approval and a round of applause interspersed with some whooping and whistles.

'Finally, they have each other and a long and happy future together. What do you buy a couple that have everything as a wedding present? Well, in the end it was easy.'

Kit pointed to the slipway where the blue VW Splitty van was now decorated in ribbons and lights.

'There you go, you two; that's why I've been away for a few days: tracking that beauty down. I wish you many happy journeys together in it.'

For a moment Shane stood with his mouth open until Kit dropped the keys into his hand and then the brothers had a rather emotional embrace which I think surprised both of them.

Shane and Rowan went to admire their new motor, flashing the headlights on and off and sounding the horn, both of them dizzy with excitement.

Then they came back to the party and Shane and Rowan switched on the new decorations. The new fairy lights looked magical; they had been looped over the café roof and along the car park railings too. One of the policemen wondered out loud if they were allowed to do that, and the other one told him to shut up and stop being so miserable because they were now officially off duty and it wasn't their problem anyway.

I felt a hand on my arm and I turned to see Kit there. He had shed his jacket somewhere. He looked adorable.

'I get the feeling you've been avoiding me,' he said with a lopsided grin.

'Absolutely not,' I lied.

'You look lovely,' he said.

He hadn't taken his hand away and I looked down at it, rather liking the feel of it on my skin.

'Thanks,' I said.

'Have you had a good day? Rowan looks very happy, doesn't she?'

'She does,' I said, 'incredibly happy, and so does Shane.'

He reached out and tucked a strand of hair behind my ear. The touch of his fingers sent a shiver down my backbone.

'So my brother has married your sister. Does that mean we're related?' he said.

'I don't know, I'm not sure,' I said, 'I don't think so.'

I sipped my wine, my mouth was suddenly very dry, and I felt giddy in a way that the alcohol had nothing to do with.

He leaned a tiny bit towards me. He was going to kiss me, I know he was. In front of all those people. I closed my eyes for a moment.

'There you are Kit. Aren't you going to introduce me?'

It was Jessica Rabbit, wiggling across the sand like some sort of slinky, plastic snake. I wondered if Rowan was still up for the 'hole in the sand' business.

31

Kit straightened up.

'Of course. Sukie George, this is Elin Anderson, Rowan's sister.'

I wondered for a moment if we were supposed to shake hands or anything, and if we did, would her skin be as chilled and reptilian as I imagined?

'Wonderful to meet you,' she said.

'Hello,' I said, trying to smile.

She had a glass of champagne in her hand, a smudge of scarlet lipstick on the rim.

'What a lovely wedding. I've never seen anything like it. So original and – oh I don't know – bohemian,' she said, making it sound as though we were a band of itinerant hippies.

'Yes, it's fabulous, isn't it?' I said. 'Unique and laid-back. Just their style.'

She smiled and didn't answer.

'Sukie has been working with me on a project for a while,' Kit said.

What would that be then? Nail extensions filed to the right degree of sharpness? Cantilevering her into that dress?

'How amazing,' I said.

'I think we have nailed it now,' Sukie said with another annoying smile.

'I hope so,' Kit said, 'it took some time.'

Sukie wasn't even looking at him. She seemed distracted, glancing around, looking over his shoulder.

'And what a lot of friends the happy couple has,' she added.

'Yes, they are a dynamic duo,' I said.

Dynamic duo? Why did I say that? What was I thinking?

'And you look just lovely,' she said with a sweeping glance down my dress to my bare feet, 'and so does the bride. What an unusual dress she chose. So elegant. It looked almost vintage, like something rare and precious. It must have been designer, Dior perhaps or Galliano? I know a great place that cleans and stores these things afterwards. Museum conditions—'

At that exact moment there was a scream behind us.

Shane had his trouser legs rolled up and was carrying Rowan in his arms. He jogged unsteadily into the approaching surf and after a moment when he kissed her, he dropped her into the water and threw himself in after her. The waves crashed over their heads and seconds later they reappeared, laughing hysterically. Each grabbing on to the other for support.

'Shane, you bloody mongrel!' Rowan yelled.

'You told me you wanted to look like a mermaid; well, now you do,' Shane said.

Rowan sloshed an armful of water at him.

'You daft dingo!'

Shane grabbed her and fell back into the water again. One of Rowan's wedding flip-flops spun into the air.

I turned to see Sukie's horrified face and I couldn't help it, I laughed.

'So, I don't think they'll be needing that storage facility after all. I mean of course I'll ask but...' I shrugged.

She didn't reply, just gave a little shudder.

I looked at Kit; he was convulsed with laughter.

Sukie coughed delicately and looked at her watch. 'Well, I think I'd better be leaving. Can Sam drive me back?'

Oh, so she knew about Sam. That indicated a certain familiarity between them, didn't it?

'Of course,' Kit said, one hand pressed to his chest as he stopped laughing and caught his breath, 'I'll come with you to find her.'

'Aren't you leaving too?'

'Good heavens no, this party is going to rock for a while yet; I wouldn't miss it for the world,' Kit replied. He put one hand in the small of Sukie's bony back and steered her in the direction of the slipway.

'Lovely to have met you,' she called over her shoulder as she went.

'Fabulous,' I called.

Then I made some sort of 'meh' noise, which was childish but satisfying. I wondered how long it would take for them to say their farewells and went off to get another drink.

* * *

Eventually, the party started to wind down. It had, after all, been a long day and once Sam returned with the limo to take the happy couple away, the spring seemed to go out of the occasion. Just in time they had remembered to cut the cake – a three tier lemon and raspberry sponge that had not been improved by the heat of the day and several inquisitive fingers. They then did the traditional 'feeding each other' photo, which resulted in a great deal of mess and buttercream over both bride and groom.

After we had waved the happy couple off to their honeymoon suite in Jackie's hotel, Kit spoke to the caterers and with marvellous efficiency they started stacking chairs and chucking bottles and cans into the recycling skip.

Lyn and Cheryl had long ago given up helping and by the looks of them when last seen, were completely plastered and engaged in a little spur of the moment face sucking activity with Trev and Baz that all four would undoubtedly regret when they sobered up.

The Silver Surfers were still in their encampment and occasionally the scent of something that I'm sure wasn't regular tobacco drifted across the night air. I hoped the policemen had gone.

It had been such a wonderful day and now, like my beautiful dress, I felt a bit crumpled. I should go back home. But by the look of it no one else was planning to leave the beach any time soon.

Banjo was trying to play someone's guitar; I think it was Wonderful Tonight, but it might not have been. Dan and Skye were sitting with them, and Maggie was swaying gently and – good grief – smoking something. I didn't really want to know so I didn't go and ask.

Honestly.

I picked up a couple of cans that had fallen out of the skip and chucked them in. The beach was surprisingly clear of any litter; evidently the guests – drunk as they were – cared about that sort of thing which was nice to see.

'Right, there you are. You keep dodging off.'

It was Kit.

'I thought you had gone?' I said.

'Of course not. I want to talk to you and I haven't had much of a chance yet,' he said.

He took my hand, casually but firmly and we walked away from everybody else towards the dark sea. The incoming tide washed over our bare feet; it was warm and refreshing.

'Have you had a good day?' he said.

'Brilliant,' I said, 'and they did too, which was the only thing that mattered really. I loved that skywriting; such a lovely thing to do.'

'Wasn't it? Shane has a romantic streak after all,' Kit said, 'I must say, your son is a nice chap I had a long chat with him. He's very bright and engaging. And Skye too, despite the death's head moth earrings. Dan tells me he wants to take a break from work and spend a few months in Australia.'

I was shocked. 'Does he? I didn't know that. Perhaps he doesn't want to spend the next thirty years teaching.'

'Can't blame him for that,' Kit said.

Behind us, the noise of the party was fading, the lights still shining out across the bay. It looked so wonderful.

Kit stopped and turned to look at me.

'So,' he said.

I almost held my breath. What should I say? I couldn't think of anything beyond this moment.

'What are your plans?'

'I don't really know,' I said, 'I suppose I'll stay on, spend some time with Dan, tidy up Rowan's house – when we left this morning, it looked as though a herd of wildebeest had been through.'

'I mean what are you plans now?' Kit said.

'You mean right this minute? I don't know,' I said.

'I want to show you something,' he said.

What sort of thing?

'Okay,' I said, 'that sounds interesting. What is it?'

'I'll show you,' he said, 'in a moment.'

And there in the sea-scented darkness, with the waves covering our feet, he kissed me.

God, what did this man do that made me feel like that? Some magic, some intuition, some mystical ability to make my insides melt.

'Come on,' he said, 'it's getting late. You're cold.'

He swung his jacket around my shoulders and I snuggled into it, as pleased as anything. Breathing in the faint trace of his after-shave. Holding his warm hand as he led me back to the slipway where the black limo was parked with Sam patiently waiting beside it. I got in.

We sat side by side in the back of the car, his hand reaching across to hold mine.

'I'm not letting you get away just yet,' he said.

Did I even want to get away?

* * *

We got back to his house and the familiar white walls rearing up against the starry sky. Inside something had changed. No, everything had changed.

Instead of the white hallway with the strange elephant/tree sculpture, there was silvery wallpaper and a beautiful marble table with an extravagant flower arrangement in shades of purple and lavender. The sitting room was different too; there were massive, pale-blue sofas and a battalion of silk cushions painted with tropical fish. The glass coffee table had been replaced with one which looked as though it had been made from sea-washed, reclaimed wood. Outside on the veranda there were now pale-grey rattan chairs with pink and white striped cushions.

Kit pointed at them.

'You were wearing a pink and white striped dress that day when I came to Rowan's house. I gave you my business card and you tucked it into the top. Do you remember?'

'Fancy remembering that!' I said.

'I remember lots of things,' he said.

We wandered from room to room; it was gorgeous. Everywhere there was colour and comfort. It looked like a home now, not a design brochure. We stood together on the veranda overlooking the dark sea and the myriad little lights from the town and the boats.

'Wow,' I said, 'this is wonderful.'

'I could tell you had reservations when you first came here and you were right. It needed colour and some heart. I have Sukie to thank for all this,' he said. My first interior designer preferred something a bit more – stark.'

'Sukie? She's your designer? I thought…'

'You thought she was something else?'

'Well yes I did. She's very touchy-feely.'

'Don't be daft,' he said, putting his arms around me, 'you know the sort of woman that attracts me.'

'I do?'

'You do,' he kissed me and then just held me against him for a few minutes, 'you do.'

He put an arm around my shoulder and we walked to look out at the ocean below us.

'Remember I spotted you at the airport. Why do you think I came over to use that particular plug socket when I had a perfectly good one by my chair? And then on the plane too. I thought you'd think I was some sort of stalker if I kept following you around.'

'I don't think I would have,' I said.

'And I didn't get your phone number; I didn't even know your name.'

'I wish you'd asked,' I said.

'And everything on that road trip was such fun. I loved every minute of it; you were such good company. I could have gone on driving and chatting forever,' he said.

'Except it wasn't your motorhome.'

'We would have been stopped by the police eventually when Banjo ran out of patience,' he laughed.

I remembered something, 'I'm sorry about the last time I saw you.'

'I knew Shane was going to propose to Rowan so I guessed you would stay on for the wedding.'

'I might not have come,' I said, smiling, 'I might not have approved.'

'Of course you would,' he said.

'You might not have approved.'

'I did. I could tell Rowan was the ideal partner for him. Shane's easily distracted and rather lazy, I'm afraid. He needs someone to keep him going with things.'

'And what will you do now the company is sold?'

'What will I do? Perhaps I'll buy a motorhome and go off exploring more of Australia. But I'd need a navigator. Someone to get me lost in industrial estates and buy me salt and vinegar crisps. Someone who will make me laugh and forget all about financial whatsit.'

'I think I know someone who can do that,' I said.

'You do? Then she'd better apply for the job! Does she have a hair tie with a pineapple? That's the official uniform.'

'She does,' I said, 'she wears it a lot. She can also be rather noisy, wants to go snorkelling on the Great Barrier Reef, has recently become a lot more decisive than she used to be, and likes koalas.'

'Then she sounds perfect. And I'd like her to be happy.'

It was funny; in our early years together, Tom had always said he wanted to make me happy. I'd come to realise that no one can 'make' someone happy. But with the right person perhaps it was possible to 'be' happy. There's a world of difference.

'So what can I do to make her apply for the job?' he continued, 'and finally get her to cook me a full English breakfast?'

'Well, we'd better arrange an interview. She hasn't got a CV with her but she's a great talker so I think you would get the idea fairly quickly.'

He kissed me.

'But would she accept the job if she was offered it?'

'You'll have to wait and see,' I said.

'I can wait,' he said, and he kissed me. 'Welcome home.'

ACKNOWLEDGMENTS

This book was inspired by a perfect road trip in the wonderful Australian states of New South Wales and Queensland. Many thanks are due to the kind and welcoming people we met while we were there who made it such a fantastic experience, particularly Tish Please who helped to show us what a beautiful country it is.

Since then a lot has happened, and this book could not have been completed without the kindness and support of many dear friends and family.

Special thanks are due to Jane and Tony Ayres, David, Freya, Claudia and James and their families. I don't know what I would have done without you.

Thank you too to the wonderful and supportive team at Boldwood, especially Emily Ruston, Amanda Ridout, Nia Beynon, and Claire Fenby.

Thank you also to friends I have made through the Ross Writers Group and the RNA, who have been so encouraging.

MORE FROM MADDIE PLEASE

We hope you enjoyed reading *Sunrise with the Silver Surfers*. If you did, please leave a review.

If you'd like to gift a copy, this book is also available as an ebook, digital audio download and audiobook CD.

Sign up to Maddie Please's mailing list for news, competitions and updates on future books.

http://bit.ly/MaddiePleaseNewsletter

Explore more feel-good reads from Maddie Please.

ABOUT THE AUTHOR

Maddie Please is the author of bestselling joyous tales of older women. She had a career as a dentist and now lives in Herefordshire where she enjoys box sets, red wine and Christmas.

Follow Maddie on social media:

facebook.com/maddieplease

twitter.com/maddieplease1

instagram.com/maddieplease1

bookbub.com/authors/maddie-please

Boldw**oo**d

Boldwood Books is an award-winning fiction publishing company seeking out the best stories from around the world.

Find out more at www.boldwoodbooks.com

Join our reader community for brilliant books, competitions and offers!

Follow us
@BoldwoodBooks
@BookandTonic

Sign up to our weekly deals newsletter

https://bit.ly/BoldwoodBNewsletter

Printed in Great Britain
by Amazon